Peter Corley-Smith

10,000 HOURS

A Helicopter Pilot
in the North

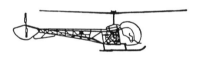

Sono Nis Press
Victoria, British Columbia

Canadian Cataloguing in Publication Data

Corley-Smith, Peter, 1923-
    10,000 hours

    ISBN 1-55039-059-7

    1. Corley-Smith, Peter, 1923-
2. Helicopter pilots — Biography.   3.
Helicopter industry — Canada — History.
I. Title.
TL540.C67A3 1985   629.133352   c85-091068-4

Revised and Reprinted Spring 1995

This book has been published with the assistance
of the Canada Council Block Grant Program.

Published by
SONO NIS PRESS
1745 Blanshard Street
Victoria, British Columbia
Canada v8w 2j8

Designed and printed in Canada by
MORRISS PRINTING COMPANY LTD.
Victoria, British Columbia

To my wife, Nina,

---

for the patience,
tolerance and love that adorn
only a few, very precious marriages.

Now — if only
she could make
good egg rolls.

Contents

Prologue

FROM THE TITLE, READERS WILL KNOW THAT THIS BOOK IS ABOUT my experiences as a helicopter bush pilot. As rewarding and enjoyable as these years were, I concluded that 20 years of damp sleeping bags and mosquitoes was enough. Consequently, in 1964 I began studying at university during the winter and flying in the summer. My flying career finally ended in 1975, when I began a new career as a college instructor. By the time this book was published, I had become a history curator at the B.C. Provincial Museum and I had begun to research and write a series of volumes on the history of aviation in B.C. I did a little on balloons and dirigibles. Then I went on to aircraft, starting with the first aeroplane to fly in British Columbia — a Curtiss Pusher piloted by Charles Hamilton, flying out of Minoru Park race track in Richmond on March 10, 1910. This first volume took me to 1930; the second chronicled the depression years, 1930-1940; and the one I am working on now will take in the Second World War and the obvious changes it brought about as well as the opportunities for aviation that emerged in the following decade.

While this exercise had been engrossing — I have been able to meet and talk to any number of aviation veterans, both men and women, and to trace to a large extent who was flying what and where — it also brought with it a touch of frustration. If only I had known when I was flying what I know now, my experiences would have been so much more interesting.

For example, in the summer of 1967, when I was flying for Vancouver Island Helicopters, I was sent on a mining exploration contract based in Chukachida Lake, some 150 miles southwest of Dease Lake in northern B.C. It was a hum-drum operation. I had to put students down at the top of drainages, then pick them up an hour or two later after they had worked their way back down to the valley taking soil samples on the way. At the southern limit of our area was

Toodoggone Lake and an old abandoned mining site which had a pleasant grassy meadow facing the Toodoggone River, with the lake on the left: an ideal place to sit and have a sandwich lunch and enjoy the view if there was enough breeze to keep the mosquitoes down. I recall vaguely that someone had told me this was the first mine in Canada to be installed and supported solely by aircraft and I was curious but at the time had no way of finding out anything further.

Jumping ahead now some 27 years, I began to research the early career of Grant McConachie, a young man trying to break into aviation at the beginning of the Great Depression. In 1931 he sought the help of his Uncle Harry, who made his living as a salesman with a travelling midway, selling "Sur-Gro, the miracle hair tonic." Evidently he was very good at it because McConachie was able to persuade Uncle Harry to put up $2,500 for a used Fokker Universal bush plane, conveniently located at Edmonton, where he lived. McConachie's first company, with Uncle Harry as president, was called Independent Airways.

After a spell of unprofitable barnstorming, and an equally unprofitable winter of hauling white fish from northern lakes to the nearest railhead for the Chicago market, McConachie was rapidly heading for bankruptcy, and here the story begins to take on a glamorous tinge. Apparently, in the spring of 1932, McConachie met royalty: a Princess Galitzine, the wealthy Maltese wife of White Russian refugee Prince Galitzine. The Princess owned two aircraft — a de Havilland Puss Moth and another Fokker Universal.

So the Princess, as vice-president, and her two aircraft joined Independent Airways. Then, in November 1932, taking off from Edmonton to start a new fish-hauling contract, McConachie had an accident, suffering painful injuries. So, although he was only out of action for a month or two, the aircraft was a write-off, and this left the company with only two machines and brought it close to bankruptcy for the second time, when, once again, McConachie made another fortuitous contact. He was approached by Barney Phillips, a mining promoter.

This is where the romantic creeps in, with a story that is familiar to most bush pilots — one that was sometimes music to their ears because it meant a good deal of revenue flying — the story of a lost gold mine. A prospector had rediscovered the mine after a two-year search, then only just made it back to civilization to present his grubstakers with a map before he died. Barney Phillips had bought the map from them.

Phillips, a canny operator, knew that Independent Airways was in serious financial difficulty, and he had chosen McConachie to take him in to the site for the first time because McConachie would then be obliged to maintain the strictest secrecy about where they were going or lose the chance of a lifetime to revitalize his failing company. The only aircraft available was his Puss Moth and, with it, early in the spring of 1933, McConachie made several trips to move Barney Phillips and three miners into the lake — a remote one in British Columbia, not far from the headwaters of the Stikine River — with enough supplies to last them for a couple of months.

When McConachie returned to Edmonton, however, he found that the one remaining Independent Airways' Fokker had been seized by a sheriff on behalf of creditors. The sheriff promptly seized the Puss Moth as well.

Now McConachie was the only person who knew where the crew was; yet he had no means of getting back to resupply them. After many weeks of harrowing anxiety, at the end of July, when the supply trip was more than six weeks overdue, McConachie finally managed to persuade Ken Dewar, a Consolidated Mining & Smelting pilot, to fly in supplies. Barney Phillips and his three-man crew were rescued in the last stages of starvation.

Despite this discouraging start, Barney Phillips, who had proved enough gold at the site to warrant a mine, decided to stick with McConachie. He purchased two Fokkers to be operated by McConachie thus enabling McConachie to set up a new company, United Air Transport. (From there, McConachie went on to become, in 1947, the president of Canadian Pacific Airlines—one of the two dominant airlines in Canada.)

The mine to be installed and serviced by the two Fokkers — with the help, a little later, of a much bigger Ford Trimotor — was the Two Brothers Valley Mine, situated close to the lake of that name; but when I looked for it on my collection of old aviation maps, I couldn't find it. I did, though, find Chukachida Lake, and eventually I discovered that Two Brothers was now named Toodoggone Lake. The derelict mine site was the one I had sat in to enjoy my peaceful and solitary lunches. I'm not quite sure why, but I wish I'd known this at the time. I suppose it was because then it was just another old, abandoned mine site; yet if I had known how it came to be there, it would have come to life for me. So it was in many other places. Now, if only I could go and visit all of them again . . .

P. C-S, 1995

Foreword

READERS WHO ARE IN THE HELICOPTER BUSINESS, OR WHO have been, may cock a derisive eyebrow at the title of this book. I am aware that 10,000 hours of helicopter flying is no milestone; many have flown more. The truth is that I was unable to find a title for myself and I turned to my friends for help. They were kind enough to provide a number of suggestions (many of which, unfortunately, are unprintable), but the consensus among them was that *Chopper Jock* was a suitable title. I vetoed that. Another, I think more imaginative one they suggested was *Gay Blades in the North*. The publisher vetoed that. In the end, we settled on *10,000 Hours*. It is my hope that readers will not regard this as a boast but as a simple statement of fact that has the merit of being short enough to fit on the spine of a book. And, because I derived a great deal of enjoyment flying those hours, it is also my hope that the reader will share at least a measure of that enjoyment reading about them.

I must acknowledge in particular the help of three of those friends who offered suggestions for a title, Dave Parker, Bob Turner and Charles Lillard, for they did much more. They were generous with their criticism, careful to ensure that my vanity remained in check. They spent many hours helping me across patches of contorted prose or rescuing me from plunges into logical absurdity. My sons, Gerald and Graham, were similarly unstinting with their criticism and, because they were present during some of the events described, they have brought a sharper memory to bear on details. I must also pay tribute to my publisher. I have a little experience with publishers now; enough to know that Sono Nis has achieved a rare balance between stern professionalism and sensitivity to the writer's intentions. From the beginning it has been a joy to work with them.

Victoria, B.C., 1985

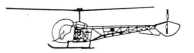

CHAPTER I

A Beginning of Sorts

EARLY ONE SATURDAY IN THE FALL OF 1954, I LEFT OTTAWA to drive the 10 or 12 miles to the airfield at Carp. I was feeling very much master of my fate. After some 18 months of frustration and discouragement, I was on my way to start my first bush flying job. I had lived a rather untidy life up to then, responding to whim and expedience rather than to well-planned objectives; yet I had achieved one abiding ambition. I had wanted to fly, to be a pilot. I don't know when the ambition was conceived, but I cannot remember not wanting to be a pilot.

In any event, the Second World War allowed me to become one in the R.A.F. Not only that, I also found myself performing one of the most interesting and exciting tasks available: special duties missions over German-occupied Europe. As captain of a crew of seven, I flew a four-engined Stirling in support of the European resistance forces. We parachuted supplies, and sometimes agents, into France, Belgium, Holland, Denmark, Norway — and even on two occasions into Germany.

Unlike the bombers, we did not operate in large groups. Instead, we worked individually on moonlit nights. We flew as low as visibility permitted, map-reading our way across Europe. The peak of concentration came when we approached our destination. Then we climbed to 400 feet and, from a feature on the ground chosen because it was easily recognized, we opened the bomb doors, lowered the flaps and flew a slow, steady course, worked out by the navigator, to the "Reception," where we hoped to find a prearranged pattern of lights, perhaps a T or an L, on the ground.

This was known as pucker time. We were exceedingly vulnerable. If a night fighter jumped us when our bomb doors were open and our flaps down, we'd stand little chance of getting away from him.

And there was always the possibility that the Gestapo had learned about the drop and prepared a "Reception" of their own. At the same time, it was vitally important to make the drop on the first run. If we had to circle even once, German troops in the vicinity would be alerted; they could move in, endangering the resistance people. This was always an anxious few minutes but, by the same token, the feeling of exhilaration after a successful drop was vivid.

The more so, perhaps, because there was sometimes a considerable pause between operations. For reasons of safety, we had to fly as low as we could. People on the ground had little time to aim weapons and shoot at us. Night fighters were reluctant to follow us down to the tree tops. And we had to be able to map read. Consequently, we could only operate in good weather and within three or four days on either side of a full moon. A tour of duty was 35 trips. It took me nearly 18 months to accomplish this.

Few sorties failed to provide some element of surprise to test our alleged skills as a highly trained, highly disciplined crew. On one trip to the east of Oslo, in Norway, we ran into cloud on the coast. After flying over it for awhile, breaks appeared and I dropped down. The bomb aimer, who did the map-reading as well as the dropping of the supplies, picked up a lake he recognized almost immediately. He was satisfied that we were only a few miles off track. If I altered course 10 degrees to port, we would very shortly pick up our recognizable run-up point to the "Reception." Ah, yes; there it was.

I swung onto the course the navigator gave me, opened the bomb doors and lowered the flaps. A minute or so later we spotted lights and I turned a few degrees to line up with them. After another 30 seconds I had to make a second correction, then a third. This time I muttered about navigators who couldn't plot a simple course from A to B. The navigator reacted testily: something about reproduction, illegitimacy and pilots who couldn't hold a course for two minutes without wandering all over the sky.

At about this time, other lights began to appear on the ground — quite a few of them. There was an animated burst of commentary from the whole crew. I had to shout for silence so that the bomb aimer, the navigator and I could discuss this phenomenon. Eventually, the truth dawned on us; we had crossed the border into Sweden; the lights of the "Reception" I had been trying to line up on were those of a moving train.

At this discovery the rest of the crew felt free to comment again. They waxed sarcastic. But it was the rear gunner who was most outspoken. He proposed that the bomb aimer should bail out while we were still over Sweden and allow himself to be interned for the duration. Then the rest of us could go back to base and find a replacement who could at least tell from the map what country we were flying over.

After this sort of excitement, the prospect of driving an airliner from one airport to another seemed so unappealing I accepted, soon after I was demobbed, the first job that seemed to promise a decent salary and some sense of adventure. I became in turn a mill shift-boss, a surveyor and Chief Sampler of a gold mine on the Gold Coast in West Africa. It was a fascinating experience, but the gold was fast running out in that particular mine and so were the days of the white man's privileged position. Kwame Nkrumah was leading the country to independence. I wasn't all that taken with being privileged, but I was even less enthusiastic about being under-privileged. It was time to move on. I went back to England to seek an alternative. Eventually, I found another mining job in the Copperbelt of Northern Rhodesia. During the several months it took me to land this job, I met Nina, who was to become my wife. Friends of mine had opened a private school for boys and she was the matron there. Matron, however, in this context is an unfortunate word; it has connotations of a motherly, middle-aged figure. Nina was neither; she was an extremely attractive young woman who had served as a nurse in the Far East during the war. We were engaged before I left and, a year after I had settled into my new job in the Copperbelt, and qualified for a bungalow, she sailed for Capetown and I made the long train journey south to meet and marry her. It was the one unquestionably sensible thing I ever did.

Unfortunately, though, after another three years of relative contentment, I discovered that I preferred working above the ground to working below it. I wanted to fly again, and now another ambition which had been lurking in my subconscious began to nudge at me. I had been to school at Dover College, one of the smaller English public schools that are in reality private schools, and there, on display in a glass case in the main hall, was a photograph of an "old boy," 17-year-old Edgar Christian, placed above a large diary he had kept during the last year of his life.

Edgar Christian's career was brief and tragic. It was also, to my adolescent perception, poignantly romantic. He had an elder cousin named Jack Hornby. Hornby, the younger son of a well-to-do English family, failed to pass the required examinations for entry into the diplomatic service in 1904. He took his disappointment to Canada, where he turned eventually into a drifter. Attaching himself to a fur-trading venture centred around the northeast corner of Great Bear Lake, he became eccentric and unpredictable, going off to travel with bands of Indians without bothering to notify his white companions. By the 1920's, however, he had gained a measure of fame — or notoriety, depending on who you spoke to — by making several trips into the far north, all of which had nearly ended in disaster.

Jack Hornby was apparently beguiled by the old cliché, the Challenge of the North. He possessed, in almost equal measure, remarkable stamina and astonishing luck. This led him to believe he was infallible. He took immense pride in his capacity to live off the land, no matter how remote and sterile that land was. As a consequence, he never troubled to outfit himself adequately to allow for emergencies. While many experienced northern travellers admired his stamina and his ability to withstand privation, they confidently predicted that his luck was due to run out.

This is precisely what happened. At the end of one of his curiously improvident odysseys, during which he and his companion, James Critchell-Bullock, had come within an ace of starving to death, Hornby learned that his father was dying and he returned to England in 1925 just in time for the funeral. He stayed with his mother for a few months before returning to Canada, and it was then that his young cousin Edgar Christian became enthralled by Hornby's descriptions of his adventures in the far north — so enthralled that he decided to leave school and return with Hornby in 1926.

They travelled by sea and rail to Edmonton with vaguely formulated plans to prospect for silver and trap for fur in the area Hornby had passed through on his last expedition, one of the remotest and most forbidding areas of what the early explorers called the Barren Ground, the Arctic tundra. They would have to travel up through the Athabaska country to Great Slave Lake, and then up into the Barrens to build a cabin on the Thelon River. Along the way, a number of the people who regarded Jack Hornby as something not far removed from a dangerous lunatic, tried to persuade Edgar to abandon the trip. It was all very well for Hornby to risk his own life on foolhardy expeditions, but it was quite another thing to take a totally inexperienced youngster with him. By now, however, it was too late to sway young Edgar. In his eyes, Hornby had become an object of hero worship, someone he trusted implicitly. To make matters worse, they picked up another disciple in Edmonton: 22-year-old Harold Adlard.

Edgar Christian's diary, which he put among the cold ashes of the stove after the last fire had gone out in the little cabin on the Thelon River, just before he died in June of 1927, provided a grim record of slow starvation and dwindling hope. They had arrived to build the cabin at a site Hornby had picked out on his previous trip — a little grove of spruce trees at the outer limits of the tree line — in October, a month too late for the annual caribou migration. Their only hope of survival in that country would have been to lay in a good supply of meat. They had missed that opportunity. They had gone in by canoe; thus, without dogs, there was no way out until late the following summer. Edgar was the last of the three to die and, to the very end, he maintained what were then considered the principal virtues of a British public schoolboy: courage and loyalty. Never once was there a hint of self-pity in his diary; never once did he condemn the man who had led him to a death by slow starvation just after his eighteenth birthday.

The diary had obviously made much more of an impression on me than I realized at the time. It had led me to read any number of books about Arctic exploration. This in turn had prompted me to read anything I could get hold of about the Canadian bush pilots. People like Punch Dickens, first man to fly across the Barren Ground. Or Wop May, who had flown the 600 miles from Edmonton to Fort Vermilion in an open-cockpit Avro Avion in the middle of winter to deliver serum that saved a community from a diphtheria epidemic. There were a score of others who were very much among my youthful heroes. But always there was a nagging curiosity. What compelling attraction did this country have? An attraction that drew men who had suffered appalling hardships and privations to return to it again and again. Now, under the sunny Rhodesian skies, or in the blackness of an underground stope, I wanted, not of course to follow too closely in young Edgar Christian's footsteps, but to see the Canadian Arctic for myself. What better way to do this than become a bush pilot?

At about this time, too, Nina was finding life in a mining community both restrictive and monotonous, so we packed our belongings and began the long journey to Capetown, to Southampton and, after a brief holiday in England, to Quebec City. There were, as I said, many months of disappointment and discouragement to come, but finally, even if it was only for three weeks, I was to get an opportunity to fly. It was a make or break sort of proposition, but I was still young enough to be full of confidence that morning in Carp.

The morning was one of those beautiful ones that come early in the fall, when the sun shines with a peculiar brilliance, the air is crisp, and the turning leaves reflect colours more spectacular than any I had seen in my previous travels. I felt an exhilaration I hadn't experienced since the early days of the war. For the past 18 months I had been working as a cartographer for a company called Canadian Aero Services. Now I was convinced that action and adventure lay ahead, and that the dreary days of crouching over a stereoscope, making maps instead of using them to fly, were behind me.

The manager of the company I was going to work for now had phoned me two days before to tell me he had a job for me. He was not there when I arrived at the airport, but he had left instructions for me to take the aircraft out for an hour and practise take-offs and landings. The temptation to leave the circuit and explore the surrounding countryside was hard to resist until I saw that the manager had now arrived. He was standing by his car outside the hangar, watching me. When I returned, he took me into his office and gave me a briefing. It was a most interesting introduction to the realities of commercial flying in Canada.

The gist of it was to make sure that I never underbooked for the flying time. Flying time started from the moment I pressed the starter button until I shut off the engine. If it took me some time to run up the engine and check the magnetoes before take-off, so much the better. Never hurry. If I had to make a landing anywhere but at the airport, fly over that area three or four times to make sure it was okay. I might know that it was after the first pass, but the customer wouldn't. However, it was the final piece of advice that startled me. The company did not carry insurance on the pilot — only on the passenger. So, if I had to make a crash landing, remember: always kick on left rudder and let the passenger go in first. He's insured; you're not. I've often wondered if I would have had either the presence of mind or the callousness to do this. Fortunately for my conscience, I never found out.

The question of remuneration was dealt with very quickly. He was really doing me a favour, letting me get some experience. So, to satisfy the regulations, I would get a nominal two dollars an hour and I would have to pay my own accommodation expenses. By now I had progressed to a salary of 95 cents an hour at Canadian Aero.

More than double that figure sounded very encouraging to me. I had visions of flying seven and eight hours a day. I was to learn otherwise; financially, that three weeks was a resounding flop.

I met the customer after lunch. He was a young French-Canadian, and my initial impression was that he looked decidedly shifty. Later I was to realize that he was merely a young man trying to make a living in a marginal field. He had an old 35-mm Leica camera with a telescopic lens. I had to fly low and slow over the farms while he photographed them. Then he would have the film processed, enlarge the photographs to something like 24 inches by 24, colour tint them by hand and sell them to the farmers. He carried a sample with him for sales purposes. No doubt it was his best work. Fuzzy and crudely tinted, to me it looked hideous; but apparently very few farmers could resist buying one. They would pay a $25 deposit on the strength of the sample, another $25 when they received the picture, framed and ready to hang. I suppose it gave them some sense of permanence and identity to see their farms from where God normally looked.

That afternoon we did a practice run on some of the farms around Carp. I thoroughly enjoyed puttering around the countryside on a calm, sunny afternoon, and the young man declared himself satisfied except for one thing: the speed of the aircraft. The Fleet Canuck cruised at about 80 miles an hour. The young man felt that this was uneconomically slow. When we returned to the hangar and he had gone, I mentioned this to my boss. He grunted sardonically, picked up a screwdriver and went out to the machine. "Just remember," he said two or three minutes later, "you'll stall at about 70 miles an hour now, instead of 55." He had simply re-calibrated the airspeed indicator.

I had the weekend to think about this, but it made no difference because I couldn't back out now.

CHAPTER 2

The First Customer

WE TOOK OFF FROM CARP ON THE MONDAY MORNING AND headed northwest along the railway line. The young man, let's call him Claude, had no specific plans about which area he would start in. He had discovered from experience that the more isolated the farm, the more likely he was to make a sale. He noticed the change in the airspeed right away. I told him the mechanics had done some work on the machine the previous day. He looked complacent; a businessman who knew that you had to keep a sharp eye on things. As we settled down to follow the C.N.R. tracks, I had a chance to take stock of him. He was slender and wiry, a dark-haired, sharp-featured youth. Yet he was more attractive than this sounds. He was an alert and lively character. Later, even when I was most dissatisfied with his behaviour, I felt a certain kinship with him. Whatever his faults, he was an enterprising and resourceful youngster.

We flew for nearly two hours before we came to an area Claude found suitable. The farms were well separated, but not so far apart that we'd have to spend a lot of flying time going from one to the other. I had made two passes over the farm he had indicated when he suddenly turned to ask me if we could land in a field about a quarter of a mile away from the farmhouse. I had not been expecting this, and my first instinct was to respond with a brisk refusal. But as I looked down at the field he had indicated, I reflected that I was now supposed to be a bush pilot. The ability to land in farmers' fields should obviously be part of my repertoire. At the same time, of course, I was frightened by the prospect. Even with the sharpest eyesight it is not always possible to spot from the air the soft, boggy places in a field which, if you run into them just after touching down, will inevitably tip you onto your nose, smash the propeller and perhaps wreak some structural damage as well. If I did that on my first landing, my bush flying career would end where it started.

In fact I was already experiencing the classic dilemma of bush flying. On the one hand I had to worry about satisfying the customer; on the other I had to consider the risk of an accident. The field he wanted me to land in was a narrow rectangle, sloping sharply downhill at one end. I made several low passes over it. The slope suggested that it should be well drained, and I couldn't see any rocks. What I disliked was the length of it; I didn't really know if I had enough room to take off again. But there was very little wind and in the end I decided that if I landed up the hill — then turned and took off down it. . . .

The landing worked well, but when I had taxied to the top end and turned to look down the field, it seemed frighteningly short. There was a narrow strip of trees at the end of it, with another partially cleared field beyond. Somehow I would have to get over the trees and poke the nose down again to pick up speed. Claude climbed the fence and I handed him the sample blow-up. He wouldn't be long, he assured me, and I was left to contemplate the spectre of a real humiliation. If I lost my nerve now and decided that I couldn't take off, I would have to phone Carp and tell them. In which case, presumably, another pilot would take the machine off and prove my incompetence; or the machine would have to be dismantled and towed to the nearest suitable field. To make matters worse, Claude was gone for more than an hour. When he came back, he was jubilant: he had made his first sale. He pulled the little roll of bills out of his pocket and waved them at me before he reached the fence. I like to think I managed a confident smile.

We cleared the trees with something to spare. It was a significant moment for me. My mouth was dry and my heart thumping uncomfortably, but my confidence in my own judgement was restored. On the ground during the last hour I had begun to wonder whether or not I really wanted to be a bush pilot after all. If you had to suffer this sort of anxiety about the take-off after every landing, life would be intolerable. Now I knew the answer. Either you said no to a landing, and to hell with what the customer thought, or you relaxed, knowing that your perspective from the air was much more reliable than the perspective from the ground. This knowledge was promptly reinforced when, after we had photographed the next farm, Claude asked me to land again. The only field large enough for a landing was covered with boulders. He looked down as we flew over the field, then suggested that if we zig-zagged a little after landing we could get through the rocks. I studied his face for a moment, wondering if he was trying to be humorous. Obviously he was not, and I burst out laughing. Claude began to pout.

But as we flew towards the next farm, some two or three miles away, I began to do some simple arithmetic and the results were discouraging. If we were going to land at virtually every farm, and spend an hour on the ground, my flying time on short autumn days was going to be negligible. I discovered afterwards that this was only Claude's third venture into this kind of aerial photography, and it had never occurred to him before to land at each farm and consummate the sale on the spot. Once he had conceived the idea, though, he was delighted with it and determined not to give it up. A stroke of luck intervened at the next farm and solved the problem for me.

This particular farm looked a good deal larger and more prosperous than the previous two we had photographed. Adjacent to it, its fence only about 200 yards from the farmhouse, was a field that was clearly suitable for landing. Still, however, I had some reservations. To get into it, I would have to drop down right over the farmhouse because there were tall trees at the other end of the field. Then, between the field and the farmhouse, there was a large shed with a pen beside it full of what I took to be chickens; and another long, low building whose function puzzled me. I suggested to Claude that we might frighten the chickens, but he dismissed this as a frivolous objection, and as we sank towards the landing I observed with some satisfaction the panic flight of the birds into the shed. As we taxied back to the fence, I saw a figure running from the farmhouse to the chicken shed.

Claude climbed confidently over the fence with his sample picture under his arm. The farmer met him about a hundred yards away and, as I leaned on the fence, smoking a cigarette, it became apparent to me that this was no ordinary sales talk they were engaged in. The farmer's gestures were peculiarly animated; Claude was stepping backwards throughout the initial conversation. Finally, he turned and walked briskly back to the fence, the farmer right behind him. When they got there, the farmer turned to address his remarks to me. I learned that the birds in the pen were not chickens after all, but turkeys; and that when turkeys become frightened they have a tendency to pile up one on top of the other, until the ones at the bottom of the pile suffocate — and now his fornicating turkeys were piled up six feet deep and only the son of our maker knew how many were dead. And did I know what was in the other building. I confessed I was intrigued. He choked for a moment. They were mink. And did I know what happened when mink got scared? They stopped doing that for which mink are celebrated. He would lose an entire generation of valuable little minks because of our stupidity. He was a very angry man. We left him lamenting that his sons were out hunting and thus he had no gun as his disposal. Claude did not ask me to land in farmers' fields again.

We photographed perhaps another dozen farms; then Claude suggested that we go and land at a small town some ten miles up the line. It was past lunch time by now and I agreed readily enough. According to the map, the town boasted an airstrip. I eventually decided that the scraps of cloth hanging on an old pole at one end of a deeply rutted field were the remnants of a windsock and reluctantly went in to land. To call it an airstrip was an exercise in imagination. It was much rougher than either of the fields we had just landed in. But the owner was there to greet us by the time we had shut down. He promptly informed me that there was a five-dollar landing fee; another five-dollar parking fee if we intended to stay overnight. I was tempted to argue on the grounds that his field was so rough it had done at least five dollar's worth of damage to my aircraft. But the alternative was to waste more time finding somewhere else to land, and then probably going through the same exercise. I was anxious to get back into the air again, so I paid him.

The next problem was transport. The strip was some three miles out of town. We asked if we could use his phone to call a taxi. There was only one cab, he informed us, and he knew for sure that Merv, the driver, was out on a hunting trip. However, he would take us into town and charge us the same fare as Merv would have. It was no surprise to discover that this, too, was five dollars: he worked in simple economic units. I had not thought to negotiate whose responsibility such incidental expenses would be before I left base and as we drove into town in a dirty old pickup truck, which smelled strongly of dogs and cow manure, I made up my mind to phone in that night and do so. When we arrived at the one and only cafe in town, Claude made it clear that he didn't consider it his responsibility; he was out of the truck and into the cafe before I had time to blink.

During lunch, Claude advised me that we wouldn't be flying any more that day. He would have to hire a car from someone and visit the farms we had photographed. He instructed me to book rooms for us at the hotel; then I could go back to the aircraft and fetch our bags. He was obviously enjoying his position as the paying customer who called the shots. I had no intention of parting with another five dollars just to pick up our bags and I told him he could use his rented car to pick them up. He agreed rather sulkily, and left to look for his car. It wasn't until some ten minutes later, as I sat wondering what to do with myself for the rest of the day, that I realized he had left me to pay for his lunch.

The small railway towns of northern Ontario are not geared for the entertainment of visitors. I do not remember the name of this particular town, but it had a single main street: a strip of badly maintained tarmac which extended perhaps half a mile on either side of town, and then degenerated into a rough gravel road. There was a gas station, a general store, a drug store, a cafe, a bank, a hotel and an exceedingly dilapidated cinema. The bank was the only building which looked as though it had had a coat of paint in the last 20 years. I walked across the road to the hotel to book our rooms. The woman who eventually appeared behind the reception desk after I had rung the bell three or four times seemed surprised by my request. But she agreed to get two rooms ready for us.

Outside on the sidewalk I toyed with the idea of going back to the cafe for another coffee, then decided that the best way to pass the afternoon was to walk back to the machine and do some maintenance. I could pull panels and look at things . . . polish the windshield, I thought vaguely. The walk made me feel better, but I was only about halfway to the airstrip when a truck stopped to offer me a lift. It seemed churlish to refuse, so I climbed in. The driver was a cheerful-looking character of middle years with a craggy, weather-beaten face. I explained my situation to him briefly and he burst out laughing. "How much did old Gus charge you to land in that goddam cabbage patch of his?"

"Five bucks."

"He's getting a little smarter. Used to be ten." He went on to explain to me that Gus had spent years persuading the Department of Transport to declare his field a landing strip; then he had begun to gouge everyone who came to it, until now no one ever landed there.

"But where can I leave the machine, then?"

"No problem. I'll show you."

When we reached the airstrip, he parked the truck and began to walk towards the aircraft. I realized that he was literally going to show me. "What about the truck?" I asked.

"Oh, I'll get someone to run me back."

When I had taken off, he told me to fly back to the town. As we approached it, he pointed out a clearing next to the gas station, which was the first building on the main drag, right in town. "You can park her in there," he said.

I must have looked startled. "Don't worry," he said. "You see those red drums over on the left — that's avgas. Two or three pilots come in here regularly to gas up."

I looked down in growing confusion. What he said was obviously true. But there was no way in the world one could land an aircraft in that little clearing. "Yeah," I said vaguely, "but where do you land?"

It was his turn to look puzzled. "Land? On the road, of course."

"Isn't that illegal?"

He looked at me for a moment. I suppose he must have thought I was being facetious. "Could be," he said, "but it don't bother no one around here. Just make sure there's no traffic."

Once you got the idea, of course, it was an excellent one. The tarmac stretched for about half-a-mile beyond the gas station. There were no buildings along it and the hydro and telephone wires were far enough back not to be troublesome. As I turned off the road into the clearing, two or three children paused to watch, but nobody else took any notice. We were now parked some 200 yards from the hotel.

My companion, whose name was Arnie I learned from the shouted greeting of the man in the gas station, looked at his watch. "Come on," he said, "I'll buy you a cup of coffee. You obviously need some advice."

It was good advice that Arnie gave me during the next hour. He had been a mechanic in the Air Force during the war. Afterwards, he had gone into commercial aviation for a couple of years. But he found he was spending more time away from home than he was willing to and he had given it up. Now he farmed in a small way and took the odd jobs that always seemed to be available. He drove a snowplough for the highways people in the winter, fought fires with the forestry people in the summer. He would never accept a job that kept him away from home for more than two weeks at a time. He didn't earn much money, but then he didn't really need much. He had a few cows, a couple of pigs, some chickens. His wife tended a large vegetable garden. Arnie would get a moose and at least a couple of deer every fall; he'd butcher a steer in the summer. All they had to buy, really, were things like clothes and booze, gas, coffee and sugar — a few things like that.

But as far as I was concerned, I was going to discover that bush flying wasn't all it was cracked up to be — especially if I got into helicopters (I had told him of this ambition while we were driving out to the airstrip in his pickup). Helicopters were too expensive to operate anywhere where there were roads; so I would really be out in the bush. I told him that was just what I wanted; I wanted to see places few people had ever seen before. He grunted cynically. "Well, you'll see 'em all right — an' when you seen one, you seen 'em all. Right now, though, you're going to find out that everyone in these small towns thinks flyers get big money. They'll jack up the price on everything as soon as they know who you are. You staying at the hotel?"

"Yes."

"How much they charging you?"

"I don't know. I didn't ask."

Arnie grunted again. "It's $3.50 for a room. Don't give 'em any more."

"What happens if they insist?"

"Threaten to call the police. They've been keeping the beer parlour open late every night. They don't want any hassle."

In fact, I paid $5.00 for the room. I didn't have the courage to argue. But Arnie was perfectly right. People cling to the fiction that pilots get paid high salaries. While this may be true in the airlines, it certainly was not in bush flying. I have been on numerous jobs where the cook in a bush camp was earning more money than I was. And though at first I found the dickering you had to do in small towns distasteful, I soon began to appreciate the necessity for it.

But where Arnie was most helpful was in telling me what to do about parking the aircraft at night. Don't go out to the airstrip or airport and run up landing fees and parking fees and cab fares, he advised. Just find the closest field to town that I could land in. Then, if the farmer tried to give me a hard time, offer him a ride. Everyone wanted to take a look at his spread from the air. A quick, five-minute ride and they'd let me park for days if I wanted to.

"What about the machine — isn't it safer to leave it at an airport?"

"No, I don't think so. I never heard of anyone stealing anything or messing with an airplane."

Once again, Arnie was right. I followed his advice on several occasions and at least twice got a free supper as well as free parking. And as far as security was concerned, those were law-abiding days. Except in Quebec, I wasn't to feel any anxiety about leaving an aircraft unattended by the roadside for many years to come.

I would like to have spent more time with him, but Arnie had to leave. He was going to drive a Cat — do some clearing on a construction site for a few days. He borrowed a car from the gas station and I drove him back out to the airstrip to pick up his truck. I offered to try and get him a discount on a photograph of his farm. He laughed. "It's just a shack. I don't need no goddam picture of it. If you're still around when I get back, I'll take you out there — have a few beers; have dinner with us." I wish I could have taken him up on the offer. He was a nice guy. Unfortunately, we had moved on before then and I never saw him again.

When I got back to town I dug out some rags and spent an hour polishing and cleaning. By now it was almost a reasonable time for an evening meal, so I took my bag out of the machine and walked across to the hotel. I was given a key, and the room I entered with it came as an unpleasant shock. It was sparsely furnished with a narrow bed, a hard chair and a dresser with an empty frame where the mirror had once been. Everything was dark brown — the walls, the furniture, the linoleum on the floor were all the same colour. The edge of the dresser and the windowsill were scarred with innumerable cigarette burns. There was a tiny sink attached to one wall, and the holes in the plaster above it suggested that it had once boasted a medicine cabinet. But it was the smell that dismayed me. I tried to open the window but found that the sash was hopelessly jammed. I looked at the bed. The sheets at least seemed clean but I didn't have the fortitude to turn them back and examine the mattress underneath.

In fact, this was the forerunner to a number of such rooms I had to sleep in during the next year or two. Hotel keepers relied on beer parlour sales for their livelihood; they provided rooms only because it was a legal requirement. I understood then why the woman behind the reception desk had looked surprised when I asked for one. Normally, they were used only for assignations, or by people who had come back from a spell in the bush and promptly got so drunk they couldn't get home. These people would then work out the frustrations of their weeks in the bush by smashing everything in the room that was breakable. And they defaced it in other ways, too. I experienced the ultimate in this context about a year later, when I was working for the Department of Lands and Forests in northern Ontario. As I went into the room they gave me I saw what were, unmistakably, smears of excrement on the walls. This was too much, and I marched back down the stairs to complain. The man behind the desk uttered an exclamation and turned to the key rack. "Hey, Elly," he shouted through the open door beside it, "you forgot to wash the shit off the wall in 12." He turned and handed me another key. "Here, try this one," he said cheerfully.

So in the circumstances, you couldn't really blame the hotel keepers for either the austerity of the furnishings or the smell. But I was very green; I didn't know any of this yet, and I was appalled by the squalor. At the same time, I suspected that this was the sort of thing the management of Spartan (the company with the helicopters I wanted to fly) had in mind when they hinted that I might be too fastidious for bush flying. I concluded reluctantly that I was going to have to put up with it — and do so without complaint. I rinsed my hands in the minuscule washbasin and went down to have supper. On my way through the lobby I saw Claude.

He emerged from the beer parlour to go to the washroom, which was off the lobby. He was in high spirits, and from the look of him I judged that he had been in the beer parlour for some time.

"How'd it go?" I asked.

He looked blank. "Sales," I said. "How many photographs did you manage to sell?"

"Oh, I did not get a h'automobile today. I will go tomorrow."

"So we won't be doing any flying tomorrow?"

"In the h'afternoon. I will go in the morning — very h'early."

My face obviously reflected my dissatisfaction and Claude assured me that he would be more organized in future. We would do lots of flying. He insisted that I go and have a drink with him. I shrugged and followed him back into the beer parlour. We sat at a table by ourselves. A group of people at a table across the room shouted at Claude to come and pay for the round of beer he had ordered. Claude shouted back that he had to talk business with me and held up four fingers to the beer slinger. Before the beer arrived, he suddenly jumped to his feet and reminded me that he had been on his way to the can when we met. He had to go now. He did, and I was left to pay for the beer.

I gave Claude a lecture on the economics of flying when he returned. He couldn't expect me to do a couple of hours flying, then sit around for two days on the ground. No company could make money like that. The obvious way to work, I told him, was to do all the flying while the weather was good; then I could take the machine and go to another job while he rented a car and did his selling. Claude disagreed. One needed to get the feel of an area, he said. Sometimes people just didn't seem interested and you had to move on. This sounded vaguely plausible and we reached a compromise. We would alternate: fly hard one day; sell hard the next. I had a suspicion, which was soon confirmed, that Claude had no intention of honouring this commitment; but at the time, he unhesitatingly agreed.

During the next three weeks I discovered that Claude fell into the twilight zone which exists between a salesman and a con man. To begin with, there had been several aspects of his operation which puzzled me. He came from Montreal. He had chosen the agricultural country of the Gaspé peninsula for his first venture into this kind of aerial photography early the previous summer. Then he had gone well north of Montreal. Now he was in northern Ontario. Why move so far each time, I wondered. Claude's reply that he liked to get around and see the country was unconvincing. I soon came to the conclusion that the $25 deposit he collected was the only money to change hands; and that most of the photographs, when they arrived, were so bad that the farmers would have dealt harshly with him if they could have got their hands on him.

For the moment, though, he was having a wonderful time. He clearly relished the sense of prestige it gave him to have an aircraft and a pilot at his command. I heard him many times, when he was talking to people, refer to me as "my pilot." And I am sure it enhanced his feeling of superiority to have me so visibly hanging around all day waiting for him. But his greatest pleasure, after he had collected half-a-dozen of the $25 deposits, was to go into the beer parlours in the little towns we visited and sit with the locals, boasting of his previous exploits. He sought to convey the impression that he was a man of parts; a resourceful entrepreneur who had done many highly profitable things in the past. I knew from the differing versions I heard that most of this was fantasy. He told so many lies that the distinction between illusion and reality had long since become hopelessly blurred for him. He was a sort of bush league Duddy Kravitz, without Duddy's hard core of ambition.

I found all this very irritating, but there was nothing I could do about it. On several occasions, when he returned after leaving me to wait around for two full days at a stretch, I had threatened to pull out and go back to Carp. But I knew, and somehow he must have sensed, that I couldn't. If I left before my three weeks had expired I would inevitably have been labelled a quitter. So I endured some of the longest days of my life, lying on my bed in foul-smelling hotel rooms reading paperbacks, or polishing up the machine. I borrowed buckets of water and penetrated places which had never been disturbed before. I bought paint bombs and did a touch-up job. I bought a can of wax and waxed the entire aircraft. And all the time, of course, I wondered whether I really did want to be a bush pilot after all.

But it wasn't all wasted time. I learned some things that were very useful; others that were interesting. I learned how to deal with Claude's illusion — one held, I came to realize later, by nearly all customers — that pilots are very highly paid, and thus should not mind bearing the cost of any meals or drinks they shared with one. In a cafe or restaurant, I would promptly ask for separate bills; in a beer parlour, I would promptly put my money on the table and ask to see theirs. But these were small things and, much more importantly, I learned something about how people lived in rural communities. The dominant feature was the modern equivalent of horse trading. If one farmer brought his binder and helped another with his haying, the other would have to help the owner of the binder to put a roof on a new barn. But such transactions were always preceded by elaborate and lengthy bargaining sessions to make sure that the balance of effort and expense was equitable. A man's stature in the community depended on his ability to drive a hard bargain without being guilty of sharp practice. Thus if I, as a stranger, went into one of these communities and didn't do the same thing, I would be regarded as a fool and exploited. I learned very quickly that when I asked the price of anything, the quote I got was merely the opening gambit of a negotiation; and that the process of a negotiation was often more satisfying than the closing of a deal.

Yet, even more dominant in their lives was the obsession with hunting. Practically everyone I spoke to had either just returned from a hunting trip, or he was just about to embark on one. Although hunting no longer posed any risks (except for the danger of hunters shooting one another), it was still necessary for a man to demonstrate his virility by hunting. And this led to interesting social ramifications. On several occasions people suggested to me with a leer that I should land at so-and-so's farm and offer his wife a ride. So-and-so woudn't be back from his hunting trip for three or four days yet and I might get a ride in return. I smiled and talked of not wanting to become the hunted. But in fact it was common knowledge that this was the time of the year when unscrupulous people who coveted their neighbour's wives seized the opportunity to attempt a consummation. A week before we arrived in one of those towns a husband had returned unexpectedly from a hunting trip, perhaps with some premonition or perhaps because for once he had not been the last to hear. He caught his wife and her lover in the act, and in the true spirit of frontier justice shot both of them.

But my abiding memory of that trip was of crushing boredom, and when at last the fourth Monday rolled around, and I was free to go, I felt as somebody must when he has been released from prison. Claude had been missing all the previous day; there was no sign of him that morning. He had hinted that he would like me to stay at least another week. When I couldn't find him, I loaded my bag into the aircraft and took off with a good deal of satisfaction. I headed southeast down the railway line, running into increasingly severe snow flurries. I felt absurdly elated, and it seemed romantically fitting to me that I should be going home like the wild geese as the first snows began to fly.

CHAPTER 3

The Weaning of an Immigrant

MY ATTEMPTS TO GET BACK INTO FLYING HAD STARTED WHEN my wife Nina and I disembarked in Quebec City, on a spring morning in 1953, from the liner which had brought us across the Atlantic. We both felt the same odd mixture of optimism and anxiety. There was customs to go through. Nina had china packed in straw. We had learned on board that it was a serious offence to import straw into Canada; the penalty could be imprisonment. We had been told before we left England that rents were astronomical in Canada, so we had brought our own accommodation with us — a house trailer. If they wanted to tax that we were sunk because currency regulations had only allowed us to bring $400 in cash with us.

As it turned out, the customs man did want to charge us; he wanted $800 in import tax on the trailer. It took us all day to convince him that we didn't have that amount. Finally, as five o'clock, the hour every civil servant respects, approached, he let us go. He had concentrated so hard on the trailer, he forgot to look at any of our other possessions. The crisis of the illegal straw passed into limbo, and we set off with a surge of optimism. But the day wasn't over yet.

While at the dock, waiting to disembark, I had studied the road which slashed diagonally up across the Heights of Abraham with some anxiety. It looked very steep; I was worried about our car's ability to tow the trailer up it. Several people assured me that the grade was less severe than it looked. The alternative was some ten miles of driving, right through the heart of the city. I decided to give it a try.

Wolfe's troops made a better job of scaling the Heights of Abraham than we did. I believe the hill is about half a mile long, and approximately halfway up it all progress ceased. Nowadays, of course, when most people have some experience of trailer towing, it probably wouldn't seem much of a problem to back a heavily loaded trailer a quarter of a mile down a steep hill. In my case it was. I had only backed the trailer once or twice, but that was enough to convince me that it was an acquired rather than an inherent skill. I had discovered that it was very easy to turn the steering wheel in the wrong direction; whereupon, the trailer would abruptly skew away to one side or the other, and the only thing to do then, unless you were manoeuvring on a football field, was to pull ahead, straighten out and start again. The knowledge that I couldn't do this now, that I'd have to get it right the first time, made me nervous. There was also the question of brakes. I wasn't sure they would hold, and I had visions of losing control — of disappearing backwards over the edge of the road and hurtling to destruction down the cliff.

Fortunately, this vision was followed very quickly by an even more disturbing one: a vision of the customs man laughing when he heard about it. I pulled myself together and gave Nina crisp instructions to go and warn the traffic backed up for some distance behind us that I was coming down. I suggested that *sauve qui peut* was probably the most appropriate phrase. In moments of crisis my wife sometimes listens to me and she was just about to do this when a police car came down the hill. It pulled over and parked in front of us, its flashing red beacon adding to the sense of impending disaster. The policeman who climbed out of it wore the patient expression of a man who is accustomed to dealing with stupidity on a daily basis. I explained my problem to him. He turned to look at the traffic behind us and suggested I give it one more try.

Knowing better than to argue with a police officer, I started the engine and let out the clutch. The wheels spun and we didn't move. The policeman watched the little wisps of smoke from the tires dissipating for a moment, then he turned to gaze thoughtfully out over the St. Lawrence. Eventually, he turned back to me. "Do that again," he said.

"What?"

"Your front wheels were spinning."

"Yes, I know. This is a Citröen. It's got front-wheel drive."

"Son of a bitch!"

But he got me down the hill all right, walking behind me and moving the traffic out of the way as I descended. When we reached the bottom, I leaned out of the window to thank him. He was standing looking at the front wheels with a curious expression on his face. The concept of front-wheel drive seemed to have unsettled him. "Where are you headed?" he asked. He looked relieved when I told him Ottawa.

Happily things smoothed out for us after that. We were going to Ottawa because an old friend of mine had been there for the past two years, working for the National Research Council, and I was hoping for advice and job contacts. As it turned out, I didn't need any help from my friend when we got to Ottawa. Those were boom times, and I was able to find a job within a week of our arrival. I went to whatever the Manpower Office was called then and, because I had some experience as a mining surveyor, I was hired by the first company they sent me to: a firm which made maps from aerial photography. The starting salary was 75 cents an hour, but it was a job and at least I had the security of a regular pay cheque.

The next step, though, getting back into flying, proved much harder than I had anticipated. The company I had just joined seemed an ideal stepping stone. Canadian Aero Services was the subsidiary of a large American aerial survey company in Philadelphia, and it was affiliated with Spartan Air Services in Ottawa. Spartan had been founded by two ex-R.C.A.F. pilots with a war-surplus Avro Anson, a twin-engined reconnaissance aircraft. They did the actual flying and photography; the company I worked for translated the photography into maps. In 1953 both companies were expanding rapidly. By then Spartan had a fleet of several Ansons, Beechcraft and de Havilland Mosquitoes. I was confident that within a few months I would be able to transfer to them at least as a co-pilot and move back into flying.

Unfortunately, it took much longer than that, for there is an intriguing Catch-22 in Canadian aviation. It involves the mystique of bush flying experience. In order to get a flying job, one must have bush experience. In order to gain bush experience, one must have a flying job. It was a neat and apparently unbreakable circle, and I was trapped in it for a long time.

Then, too, the work I was doing during that first year in Ottawa was dreadfully tedious. The initial step in the process of making maps from aerial photography consists of picking three points on the perimeter of the photograph, pricking them with a stylus, and then transferring these pricked points to the next overlapping photograph under a stereoscope.

For me, the job was not only tedious but frustrating as well. Because all the long hours I spent crouching over a stereoscope showed me, in three dimensions, the country I wanted to fly over: the mountains and forests, the creeks, rivers and lakes that seemed somehow more romantic and exciting than any I had yet seen. By now I had taken to visiting the Spartan hangar every Saturday morning, and I would look with bitter envy at the pilots in the crew room who seemed to accept their good fortune with so little appreciation.

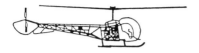

CHAPTER 4

Spartan Air Services

SPARTAN AIR SERVICES OPERATED OUT OF ONE OF THE OLD R.C.A.F. hangars at Uplands Airport. I spent a good deal of time in it during the summer of 1953, convinced that before long there would be some sort of an emergency: a pilot would be needed in a hurry and I, because I was there and fresh in people's minds, would be the one to be called. I tried not to notice that the Chief Pilot, whose name was Taylor, I think, had begun to avoid me whenever I appeared. He had been encouraging when I first saw him. I had flown Stirlings, Lancasters and Yorks during the war and he agreed that this was good flying time to have in my logbook. He took me for a check ride in an Anson and commented favourably on my ability. But there was the seven-year gap with no flying at all, he reminded me — and, of course, I had no bush experience.

So time wore on. Nothing happened, and I grew alarmed. I knew that the bush experience, or lack of it, was merely an excuse: they could easily have hired me as a co-pilot so that I could get the experience while someone else was making the decisions, and it wasn't until some months later that I learned what the real problem was.

Several months before I had begun my siege of the company, they had hired an ex-R.A.F. pilot. He had flown out from England to see them. He was a Group Captain, taking early retirement from the Air Force, and he had heard that they were a company with an exciting future. He could offer them not only his flying experience but a good deal of administrative experience at a senior level as well. He spoke the jargon of flying; he impressed everyone as a very competent individual. They hired him, congratulating themselves on finding somebody whose organizational skills were so badly needed in an expanding company. He went back to England to fetch his family and settled them into the Chateau Laurier, where they stayed for several weeks while he looked for a suitable house for them to live in.

During all this time he had never actually been in an aircraft and flown. He seemed to assume that he was going to be given an administrative, if not indeed an executive, position. After more than a month had elapsed, management grew uneasy. He was evasive whenever they tried to get him into the air. Finally, they insisted on a check ride before sending him off on a job as a co-pilot so that he could familiarize himself with the Canadian aviation scene.

Evidently it was a memorable experience. The Chief Pilot claimed afterwards that it took at least ten years off his life. He had started the engines and then told the Group Captain to carry on. The Group Captain had opened the throttles wide, executed a sharp and involuntary right turn and headed straight for a Mosquito parked on the edge of the tarmac outside the hangar. Somehow the Chief Pilot had managed to get the throttles closed and the brakes on in time to avoid a collision.

"Sorry, old boy," the Group Captain remarked imperturbably; "a little rusty, what?"

I have no record of the Chief Pilot's response.

They tried once more. This time the Chief Pilot took the Anson out onto the runway before handing over. But the same thing happened again. The Group Captain made no allowance for torque. He opened the throttles wide, the Anson swung sharply to the right, the Chief Pilot tried to take over the controls but the Group Captain, no doubt realizing by now that his future career was at stake, hung on grimly and refused to let go. Somehow they became airborne, more or less at right angles to the runway, and hurtled by the control tower some 50 feet from the noses of the startled controllers.

I never did discover what happened after that. The Chief Pilot always became incoherent.

Belatedly, the company made some enquiries from the British Air Ministry. They discovered that the Group Captain had in fact been a Flight Lieutenant and an administrative officer. He had never flown an aircraft in his life. And it was only after they had fired him and he had vanished that they received a bill for some $800 from the Chateau Laurier. He had provided for his family, and provided handsomely, at the company's expense.

It seemed unfair to me when I heard about this episode that I should have to suffer for it. But in retrospect, it was very understandable. They'd always had reservations about an Englishman's ability to withstand the rigours of Canadian bush flying. And in any case, they were busy people who had been made to look foolish and they weren't going to take any more risks with ex-R.A.F. officers.

By the fall, another complication began to emerge. I had been working very hard at Canadian Aero on the theory that this would demonstrate to Spartan my desirability as an employee. Instead I succeeded in impressing only Canadian Aero who, I learned, were now reluctant to see me transferred to Spartan. I was in the position of a husband whose only recourse to escape the drudgery of washing up every night was to start consistently breaking dishes. It was all very frustrating and I had just about decided I had better look elsewhere for a job when something new appeared in the hangar; something which made me once again determined I was going to work for Spartan. They had decided to add helicopters to their fleet.

Nearly all map making from aerial photography required a measure of ground control; that is to say, a reasonable number of benchmarks, or "fixes," had to be established by conventional ground survey methods, and these "fixes" would be marked with large strips of white cloth so that they could be seen on the photographs and used to orient the map in its correct geographical position. Establishing this ground control in remote areas was by far the most time-consuming and expensive aspect of photogrammetry. Survey crews had to camp on lakes so that they could be supplied by floatplane. This meant, in many cases, long, difficult miles of walking through the bush in the morning to reach the beginning of a traverse; and even more miles back to the camp in the evening. The use of helicopters to put crews out and bring them back to camp at the end of the day could result in an almost exponential reduction in the time required to complete a survey. Thus, in 1951, Spartan went into the helicopter business.

I do not know the details of those first two years of operation, but I do know they experienced the sorts of problems that are bound to occur in any new branch of technology. There were two makes of light commercial helicopters available at the time: the Bell and the Hiller. Spartan had both and both had teething troubles to begin with. But when I first saw the helicopters that fall, returning from their summer's operations, the experience accumulated over the past two years was beginning to amount to something. It had been a promising if not yet very profitable season. Spartan planned to buy another four machines the following spring, which would bring their fleet of helicopters up to twelve.

I conceived an instant and burning ambition to become a helicopter pilot. It was a new and exciting development. I could get in more or less on the ground floor and, like most people at the time, I thoroughly overestimated the future potential of the helicopter. I foresaw dazzling opportunities for advancement. The trouble was, of course, that for me now the equation was even more unbalanced: not only did I have no bush experience, but I couldn't fly a helicopter either; and helicopter training was very expensive. I soon came to the conclusion that I was going to have to cut adrift from the security of Canadian Aero Services and find some sort of flying job, so that I would at least have the bush experience.

The job I found — the one I have already described — was a humble one, but it was a beginning and I was in no position to complain at the time. There is a system of sorts for people who want to get into bush flying. It begins at a flying club at a small airport where the would-be pilot gets any job that is available — perhaps driving a gas truck — and lives on hamburgers and hot dogs so that he can afford to pay for his tuition. This phase usually lasts about eighteen months and, if the aspirant can stick it out, it helps to prove that he is really serious about getting into aviation. I was fortunate in this respect: I already had my commercial licence — I had only to write an examination on Canadian air regulations to get it. So it was the next stage I was concerned with, and this is the big one: getting the first flying job. There is usually a small operator with one or two aircraft who will employ you if you can stand another year of penury while you acquire the magical bush experience. Such operators make their living by accepting all the odd charter flights the larger companies do not want; the sort of trips that yield, perhaps, two hours of flying time but require another ten hours of waiting time on the ground.

An operator in this category does not believe in spending too much money on maintenance; nor does he feel too severely bound by the regulations which govern commercial aviation. He considers hiring inexperienced pilots a high-risk venture; consequently he pays only for flying time, and then at a rate no truck driver would ever accept. In addition, when the pilot is not away on a flying job, he is expected to help around the hangar; to sweep the floor or work on the gunk tank — a tank full of noisome solvent in which engine parts are cleaned during an overhaul. It is more tedious and depressing than most apprenticeships, but if you want to fly, that is the initiation fee you must pay. I was willing to pay it if necessary.

I have already told you how the operator I went to see at Carp dealt with the problems of a slow-flying aircraft. When I first met him, he struck me as brisk and impersonal. He talked to me for a few minutes, then took me for a check ride in a small single-engined two-seater called a Canuck. I had not flown a light aircraft for more than ten years, but flying is rather like riding a bicycle: you may wobble a bit if you haven't done it for a long time, but it stays with you. He seemed satisfied. He told me he had nothing at the moment, but if anything came up he would get in touch with me. It sounded like a typical "don't phone me" response and I went home thoroughly discouraged. A week later he phoned to say he had a three-week job for me in northern Ontario.

My superiors at Canadian Aero were unenthusiastic about this development, but they agreed to let me take three weeks off without pay so that it was not yet necessary for me to burn my bridge.

The rest you already know.

CHAPTER 5

New Dimensions

I VISITED THE SPARTAN HANGAR THE WEEKEND AFTER MY return from the northern Ontario job. There was a perceptible difference in the attitude of the people I talked to. Without knowing the details, they seemed to appreciate that I had been out on a crummy job and that I had not caused my brief employer any anxiety. The long, tedious hours of polishing and waxing had paid off, too. They knew about it and were impressed. The manager of the helicopter division spoke of working out something for me. We could talk about it after Christmas. He emphasized the last two words, and I decided it would be unwise to bother him again before the new year.

In the meantime, I was learning what it was to become a Canadian. Our car, a French Citröen, had disturbed the policeman in Quebec City; now it was provoking the Ottawa police, and I must confess I found this entertaining. Everything about it seemed to irritate them. For one thing, instead of flashing lights, our car had a system of turn indicators which depended on little glowing red arms that emerged from the pillars between the doors. The switch had a clockwork motor — rather like those timing devices on a camera which allow you to take a photograph of yourself — so that it cancelled itself after about 20 seconds.

One day I came to an intersection where the traffic lights had failed. A policeman was directing traffic. I signalled for a right turn. He waved me on, but when I began to turn he became incensed and ran in front of me. It was a near thing. I had not been expecting this and I only just managed to stop before knocking him down. To exacerbate the situation, he came to the wrong window. I had right-hand drive — and it seemed to make him more angry that he had to walk round to the other side of the car. He muttered something about dangerous Limey cars. I pointed out, very respectfully, that it wasn't a Limey car — it was a Frog car.

"Anyways," he snarled, "why the hell didn't you signal you were going to turn right?"

I protested that I had (by now, of course, the indicator had cancelled itself). "Yeah, well your indicator ain't working. Put it on," he commanded, beginning to turn towards the front of the car.

"No, no, it's here," I said, pointing over my shoulder. I switched it on just as he turned to look. The indicator snapped up, perhaps three-quarters of an inch from his nose. It startled him so much I'd swear his feet came off the ground.

A similar incident occurred when I was driving downtown with my wife one night. The bulb in one of our headlights had burned out, and a police car standing by the curb took off after us. He activated both his cherry and his siren, which I thought rather excessive in the circumstances — but at that time I didn't know that rabbiting was a favourite pastime with teen-agers when the police tried to stop them. In any event, I pulled over and the policeman went, once again, to the wrong window. My wife rolled it down to tell him this, but before she could speak he launched into a long lecture on the dangers of driving with one headlight. He must have been bored that night, because he spent a lot of time on that lecture. Nina tried to interrupt him several times, but he merely raised his voice and continued. He was surprised that anyone could be so unobservant as not to notice that one headlight had gone out. On the other hand, he conceded, it was a well-known fact that women were less alert and competent as drivers than men. By this time I was having some difficulty keeping my composure. I had to simulate a sneezing fit to conceal my laughter. All at once his voice faltered, and he came to a stop. "Jesus Christ," he said, after an appreciable silence, "there's no goddam steering wheel."

Nina congratulated him on his eyesight and suggested tartly that it would be more profitable for him to walk around to the other side of the car and discuss the headlight problem with the driver — who, on purely technical grounds, might be described as a man.

Instead, he turned, walked back to the police car, climbed in and drove away without another word.

Another novel experience for me was my initiation into Canadian drinking habits. On most Friday evenings after work, a group of the employees at Canadian Aero Services visited one of the two dozen or so drinking establishments in Ottawa. Few of the new immigrants did this, sometimes because they couldn't afford to, but usually because they didn't want to; they found both the Friday night crowds and the environment uncongenial after the pubs, bistros and beer gardens of their homelands. Thus it was usually the Canadian-born and veteran employees who patronized this particular lounge, and over the years of faithful attendance they had struck up a friendship with the proprietor and earned certain privileges — not the least of which was the guarantee of somewhere to sit when they got there. A corner of the huge pink and mauve cocktail lounge they favoured would be roped off and kept closed until they arrived.

I joined them occasionally because they were a pleasant bunch, cheerful and tolerant. I learned from them that Englishmen were called kippers; that nearly all Brits were effete and thus found great difficulty fitting into the rugged and virile Canadian scene; and I learned that the Brits had no sense of humour — there were a host of jokes in which the point was that the Brit didn't understand the punchline.

The hotel we frequented was a three-storey building. The whole of the ground floor was given over, without any partitions, to the beer parlour. The cocktail lounge on the second floor did have occasional chest-high, pink and mauve partitions which, though they were hideously ugly, offered some acoustical avantages. Unlike the beer parlour, it was possible in the cocktail lounge to carry on a conversation with the person next to you without having to lean over and bellow into his or her ear. The third floor provided rooms which were used a good deal but seldom, I gathered, by travellers.

So it was not an entirely disagreeable atmosphere, if you could forget for the moment that a bottle of beer cost very nearly an hour's wages. The form was for each of us to put two dollars on the table. The waitress would then fill the table with bottles of beer, and I would settle back to listen to the unfamiliar jargon of hockey and baseball and a game called Canadian football which, apparently, was played almost exclusively by Americans. It was a very masculine ritual. Often we would be joined by two or three of the local hookers, who stopped off for a sociable drink before starting work. The proprietor would pause for a chat. Supper would be forgotten. Memorable episodes on field survey trips would be related. They seldom got home before midnight, and I would learn on Monday morning that nearly all of them had forfeited conjugal privileges over the weekend.

But the particular night I am recalling was more festive than usual. Herbie, the proprietor, was in an indulgent mood. His daughter was to be married the following day, and she was obviously marrying to Herbie's satisfaction. He visited our table several times, bought us a round — which he normally did only at Chirstmas, I was told — and eventually, late in the evening, came and joined us. He was in a mood to review his life, and clearly he found his recollections gratifying.

"I got it good now," he told us, "but don't think I didn't have to sweat for it. Took me seven years. Fourteen . . . sixteen hours a day for seven years before I had the hundred-thousand I needed to start this place."

"Is that what this hotel cost?"

Herbie looked at me in surprise for a moment, then burst out laughing. I suppose he was amused at my naivety. "Shit, this joint cost a quarter million bucks," he said complacently. "But I didn't have no trouble raising it once I got a liquor licence."

Somehow this gave me a much better idea of why bootlegging had flourished in Canada.

Back at the office, things had improved, but not much. I was no longer a slave to the stereoscope; I had other tasks: I drew grids for base maps or made templates or gathered data from other agencies to supplement our own. It would have been a dreary winter if the people in Canadian Aero had not been so pleasant. In the new year, though, I suffered a cruel disappointment. A new system for establishing ground control in aerial photography had been developed. It was called SHORAN, which I think stood for Short Range Aerial Navigation. In brief, it was now possible for the aircraft doing the photography to get continuous and accurate fixes of its position electronically. This did away with the necessity for extensive ground surveys and, as a consequence, Spartan decided to hold back on the four additional helicopters they had intended to buy that season; and this in turn did away with my ambition to fly one of them. I understood then why, in the last century, mobs of millworkers had attacked and destroyed the newly invented cotton gin. If I could have got my hands on any SHORAN equipment, I would cheerfully have done the same.

This seemed to leave me three alternatives — two of them costly, the other very tempting. I could do some more jobs like the one I had done for the operator in Carp; I could pay for my own helicopter training, with little prospect of a job afterwards; or I could go into the heavies. Construction of the Distant Early Warning radar line was just getting into full swing at the time, and several new flying companies had sprung into existence. I had the right kind of experience to get a job with one of them; but the problem with these new companies was that they were nearly all strong on ambition, short on capital. They bought war-surplus aircraft and put them into service with a minimum of preparation. In the spring I was offered a job as a co-pilot on a York, the civilian version of the Lancaster bomber. I went for advice to some of the pilots I had got to know in Spartan. They shook their heads and told me I would be a fool to accept. It was a widow-making operation. Reluctantly I heeded their advice and turned the job down. I am very glad I did. For in the next two years the Canadian Arctic became littered with the wrecks of aircraft which had received very little maintenance and whose navigational equipment was totally inadequate.

If the historians ever deal with the airlift for the DEW-Line construction, they will have a black story to tell. The smell of big money was in the air, and in their eagerness for profits, the newly established operators made turn-around the only thing that mattered. Pilots would come back from a trip to the DEW-Line with a list of malfunctions on the aircraft. When they returned to start the next trip, they would find that only one or two of the simplest of these malfunctions had been rectified. If they refused to fly the aircraft, they were promptly replaced by another pilot who had been seduced by an offer he couldn't refuse.

But there was more than just poor maintenance to worry about. Loads well above legal limits for the aircraft became standard practice; and the pilots seldom knew until they were out on the runway and committed to take-off how seriously they were overloaded. In one case a York travelled the full length of the runway at Edmonton Municipal airport, went through the fence, across the road, through another fence and then blundered some 300 feet through a railway yard before it disintegrated and burst into flames. It was discovered later that, after the pilots had checked their load and gone forward to the cockpit, the ground crew had loaded an aircraft engine weighing more than 2,000 pounds into the remaining space in the fuselage. Had the runway been half as long again, that aircraft would never have got off the ground. But this was academic information as far as the pilots were concerned. They were both killed.

So in retrospect I have no regrets about my decision to pass up the apparent bonanza of the DEW-Line airlift — not only because of the risks but because, after it was over, there was nowhere to go. The pilots who had survived found themselves at a dead end and they had to drift into other occupations. For my part, I decided to live as frugally as possible for the rest of the year and then to pay for my training as a helicopter pilot. It was a distressingly expensive solution, but I still had great faith in the future of helicopters, and I was confident it would be money well spent in the end.

By the autumn of 1954 I had made a deal with Spartan to be trained as a helicopter pilot. One needed 25 hours of training to get an endorsement on one's commercial licence, and helicopter tuition cost $75 an hour. I was to pay $1,000 in cash and the remaining $850 when I had found a job. By my standards, those were huge sums of money but that was the best deal I could get, and in November of that year I finally stepped into a helicopter for the first time. It was a disconcerting experience. I had enjoyed the illusion that helicopter flying would merely be a slight extension of my skills as a fixed-wing pilot. Not so, I discovered; it was much more than that.

My instructor was Spartan's chief helicopter pilot, John Theilman. He had been a regular officer in the R.A.F. before the war, and had flown autogyros in the thirties. Later he had flown helicopters, and when he left the Air Force, he joined British European Airways as their chief helicopter pilot during B.E.A.'s brief experiment in commercial helicopter operations. B.E.A. quickly discovered that, where there were alternative means of transport, the helicopter was not yet economically feasible. They closed down their operation and John came to Canada to join Spartan.

On my first flight, John took off and once we were in the air he gave me the controls. I found this very reassuring because, in forward flight, a helicopter behaves just like a fixed-wing aircraft. But in order to take-off, and before you can land, you have to hover — and this is the sweat and tears for the beginner. The best description I can give is that it is like balancing on a large, inflated ball which is floating on water. Each time the ball tends to roll, you have to adjust your balance. Given sufficient time, anyone can learn to do this; at first, though, he will be inclined to overcompensate until he loses his balance.

There are three controls in the helicopters I flew. The first is called the Cyclic stick, which you operate with your right hand. The stick is vertical and the machine moves in whichever direction you push the stick. The second is called the Collective stick. It lies horizontally below your left hand. If you pull it up, the machine rises; push it down, and the machine goes down. At the end of the Collective is the twist-grip throttle, just like the one on a motorcycle. The third control is, or are, the rudder pedals which make the machine rotate. Every time you move one of these controls, the others have to be moved too. It takes a long time to develop the conditioned reflexes to co-ordinate all these movements without having to think about them. Those were cold November days when I began my training, but I was never cold. I sweated in my shirt sleeves as I struggled to get all my limbs to do the right things simultaneously.

This doesn't mean all this is so difficult that only exceptional people can fly helicopters. That's nonsense. But, to the beginner, for the first few hours, it certainly seems so. And, as I mentioned earlier, I approached the exercise with some arrogance. A fixed-wing pilot, during training, learns to worry about his air speed. If he lets the air speed drop below a certain figure, he will stall and crash. With that anxiety out of the way, I thought helicopter flying would be simple. But the helicopter pilot has an equivalent and, in many ways, a more critical anxiety. The rotor blades on a helicopter rely a great deal for their strength on the centrifugal force imparted to them by rotation; thus if you allow the revs to drop below a certain figure, the rotor blades will simply fold upwards and collapse like the spokes of an umbrella in a strong wind. Conversely, if you exceed the specified revs appreciably, you can damage the machine. So each time there is a small variation of wind or turbulence, you have to adjust the throttle to maintain the revs at a set figure. And each time you do, you have to move all the other controls in compensation. It seemed a constant juggling act and, for the first few hours, despite intense concentration, I began to wonder whether or not all this was beyond my capabilities.

Paradoxically, after about 12 hours, when I had become reasonably proficient at hovering, the rest of my training was something of a bore. I had to take off, circle and land for the next ten hours. Obviously it was practice that I needed, but it was tedious. And after that, the remaining hours were taken up with autorotations, or forced landings. In this respect, there is another significant difference between the fixed-wing aircraft and the helicopter. In the fixed-wing, the propeller is connected to the engine through gears and, if the engine fails momentarily because of a fuel blockage, or some ice in the carburetor jets, the propeller continues to turn the engine, which will pick up again when and if it clears itself.

With the helicopter, this is not the case. The engine, when it fails, has to be disconnected immediately so that the blades will autorotate fast enough to provide the equivalent of a glide. Thus the helicopter has a centrifugal clutch between the engine and the rotor blades; and if the motor fails, it immediately stops turning, making it very unlikely, at the usual operating heights of helicopters, that the pilot will be able to start it again, and get the clutch engaged before he reaches the ground.

The first thing you have to do when the motor fails is to bang the Collective right down on the floor to put the blades into fine pitch so that they will autorotate. Autorotation is not actually windmill-ing — it is more complex than that — but for our purposes that will do: the blades continue to rotate and the helicopter glides down steeply. When it reaches the ground there is enough mass in the blades, enough inertia, for the pilot to pull up the Collective and stop all motion before touching down.

Naturally, this manoeuvre calls for precise timing. If you pull up too late on the Collective, you thump hard into the ground. If you pull up too early, the inertia in the blades is exhausted and, once again, thump. At first the rate of descent in an autorotation seems scary, but it is not a difficult thing to do if you have a half-reasonable landing spot to put down in.

My training ended in a check ride with Bill Glenny, a young pilot-inspector with the D.O.T. I think then he had a little over 200 hours of helicopter time. The machine we used had dual controls, of course, and Bill had his hands on the controls, presumably be-cause he was nervous about my ability to handle the machine. I quickly discovered that he was actually initiating movements and doing the flying; so I relaxed my grip, sat back and enjoyed what must have been one of the easiest check rides in history.

There followed a period of uncertainty. John Thielman seemed equivocal about my performance. I don't think he dismissed me as a failure; but neither, I suspect, did he endorse me with any en-thusiasm. The sensible thing to have done would have been to go and look for a job with another company. But in those days the only real alternative to Spartan was Okanagan Helicopters, who were based clear across the continent in Vancouver. Our first child, Ger-ald, was only six months old at the time, and I just didn't want to move. In the end, after I had practically driven everyone up the wall in the Spartan hangar, they reluctantly signed me on as a pilot some time in January, at a salary of $250 a month.

In order to fly commercially, though, you had to be insured; and the insurance companies would not provide coverage for a pilot until he had 75 hours of flying time. So, for the next two months, I flew the fields to the west of Ottawa, performing what seemed at the time an endless succession of circuits and autorotations. Then, all at once, things moved fast. At the end of February, just as I was finishing my 75 hours, I was told I was going out on my first job. I remember being very excited about it because we were going to work in the Ungava Bay area of Quebec: the Barrens, Arctic stuff, first time out. I felt — well, I felt intrepid.

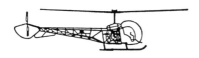
The Barrens — First Time Out

I WAS NOT THE ONLY ONE EXCITED; THERE WAS A GENERAL air of excitement about that operation. The company had succeeded in persuading the customer to begin a project in the north at the beginning of March, instead of waiting until the break-up in June. This meant a seven-month contract, rather than the customary three or four months. We were making a significant commercial breakthrough, and although nobody had any experience operating helicopters in the Barrens under winter conditions, we had no misgivings. On paper, it looked good. We would be doing all our flying more or less at sea level — which meant good performance from the helicopters. Better still, the air would be cold and dense — which meant even better performance. We would be well equipped. We had cowlings to keep the engines warm in the air, covers to protect everything from the weather on the ground, portable ground heaters to start up with in the morning. We were not only confident; we were elated.

Our customer was a branch of the Quebec provincial government. I forget what their exact title was — the word *Hydraulique* was in there somewhere — but they were investigating water resources in the province. The tides in the Ungava Bay area rise to spectacular heights, and our task was to put in ground control to produce very accurate contour maps so that they could examine the potential harnessing of these tides to generate electricity. The electricity, in turn, would be used to exploit the newly discovered Ungava iron ore deposits. SHORAN was not practicable on small-scale projects like this, so we were to use conventional methods: theodolites for positions, barometers for elevations.

It was to be a two-machine operation. Nels Bentley, the senior pilot, was the manager, and Jim McCann the maintenance engineer. The fourth member of the crew was Ted Blanchet, an apprentice engineer. This crew was to handle the first three months of the contract. We were to fly the helicopters to Montreal where, after removing the tail booms and the main rotors, we would load them into a DC-6 for transport to Fort Chimo. There the helicopters would be reassembled and we would fly them to the camp at a place called Tom's River.

Nels and I left to fly to Montreal early one morning at the beginning of March. The weather was fine; we had an uneventful trip. We parked the machines outside the hangar in which they were to be disassembled and went for an early lunch. The engineers were driving over in a rented truck, bringing the spares and equipment we would need. They arrived before noon. We wheeled the helicopters into the hangar and started work. Larry Camphaug, one of the supervising engineers, was coming as far as Chimo with us to help out. He had considerable experience at this sort of thing, and by three o'clock we were ready to load the helicopters into the DC-6.

But while we worked, we had been observing a ground crew loading another aircraft, a York, out on the tarmac. This was one of the new companies which had sprung up to supply the DEW-Line construction phase, and that particular loading crew was as rough and destructive a group of stevedores as I ever want to see. When they dropped a package or a piece of equipment, which happened frequently, they all roared with laughter. The youth driving the forklift was trying to run the loads at the loading door, then jam on his brakes in order to slide the load onto the deck of the aircraft. The battered sill of the loading door demonstrated his failures.

We had no difficulty deciding that we were going to do our own loading. The loading door of a DC-6 is high off the ground, and with that crew there was a very real danger they would end up dropping one of our helicopters. But when Larry went to borrow a forklift all hell broke loose. The foreman of the loading crew refused point blank to let us do the loading. What were we trying to do, he snarled, put them out of a job? We suggested that if what we had just witnessed was called a job, it would be a damn good thing if somebody did put them out of it. They were offended and they responded with a great deal of profanity.

The exchange became so abusive I began to anticipate a fight. We outnumbered them five to four, but even so — at least two of them had biceps much the diameter of my thigh. Fortunately, higher authority intervened before it came to blows. The dispatcher came out of his office to see what all the shouting was about. When he got a grasp of the situation, he turned out to have a better voice than any of us. There were two more aircraft waiting to be loaded, and the thought that his crew was trying to prevent us from voluntarily loading our own made him ferociously angry. He was so incensed that in the end he took a run at one of them, beating him on the shoulder with the clipboard he was carrying. They retreated sullenly to load another aircraft.

It took us about two hours to get the helicopters in and securely tied down. We had learned that we were not taking off until the following morning, and by now it was an agreeable time to go and find a hotel and have a drink before supper. After we had eaten, Jim McCann discovered that he had inadvertently loaded a suitcase he needed onto the DC-6. It was a little early for bed, so Larry and I decided to drive out to the airport with him. When we got there, we found the doors of the aircraft open. Inside, one of the members of the same loading crew was busily undoing the tie-downs on the helicopters. We converged on him with such bellows of spontaneous outrage that he grew confused, retreated and climbed down onto the tarmac. As we followed him down, the rest of the loading crew arrived with a forklift.

In the ensuing commotion, it was some time before any communication took place. But in the end we understood that somebody in a remote office had decided that the DC-6 could make a trip with DEW-Line equipment to Frobisher Bay and return by morning. The crew had been instructed to make the loading change. Over our dead bodies, we advised them. So be it, they said (or words to that effect), and the shouting began again with renewed vigour.

Eventually I left Larry Camphaug standing like Horatius on his celebrated bridge while I sprinted for the phone to alert Nels Bentley. Nels promptly phoned Ottawa and, for the next two hours, we had a standoff while the battle went on by phone at higher levels. Just before midnight a message came through to leave the goddam helicopters on board. Apparently no one had been able to locate the two pilots who were supposed to make the trip to Frobisher. It was a typical example of the greed, confusion and stupidity that prevailed during the DEW-Line airlift.

The two pilots who were to fly us to Fort Chimo did not arrive at the hangar until nearly ten o'clock the following morning. And when they did, it was obvious they were badly hungover. Even though it was a dull morning, they both wore sunglasses. And they, in turn, had their shouting match; this time it was with the maintenance crew. None of the snags they had booked when they landed the aircraft had been rectified. They had an oil-pressure problem on the number three engine; the pitch change mechanism on one of the other engines was balky; the hydraulic system was sluggish; the artificial horizon was wandering. But nothing came of their altercation with the maintenance crew. In the end we climbed in, strapped ourselves into the narrow canvas bench along one side of the fuselage, and I sat with my foot braced against one of the helicopter tie-downs, wishing I had been a more conscientious Christian.

There was a little window behind me but, since we flew over cloud most of the way, there was nothing to look at except the number three engine, along the whole length of which oil was bubbling and trickling. I went forward to warn the pilots. The captain shrugged. "We got a light load," he said, "and we sure got all kinds of practice landing on three." I went back to my seat feeling thoroughly depressed. I had been cherishing fantasies of bright-eyed, debonair pilots, eagerly challenging the north. These two looked defeated, almost fatalistic; as if they knew that they were going to die anyway. Less than a year later I read in the newspapers that one of them did die in a crash at a DEW-Line site.

As it turned out, we landed at Fort Chimo without incident. But then we found we had problems. There was no forklift available, so we had to use a flat-bed truck, loaded with empty gas drums with planks on top of them to provide a platform. Even so, the platform was nearly a foot below the sill of the loading door, and we virtually had to lift the helicopters down onto it by hand. And now, of course, the trick was to get the helicopters down off the truck and onto the ground. Fortunately, there was a building large enough for the truck to back into. It had big beams supporting the roof, and we were able to rig a block and tackle to one of them. It was a cold day, well below zero, with a brisk wind. I remember sweating in my brand-new parka, and then shivering as we waited for the next phase to begin. The whole thing took about four hours, and although we were very tired at the end of it, we were elated too, because the helicopters were under cover and we would be able to reassemble them comfortably protected from the wind and blowing snow.

Fort Chimo had been a military airport during the war; I think it was used as an alternate fuelling stop for transatlantic ferry flights when Gander was socked in. The equipment was nearly all American, and there were vast quantities of it lying everywhere in varying stages of decay. What still sticks in my memory were the acres of empty gas drums. There were at least 10,000 of them, stacked haphazardly as far as the eye could see. And here and there among the stacks, a bulldozer or a crane or an old military truck. They looked curiously incongruous in that flat desert of snow.

Fortunately for us, some enterprising individual had taken note of the flurry of exploration activity prompted by the iron ore discovery, and of the DEW-Line airlift, and restored one of the buildings as a hotel. As such establishments go, it wasn't much. He had patched up the windows with cardboard and plastic. He had managed to get the fuel-oil stoves to work. He had dug out some old iron bedsteads, with mattresses of a sort on which to lay your sleeping bag. He charged about as much as a luxury hotel in Miami. But to give him his due, he fed us well; and it was still much more economical, and far more convenient, than if we had had to set up our own camp.

Reassembling the helicopters took far longer than it had to dismantle them. We didn't have them flying to our satisfaction for another three days; and when we did, the weather held us up for another four. I was impatient, eager to get to work and start building up some flying hours. But Nels was unperturbed. I still had much to learn from him.

We were to be supported by a Norseman, a single-engined bush aircraft, flown by Hartley Marsh, a young man who was vastly amused that we were up here at all at this time of the year. He was based at Fort Chimo, and had been for the past eighteen months. He and Nels agreed that the Norseman should act as a guide dog to lead us to our destination. I was outraged, and I made sardonic remarks about needing a chaperone to go a hundred miles across the country. Hartley laughed, and Nels, who was at that time one of the most experienced helicopter pilots in the business, smiled his gentle smile and said, "you'll see."

So we sat around much of the time in the lounge-cum-dining room of our hotel, playing cards and relating anecdotes. The weather was grim, so we did not venture out very often. It was a ghostly sort of atmosphere. We found rooms full of new equipment, some items still in their original wooden crates. The owner of the hotel, who acted as a radio dispatcher and expeditor for the flying companies operating in the area, told us that the Americans had driven more than 50 pieces of heavy mobile equipment, many of them bulldozers, out onto the ice of a lake some three miles away. They had all pulled out for good and left the vehicles to sink to the bottom of the lake when the ice broke up.

For the most part, though, everything had been left as it was. Now there was a small Department of Transport crew, who operated a radio and weather station, and kept the one main runway cleared with a rehabilitated snowplough. They were a curiously ungregarious lot, and we saw very little of them. Besides Hartley, I think there were only six other permanent white residents at the time: two Mounties, a Hudson's Bay factor; the Anglican minister — a melanacholy individual who looked as though the life here-after was becoming increasingly attractive to him; and two nurses who ran a clinic, principally to serve the 40-odd Eskimos and Indians, each in two distinctly segregated camps. I was told the Eskimos and Indians disliked each other to the verge of active hos-tility.

One of the things I remember most clearly about Chimo was the stove which warmed our lounge. It was an oil stove, fed by gravity and controlled by a single carburetor. At irregular intervals it would be seized by an alarming malfunction; it would begin to re-verberate, making a "whoom, whoom, whoom" noise. This noise would continue for a minute or so, then culminate in a sort of explosive sneeze which rattled the entire stove and filled the room with smoke, after which, it would settle down to function normally again. These manifestations made me nervous. I would invariably back away from the stove when it happened, and my companions mocked me. The north was no environment for poultry, they ad-vised me; if I was going to work in the Canadian bush I would have to toughen up.

We made a practice, during our stay in Chimo, of firing up the helicopters at least once a day — bringing them up to operating temperatures and then lifting them into the hover for a minute or two, just to make sure no snags had developed. I was walking back to our quarters after having done this one day, when I noticed puffs of black smoke issuing at regular intervals from the stove pipe in the roof. It reminded me of one of those cartoons of an Indian sending up smoke signals, and it was just occurring to me that this must be the product of the "whoom, whoom" phenomenon when there was an explosion so violent that it blew the cardboard and plastic out of the windows and burst the door open. Perhaps two or three seconds later the doorway was jammed with five or six people, all trying to get through it at the same time.

I suppose I shouldn't have laughed. They were badly frightened; the incident might have had serious consequences. Besides, the snowbank they threw me into contained a lot of mud and gravel.

Fortunately, someone remembered seeing some new stoves in one of the buildings. It took us several hours to repair the windows and install one. For the rest of our stay the stove functioned without incident, but I felt it reasonable to point out to my companions that they now appeared more nervous about the new stove than I had been about the old. Chickens did not prosper in the north, I reminded them, and if they were going to work in the Canadian bush they would have to cultivate a much stronger moral fibre.

At about this time I found myself beginning to worry about Nina. Here was I having a whale of a time. Everything was new, stimulating; yet Nina was sitting in a little bungalow in Ottawa with our son Gerald feeling, I couldn't help suspecting, more than a little lonely. There was no easy answer to this problem, and there wouldn't be for some years. To be a bush pilot you had to be out in the bush. In those days it wasn't feasible to take your family with you, and my enjoyment was always tempered by a sense of guilt.

Six days after we arrived in Chimo, the weather at last showed signs of improvement. In the afternoon a DC-3 landed, on its way south from somewhere. The pilot said the weather to the north of us was not too bad. Larry Camphaug left on the DC-3 to return to Ottawa. We awoke the following morning to find a thin sun filtering through the overcast. It was windy still, but the visibility was good and I was eager to be off. Yet even now, Nels and Hartley hesitated. We waited until nearly 11 o'clock before they finally decided to give it a try.

54

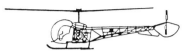

CHAPTER 7

A Tablecloth for a Map

FLYING OUT OF FORT CHIMO, IT TOOK ME NO MORE THAN TEN minutes to discover that the caution Hartley and Nels had displayed was more than justified. By myself, I could never have found my way across that country. The lakes, the drainages and rivers, even in places the shoreline of Ungava Bay, had been totally obliterated by the snow. The only way one could navigate, without some electronic assistance, was to have done what Hartley had done: fly the country in the summer, through the freeze-up and into the winter. Then one could recognize certain pin-points that no map would represent: a cluster of rocks that always for some reason remained free of snow; a distinctive curve or pattern made by early snows which had been driven by the wind and then frozen like concrete; a large expanse of ice which mysteriously stayed visible in its green and blue starkness. But to recognize these things, one needed good visibility and I knew now why Hartley had insisted on waiting for the weather to clear.

For Hartley, it must have been a tedious journey. The Norseman was known as the aircraft that had only one speed: it took off at 90 m.p.h., cruised at 90 and landed at 90. Even so, he was travelling some 25 m.p.h. faster than we were, so that he had to keep circling back. We landed after an hour and a half to refuel. I still have the photograph I took of the engineers standing on the cargo racks, pouring gas into the tanks. No horizon was visible; the ground was concealed by drifting snow. It was a scene as bleak as any of the photographs I have seen of the moon.

Some 40 minutes later we reached our destination, the camp at Tom's River. As I discovered later, the camp was at the confluence of two rivers — the Payne, which flowed east, and the Tom's, which flowed south to join it. I never did discover who the intrepid Tom was, but the river that bears his name was invisible when we arrived, as was the lake on the shores of which our camp was set. The camp consisted of three large octagonal huts, joined together by corridors. They were painted bright orange but, when I first saw them, only the roofs were visible, poking up through the snow unexpectedly like three gay beach parasols. The weather was beginning to close in as we landed. We helped Hartley unload the Norseman, and he promptly took off again to get back to Chimo while he could. He had brought mail for the crew. There were about 12 people in the camp, and they immediately disappeared into their quarters to read it, leaving us to look around in some dismay. Nels Bentley blew out his cheeks and shook his head. "Be another two months at least before we can do any work around here," he remarked sombrely.

During the next two or three weeks we tried everything possible, but it was a lost cause. The job we had to do was the one I have already described: lay out the ground control for a map to be made from aerial photographs. The map was to cover an area approximately 50 miles long by 30 miles wide, and the first thing to be done was to put in a series of conventional ground traverses from known points, so as to increase the number of surveyed reference points we had in the area. Unfortunately, we could only identify two or three of the original topographic survey benchmarks with absolute certainty, so this network of traverses could not be done. Next, we had to fly the entire area, landing every half a mile to take a reading on a sophisticated and highly accurate barometer. The system was to put out two base instruments, each with an operator to take readings every five minutes, some fifteen miles apart; then the helicopter would fly between the bases, taking a reading every half a mile or so. The map was to have contours at $2\frac{1}{2}$-foot intervals. To achieve such a scale of accuracy, it was essential to mark the points at which we took our reading with pin-point accuracy on the photographs. In fact it was impossible to tell within half a mile where we were — often considerably more than that. We had aerial photographs of the area, but they were meaningless. We might as well have had blank sheets of paper to represent the blank countryside.

A young French-Canadian called Paul was flying with me, and he carried one of those small, collapsible shovels with which the Americans had dug their beloved foxholes during the war. On several occasions we were convinced we had found a particular lake and we dug enthusiastically through the snow, only to discover rock or caribou moss beneath it. We would return to camp and the habitually rather sad face of Yves, the party chief, would grow even sadder.

But the truth was that we could only fly on average perhaps one or two days a week. The rest of the time we would be in a white-out. This is a condition which, to someone who has not actually experienced it, is almost impossible to explain. In a true white-out, when the sky becomes overcast and there are no rocks or other objects in sight, the horizon disappears and even the ground beneath your feet disappears. It is a frightening sensation at first, not to be able to see the very ground you are standing on. Besides this, there is the loss of perspective. For example, if you look at a rectangular object, it is impossible to determine whether this object is a matchbox lying 50 feet away or a cabin two miles away.

Our two helicopters possessed no flight instruments except for an air-speed indicator; thus we had to rely exclusively on eye contact with the ground for orientation. In a true white-out there was no possible way we could do this; we were bound to lose control and crash. But as Nels Bentley knew, and I guessed, you cannot convince anyone of this unless or until he has experienced it for himself. We would be suspected of incompetence if not cowardice during the weeks ahead.

The party chief, Yves, could see for himself what the physical realities were, so we had no problem with him. But he was bitter with our company because he felt they had misled him. He had come up with a small party to set up the camp and do a reconnaissance of the area in July of the previous year. Spartan had sent up a helicopter flown by a pilot who had just been hired. He had some 400 hours of helicopter flying time, all of it over the green fields of Texas. Arriving for a week's flying in Ungava in July, when most of the snow was gone, he experienced no difficulties — the country was a helicopter pilot's paradise: it was so flat one could land almost anywhere — and he confidently advised Yves a helicopter could fly in any weather. When Yves questioned him about the possible difficulties of winter flying, he dismissed them airily. Snow on the ground merely smoothed out the terrain and made it possible to land anywhere one wanted to. They could fly the year round, so long as they were properly equipped, he advised them.

On the strength of this advice, the Department had moved the intended date for the beginning of this year's operation from June to March. People with local experience had tried to dissuade them;

they told them nothing could be accomplished in this country until at least June, but the helicopter was new magic, and the locals were ignored. As a matter of history, the same pilot, a month after he left Ungava, was flying with Larry Camphaug in Labrador, where he encountered another of those visual phenomena of bush flying: glassy water.

Glassy water, as the term suggests, is water undisturbed by any ripples caused by wind or current. When this happens, it is impossible to see the surface and fixed-wing pilots, when they have to make a landing on a lake in these conditions, do so on instruments. They set up a rate of descent of 50 feet per minute until the floats contact the water. Helicopter pilots, unless they are very green, keep well away from the lake. This particular pilot set out to fly across the lake and quite simply flew right into it. The helicopter flipped and hung upside down in the water, suspended by its floats. Larry had a pocketknife on him. He cut the straps from one of the floats and he and the pilot paddled ashore, where they waited until the following day to be rescued.

I often wondered if I would have tendered the same advice if I had been in that pilot's place. In any case, I remember wishing fervently that he, and not I, had been trying to fly that first few weeks of March and April. I wanted so badly to get started and prove myself on the job; instead, I spent most of my time in our quarters which, fortunately, were very comfortable. I had brought a portable typewriter with me, together with a book on how to learn touch-typing. I became reasonably proficient as a typist and wrote some atrociously bad short stories. But my main interest, during those first few weeks, was in the Eskimos.

Two of them were employed as rod-men on the survey crews. They had their families with them, living in tents behind our camp. Both families had dog teams, and they made frequent trips to the settlement of Payne Bay, which was about 30 miles to the east of us, on the shores of Ungava Bay. These were no demoralized remnants of Farley Mowat's *People of the Deer*. They were healthy, intelligent and very charming people. Although they were beginning to adopt the white man's ways, they still had most of their ancestral skills. The men still made the frames, and the women sewed the skins, for the kayaks in which they hunted seal, walrus and beluga whales. But to me the most intriguing aspect of the Eskimos was their indifference to time or space.

The white man is always concerned about where he is; he panics very quickly when he gets lost. The Eskimo, it seemed to me, was totally unconcerned about where he happened to be as long as there was a prospect of food in the not-too-distant future. Similarly with time: the white man is always anxious about time. What time it is now; where he should be at a certain time in the future. The Eskimos found this a curious concept. And when we fretted about the weather and the fact that time was passing without any progress, I am sure they were genuinely puzzled. Weather was weather, and a sensible person merely relaxed until it improved, then went about his business. As far as they were concerned, we had solved the only anxiety they ever experienced: an adequate supply of food. This being the case, there was all the more reason to relax. They undoubtedly regarded our endeavours as singularly inconsequential, and they shook their heads and smiled in perplexity as we fumed and swore because the weather prevented us from working.

In the meantime, when we did any work, they were fun to work with. People have often, in writing about Eskimos, remarked on their almost unfailing cheerfulness. I must agree, and add that they are also unfailingly courteous. Some years later I went to pick up a small community of about 12 Eskimos near Chantrey Inlet who were reported to be in trouble. When I arrived I could see that they were quite unmistakably suffering from prolonged starvation. Even so, they struggled to their feet and smiled. All of them insisted on shaking my hand. They waited patiently while I decided who was to go first and who would have to wait.

But in Ungava that year, there was no sign of malnutrition among the Eskimos, and there was nothing, I think, they enjoyed so much as flying in a helicopter. On one occasion, we had five people — three white, two Eskimo — out doing a ground traverse when the weather suddenly began to close in. Nels and I went rushing off to pick them up. The machines we were flying could only carry two passengers. This was not a weight limitation; we were practically at sea level and the temperature was still below zero most of the time, so we had plenty of lift. But the bubble on those early machines was just too narrow to accommodate more than three people. Nels picked up two of the white men; I was left with one white and two Eskimos, trying to make up my mind whether to take two people and leave one behind, or vice versa. It had begun to snow and it seemed very unlikely that I would be able to get back again. Suddenly it occurred to me to suggest that two of them should lie on the cargo racks on either side of the helicopter. The white man refused at once. The two Eskimos had not really understood what I was suggesting to begin with; but when I pointed to them and then demonstrated what I meant by lying face down on the rack and gripping the sides with my hands, they unhesitatingly agreed.

I took a couple of wraps around their waists with the sash cord I used for tying down loads; then I took off gingerly, meaning to fly low and slow in case they panicked. As we moved off, I kept a close eye on the person on my side of the machine. I could look down at him over my left shoulder. At first he kept his head down, but soon he lifted it and started to look around. Before long, he twisted his head and looked up to see that I was watching him. His moon-shaped face was promptly transformed into one of the widest grins I have ever seen. I leaned forward to look past my passenger at the Eskimo on the other side. He, too, wore a huge beam of pleasure on his face. I poked the stick forward and flew back to camp at full speed. After that, I had difficulty keeping them off the racks whenever they flew with me.

But if the Eskimos were happy during those first few weeks, the white man was not. Recriminations flew back and forth. The customer blamed our company for misleading them. Our company hinted that it might be necessary to replace the pilots, and we experienced the frustration and bitterness of being criticized by people sitting in warm, comfortable offices, more than a thousand miles away in Montreal and Ottawa; people who had no experience of the difficulties facing us. We had pushed the limits of safety too many times; yet still we were being regarded as timid pilots. It was very upsetting. The sensible thing to have done, of course, would have been to pull everybody out and come back again at the end of May. But the powers to the south obviously did not believe us when we told them we couldn't accomplish anything. So we stayed. It was about as unfortunate a start to my career as a bush pilot as I could visualize, and it was hard not to become demoralized under these circumstances.

CHAPTER 8

The Eskimos

IN THE MIDDLE OF APRIL, THE DECISION WAS MADE TO MOVE our camp to Payne Bay. Some features along the coast were identifiable and we could do a limited amount of work. There was a vacant building there which I believe had once been used by the defunct trading company, Revillon Frères. It was in reasonable shape and the mere change of environment was a blessing. There was an active Hudson's Bay store in the settlement. The factor's name was Jimmy — by now the term factor was being replaced by manager, but most of the old-timers liked to retain it. Jimmy was getting on in years; he had lived in Payne Bay for more than 20 of them. He had an Eskimo wife and several children, and he was so contented with his life there that he no longer took the trouble to go south for his vacations.

The only other white man was Jimmy's assistant, Mark, a naive young man who took his position very seriously. He had only arrived a month or so before we had, but already he seemed to regard himself as something of an Arctic veteran. As for the Eskimos, I think there were about 40 people belonging to some 10 or 11 separate families. It was pleasant to be among them after the static boredom of the Tom's River camp, because these were active people and there was always something going on. Somebody would be building a new kayak, or repairing an old one. A group of people were making a komatik, or sled. And always there were the dogs: masses of dogs who seemed to be constantly snapping and snarling and fighting each other. I was warned never to fall over when I was near dogs. If you were on your feet they would never attack, but if you went down they would — and once that happened, it was all over in a few seconds.

I wanted to go on a seal hunt with the Eskimos, but to do this I would have had to paddle my own kayak and I didn't trust myself in the few leads of open water along the coast. There were fierce tides, the ice was in constant motion and it required considerable skill and experience to handle a kayak in these conditions. So instead, I went on a ptarmigan hunt.

On several occasions I had seen one particular Eskimo going off over the little hills behind the settlement, and one day I made signs to indicate that I wanted to join him. He seemed delighted, and we set off together. He was armed with a single-shot .22 Cooey, the cheapest rifle then available. The ptarmigan still had their white winter plumage and they were difficult to see. But once you did spot them you could approach to within about 30 yards of them before they would fly off.

The Eskimo used about 15 rounds and hit two birds — and then they were only clipped; we had to chase them down. I was surprised. I had thought sheer necessity would have made Eskimos crack shots, but I learned later that my companion was not one of the sharper members of his community. He wasn't the village idiot, but neither was he very bright. That was why I had seen him hunting ptarmigan instead of going on the more demanding seal or walrus hunts. I pointed to myself and reached for the gun to indicate that I would like to have a try. He gave it to me without hesitation. We came up on a solitary bird. I fired and saw the shot hit the snow well above the bird's head. I tried correcting, but still went over the top and the bird flew off. I turned to the Eskimo and tried to suggest by sign-language that I would like to take the gun back to camp and have a look at it. I am sure he didn't understand, but he cheerfully followed me back to camp.

I got hold of a large cardboard box, marked a target on it and lay down to see if I could get a group. Our crew stood around making derisive comments about my pretensions as the great white hunter, sighting in his rifle. But I persevered and the gun produced a tolerable group about five or six inches above the target. The bead on the foresight had broken off. The backsight had no adjustment on it, so I borrowed a file from Jim McCann's toolbox and filed the V as deeply as I could. This worked well: the next group was hitting the top of the target. I gave the gun back to the Eskimo and we set off again. The first covey we found was five strong and he bagged four of them without a miss. I left him then and he headed off across the rocks and snow grinning like a Cheshire cat.

Apparently he had a good afternoon. For the next few days, every time I saw an Eskimo he or she would make a gesture of shooting and utter complimentary noises. I brought to my crew's attention, with some repetition, my improved status in the community.

About ten days after we moved to Payne Bay, we heard that a senior member of the Water Resources Department was coming up to visit us. He was one tier below deputy minister in the hierarchy — a big shot — and we anticipated some interesting recriminations. The day on which he was due to arrive started well: we put both ground survey crews out to work. But by noon the weather began to close in, and we had to bring them back into camp. An hour later, just after we had finished our lunch, Hartley's Norseman arrived with our VIP on board. By this time we were pretty well into a complete white-out. Hartley had to do a long, slow let down — obviously, he was using the glassy water technique, and no pilot likes to do this because there may be large ridges of packed snow where he touches down, and they are invisible.

We went down to the edge of the shore ice, about a hundred yards below the Hudson's Bay store, to meet him. When Hartley had cut the engine, he stuck his head out of the window, shaking it and grimacing at the weather. But when the VIP emerged from the passenger door, he lived right up to our expectations. He jumped down onto the snow and looked around at us. "What the hell goes on?" he demanded. "Why isn't anyone working?"

Nels suggested mildly that the weather conditions were unsuitable for flying, and then our VIP really flared up. "What do you mean — not fit for flying. For Christ's sake, I've just been flying, and I was in a fixed-wing. We were told helicopters could fly in any weather. What do you guys think this is — a goddam vacation camp?"

He was a youngish man, no more than 40 years old, dressed in brand-new bush clothes, right down to the yellow bush boots. He had the plump, well-fed look of the executive. In his own eyes at any rate, I am sure he would have included himself in the category known as the shakers and movers. Stung by the unfairness of it all, I demanded that he come with me right now and see for himself what the conditions were.

"Goddam right we'll go back and look," he said, and marched up the hill. I caught Nels' eye and saw him looking anxious; he was afraid I might get into difficulties trying to prove a point; but Hartley had a big grin on his face.

The helicopters were parked up on a bench, behind the small hill above the camp. When we reached the bench, we were in total white-out. I had learned by then to take the high steps which, though they look absurd, help you to get over the invisible ridges and furrows in the snow. It gave me considerable satisfaction to see the VIP trip and flounder several times before we reached the helicopter.

He climbed straight into it while I was untying the rotor blade. When I had started up, and while I was waiting for the engine to warm up, I dug the photographs out from behind my seat; they were the ones we had used that morning. I showed him where they started, some five miles from camp. He began to go through them one by one, nodding his head after he had studied each one. It was obvious that he would not need the photographs once we took off; he was imprinting them in his memory.

As I lifted off, he was still studying the last two photographs. I watched him, and when he finally looked up, his eyes widened and he began to swing his head from side to side. I was moving very slowly and I had the gas drums as well as the other helicopter in sight over my left shoulder. But he couldn't see anything, and I was really beginning to enjoy myself as I watched his increasing dismay out of the corner of my eye. "Well, which way do we go?" I demanded. "You've got the photographs." He shouted a couple of words which I didn't catch, and then something very unpleasant occurred: he froze.

I saw this happen to passengers only twice more in my career, but then it was in the mountains, when I had flown suddenly over a cliff with a sheer drop of hundreds of feet. The freezing is quite simply a type of catatonic seizure: the person goes absolutely rigid, his feet jammed against the footrest, his shoulders jammed against the seat-back and his hands reaching down behind him for something to grasp.

At the risk of flogging a dead horse, I repeat that one's first experience of a total white-out can be very frightening. There is no vestige of distinction between sky and ground, no vestige of anything to be seen. Only a moment before I had been gloating over his discomfiture. But it is a shocking sight, and an embarrassing one, to see someone quite literally paralyzed with fright. I swung the helicopter round, moved back and plunked it down by the drums, keeping them on his side so that he could see them.

It must have been about ten minutes before he was ready to walk back down to the camp. I threw one of the seat cushions towards the edge of the bench we were standing on. We used that to walk until we could see the camp buildings. When we got there, Hartley was having his lunch. The VIP walked straight up to him. "Come on," he said, "let's get back down to Chimo. We're wasting our time here."

Hartley had his mouth full. He studied the VIP's face while he emptied it.

"You out of your tree?" he said eventually. "Your face's as white as a sheet. You've just been out there and seen what it's like. We're not going anywhere until the weather lets up."

It was a low moment. This country got you whichever way you turned. I had been hoping to return with a person chastened and perhaps even a little apologetic about the injustice of the criticism he had hurled at us when he arrived. Instead, I came back with someone who had been thoroughly humiliated, and I felt as though I had done something discreditable. The poor guy had to wait another two days before the weather cleared and Hartley took him out.

But in spite of the frustration, those first two months in Ungava were interesting and very instructive. I had read about bush pilots operating in the winter; about removing the sump plug and dropping the oil into the snow; then putting the congealed block of oil in a pail and heating it up on the stove in the morning, while a blow pot warmed the engine. Our equipment was more sophisticated, but it still took a lot of work to get a helicopter started in the morning. Overnight, we had to cover the bubble with a fabric glove, slip fabric covers over the main blades to protect them from a build-up of frost or ice — which was very hard to remove in the mornings; slip similar covers over the tail-rotor blades. Then in the morning we had to fit a sort of large tent over the centre section. We had gasoline-driven heaters, and we put the elephant's trunk hose of the heater under the tent for half an hour or so to warm things up enough for a start.

We soon learned that it was worth the effort of dragging the Stewart-Warner heaters into our quarters at night; otherwise, we would spend the first hour in the morning trying to start the heaters. We also learned not to leave the helicopters unattended during the warm-up period. One morning we came back to find the tent smouldering briskly; so after that we had breakfast in shifts. A year or so later one of the company's helicopters was completely burned out in a similar accident.

The floats gave us another interesting problem. At that time everyone operated on floats unless they were working in the mountains. And floats in cold weather could be tricky. I am not sure what the physics were but, when you landed in the evening, heat would be generated under the floats causing a slight melting of the snow. During the night, this film of water would freeze hard. The danger was that when you tried to lift off, one float would sometimes break free while the other did not. I very nearly turned on my side the first time this happened. After that, we had to run the heater hose all the way round the floats before we tried to lift off in the morning.

The helicopters we were operating were the next generation to the B model Okanagan had used in British Columbia. The Bell 47D (I don't know what happened to the C; perhaps it died on the drawing board) was very similar to the B. The main differences were that the tail boom was no longer enclosed — we had the now familiar triangular trellis-work of tubes — and instead of a plastic windshield, the pilot and passengers were now totally enclosed by a plexiglass bubble. The advantages of the enclosed bubble are obvious; the disadvantages of an enclosed tail boom perhaps less so. Pilots had quickly discovered in the B model that the tail boom acted as a significant keel surface which made it very difficult to hover in a cross wind. Removal of the covering alleviated this problem, and it also made it much easier to monitor the tail-rotor cables, which often tended to wear out much more quickly than the manufacturer claimed they would.

The particular helicopter I was flying, CF-FCK, was a converted B model. The top of the bubble had been clamped to the existing windshield and this left an irritating line of metal right across my line of vision when flying. But the biggest drawback to those early models was the narrowness of the bubble. A pilot and two passengers, all in winter clothing, made a tight fit on the single bench seat, and it was very uncomfortable flying with your left, or Collective, elbow jammed against the bubble.

Another inconvenience had to do with balance and centre of gravity — a sensitive factor on light helicopters. The gas tank on a model D was mounted laterally on the frame, behind the rotor mast. This meant a tail-down attitude when it was full; a nose-down attitude when it was nearly empty. Worse yet, there was the battery placement to worry about.

The battery, which was the size and weight of a conventional car battery, had two locations: it was in front of the instrument pedestal in the bubble when you were flying solo; it had to be moved to a platform on the tail boom when you picked up two passengers. This exercise alone kept the pilot in good shape when we were moving crews all day, and at about that time a photograph was published in *Life* magazine which helped us not to forget. A pilot had landed on a skyscraper rooftop in New York to drop two politicians for an opening ceremony in the building. The two passengers were stepping forward, waving and smiling their politician's smile; while in the background the helicopter, whose pilot had forgotten to change his battery before taking off again, was hanging vertically in the air. The machine slid down the building into the street some 30 storeys below. The pilot was killed.

A further difficulty in those early days involved the fuel we used and the spark plugs. For technical reasons which I have forgotten, and which in any case never made much sense to me, the Franklin engine would not run on 80/87 or 100/130, the two octane ratings used by all other piston-engined aircraft at the time. Instead we had to use a mixture of the two, called 6V4 (I believe this was the maker's engine designation); and even then, we had constant plug trouble. I wish I had a dollar for every spark plug I changed on a Franklin engine.

But quite apart from these small operational difficulties, there was the ever-present problem of people. When a helicopter is on the ground with its rotors turning it is manifestly a dangerous beast. Unless you are on perfectly level ground, a person can walk up the slope into the rotor blades. And even on level ground, a strong gust of wind can bring the blades down low enough to decapitate him. The pilot has to issue constant warnings to people to duck as they walk away from the helicopter. Then there is the tail rotor; this is always in a position to annihilate anyone who forgets that it is there and walks into it. No matter how often you caution people, they are always trying to cross behind the machine.

A particular hazard early on that operation was presented by the 12-foot sighting rods carried by the survey crews. There was a constant temptation to take these off the racks and swing them from the horizontal to the vertical position — to the inevitable detriment of the main rotor blades, the rod and the person holding the rod. This happened fairly early on. Fortunately, the only damage was a severely bruised shoulder for the person who did it, and people were more careful after that.

Nevertheless, you had to be constantly on the alert. On one occasion, Paul took an apple out of his bag while we were flying between points. He bit into it and pulled a face — it must have been a very sour apple. Then, before I had time to react, he opened the door and flung the apple over his shoulder. Paul was huffy when I shouted at him, but if the apple had struck the tail rotor, the tail rotor would undoubtedly have disintegrated. On another occasion, I landed on a bench. The ground rose fairly sharply on Paul's side. I locked the controls, jumped out and walked to his side to make sure he didn't walk up it. He had several things to carry, including a large clipboard he had fashioned out of $\frac{3}{8}$-inch plywood. He turned and, once again before I had time to react, sailed the clipboard up onto the bank. It went right through the rotor disk, miraculously without touching either blade. This time I really did shout at him.

I think it is reasonable to claim that the helicopter is a very unforgiving machine to people who lack concentration. And although I was bitter about the slow start we made, in retrospect I know that I was really very fortunate because I had time to assimilate the lessons I had to learn. After a year or two I was able to anticipate many of the unexpected things people do around a helicopter, but never all of them.

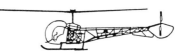

CHAPTER 9

Willie

PAYNE BAY, AS I'VE TOLD YOU, WAS FUN; THERE WAS ALWAYS something going on. We socialized with the Eskimos a good deal, by turns inviting families into our cookhouse for tea and cookies and visiting their tents. When we visited them, we were always offered tea and there was a certain amount of ceremony about the occasion — which was fitting, for tea, after all, is as much a symbol as a beverage. When we reached the tent, we would bat on the canvas. I used to know then what the Eskimo equivalent of "come in" was; I have forgotten it now, but when we heard it we would duck through the fly of the tent to be greeted by a flurry of activity. Children would be dumped on the floor and the boxes they had been sitting on offered to us. The woman of the family would hasten to pump up the Coleman stove and put a pot of water on to boil — they invariably used a saucepan, dumping in a handful of tea leaves when the water boiled. The tea was very strong; no attempt was made to strain out the tea leaves, so you invariably got a generous helping of them, the whole sweetened with a big dollop of condensed milk.

Then, as we burned our lips trying to sip tea from tin mugs without touching the rim of the mug, the family would sit in a semicircle, smiling pleasantly at us. Conversation was not easy. They had a few words of English, we even fewer of Eskimo, but it is surprising how little this bothered us. I never felt any sense of strain or embarrassment. We learned, though, to be cautious about admiring any of their possessions; they would immediately insist on giving them to us if we did. After half an hour or so, we would put down our mugs, thank them and leave.

I know that the Eskimos are very courteous people and that they would not have revealed their distaste even if they had not enjoyed these visits. But, in fact, they did; and we had to be careful to visit all the families or feelings would be hurt. To me their only weakness seemed to be that they were too indulgent with their children. When I looked out of the window at dusk — which occurred at about ten o'clock at that time of the year — and saw very small children still out playing in the snow, my puritan instincts were disturbed. They should have been in bed long ago. But of course, Eskimo children are not burdened with the incubus of time: when they are tired, they sleep; when energy bubbles, they play, regardless of the time; and they are just as quaint and fetching as children of all races are, watching us shyly, but sharply, with their brown, almond-shaped eyes.

Many people have commented about the smell of Eskimos. The ones I met smelled almost exclusively of seal blubber, at first a sharp and rather acrid smell. Yet after about a month, I found myself unaware of the smell. It had become part of the environment and was in any case far less objectionable than, for example, the smell of a pulp mill. As well, these Eskimos I discovered were not dirty. They washed both themselves and their children very frequently. Mothers used to carry the very young children in a pouch beneath the hoods of their sealskin parkas — though some of them by now used Hudson's Bay cloth parkas. They had solved the diaper problem by putting a handful of caribou moss, which is both soft and absorbent, into the pouch. And I saw them on many occasions cleaning up their children, just as a white woman has to when she changes diapers. Then they would sit with a bowl of water and a cloth and give the child a comprehensive flannel bath.

One morning, after a day of bad weather and too much sleep, I awoke before five, got dressed and went for a stroll before breakfast. As I rounded one of the Eskimo tents I came upon Louisa, the young wife of one of the Eskimos who worked on our crew, and another young woman. Their clothes were piled on a snowbank; they were stark naked, standing, scrubbing themselves with handfuls of snow. They burst into a serenade of giggles when I appeared but made no attempt to cover themselves and I walked on in some confusion, reflecting that people who scrubbed themselves with snow in this temperature certainly weren't unsanitary.

I suppose nearly all communities have at least one person who stands out from the others, and Payne Bay was no exception. His name was Willie, and Willie was undeniably a character. I always found it difficult to estimate an Eskimo's age, but I am reasonably sure Willie had passed his fiftieth birthday. He had a round, ingenuous face that broke up into a mass of intersecting wrinkles when he smiled — which was nearly all the time. His main distinguishing feature was that he was the only Eskimo in the community with a beard. It was a wispy affair — a few straggling grey hairs — but Willie was very proud of it.

By this time I was six weeks into my first beard, and it was not unsuccessful. By gesture I would make odious comparisons between Willie's beard and mine. From there on I am afraid it degenerated into a series of exaggerated claims, still by gesture, of relative virility. When I reached, by symbolic means, a representation of superlative potency, Willie would chuckle fatly and say, "Ayiee, na," which I interpreted to mean "No way."

He was a very sociable person with a good sense of timing. He would invariably pay us a visit just as we were finishing supper. The cook would feel obliged to offer him a bite to eat, and Willie always gave the impression he was only accepting as a courtesy; he did not want to hurt the cook's feelings. But when the plate was put in front of him he dispatched the food, rather noisily, with an awesome efficiency. The next time he came, the cook increased the helping; but the same thing happened again. To the cook Willie obviously posed a challenge. During the next few days, Willie continued to display an astonishing capacity as a trencherman. No matter how large a helping the cook put in front of him, he would polish it off and then sit back, as Eskimo etiquette demands, to belch appreciatively.

The cook became broody and preoccupied. I don't think he had ever had to go more than two or three rounds to win this particular contest before; the chill wind of defeat was a new experience for him. Finally, he decided to go for a knockout. He got a serving platter, much larger than a dinner plate, and piled food onto it to a height of about ten inches. There must have been the best part of an entire turkey, nestling on a vast mound of potato, stuffing, peas and gravy, on that platter.

Willie's smile never faltered. He moved in, making a noise like a cement-mixer handling a rather dry mix. The rest of us affected not to notice that anything was going on, but we were all watching him out of the corners of our eyes with mounting excitement. He didn't succeed; but it was a magnificent failure. The pile of food had diminished to within an inch of the platter when he suddenly ground to a halt, pushed it away and belched, this time involuntarily.

"Whoohoo, goddam too much," he said sadly, and a look of profound relief stole across the cook's face.

At first I had Willie pegged as a mixture of clown and con man, but he was much more than that. He was intelligent, creative and talented. On one occasion he sat watching Marcel, the radio operator, trying to reassemble an alarm clock he was repairing for someone. Marcel was having trouble with it; he put the pieces down in frustration and went to keep his evening radio schedule with Fort Chimo. Willie, who had been watching him intently, slid along the bench and got to work. By the time Marcel got back, some 20 minutes later, the clock was sitting on the table, working.

One evening I took him for a ride in the helicopter. He had never flown in any aircraft before, yet he was completely relaxed as he sat watching while I started the engine and waited for it to warm up before taking off. When we were in the air, he was fascinated by the unfamiliar perspective of his country. I reached round behind my seat cushion for the aerial photograph of the area we were flying over and gave it to him. He studied it for a moment, then twisted it around two or three times before grunting as he found his orientation. He pointed to features on the ground, then identified them on the photograph, beaming with excitement as he did so.

Not only had he never flown before, I think it is extremely unlikely that he had ever seen an aerial photograph before. Because of the snow on the ground, it was very difficult to identify features; yet, within a matter of perhaps two or three minutes he was map-reading very competently. To me it seemed almost uncanny.

Another of Willie's talents was carving in soapstone. I had seen about five or six carvings on a box in his tent, and although perhaps from an artistic point of view they were a little too representational, to me they were very attractive. They were beautifully detailed and in perfect proportion. He had a kayak and a walrus which I coveted. But I knew that if I displayed any interest in them, he would immediately want to give them to me; so I approached the transaction warily.

We sat and drank a mug of tea and smoked a cigarette in his tent, while his wife sat cross-legged on the bed, sewing a sealskin mukluk. Willie indicated to me smugly that he had succeeded three times the previous night. I demonstrated, with roars of laughter, that I knew he was fantasizing. I pulled at my beard and held up a bent finger to mock his age and incapacity. Willie appealed to his wife. She chuckled and shook her head and said something. I am sure it was something like: "You men — don't you ever think of anything else?" It was a very congenial atmosphere.

Eventually, I picked up the two carvings I wanted, examined them indifferently, then set them down apart from the others on the box. I dug out my wallet and slapped five dollars down with an air of finality. But I am afraid Willie felt insulted. He pushed the money back at me angrily, slid the carvings towards me and gestured that they were mine. I knew that he would get about a dollar apiece for the carvings in the Hudson's Bay store — a couple of dollars for sugar and tea and other small items the Eskimos regarded as luxuries — and I was determined to pay for them. The problem was how.

We argued for awhile, but soon reached an impasse. Finally, it occurred to me to offer cigarettes. I don't think I ever met an Eskimo who doesn't smoke if cigarettes are available, so I pulled out my packet of cigarettes and held up three fingers. I was being deceitful; I meant three cartons and Willie obviously thought I meant three packets. After a little more argument, he finally agreed to accept them.

I went back to my room and returned. There was another uproar when he saw the three cartons, but I dumped them in his wife's lap and carried off my trophies. It was an interesting business. Willie was a very intelligent man and he knew that the cigarettes were not very important to me. So, the idea of giving to somebody anything of yours that he admires must be a very strong cultural imperative.

As a matter of fact, the transaction had an interesting repercussion a day or so later. Mark, the young Hudson's Bay assistant, heard about it and came to see me. He was very angry. He waved a finger in my face and told me I had no right to trade with the Eskimos. If I wanted to buy any carvings from them, or anything else, for that matter, I was to go to the store. He was only about 19, and his assumption of authority irritated me. I pointed out to him that I had in effect paid a good deal more for the carvings than the store would have done; yet I still got them for a great deal less than I would have paid in the store.

That was irrevelant, he snapped. I was perverting the balance of trade between the Eskimo and the white man. I responded with some heat that the only balance I was perverting was the excessive balance of profit made by an exploiting company. I reminded him of the Hudson's Bay rifles, against which furs were stacked to determine how many would be needed to purchase the rifle; and how, over the years, the barrels had grown longer and longer until, in the end, they were damn nearly as long as the barrel on a six-inch howitzer and it required four times as many furs to purchase an article which had become so cumbersome it was useless. The Gentlemen Adventurers trading out of Hudson's Bay, I snarled (a little breathlessly), may have been able to bully people and exploit them in the reign of King Charles, but they weren't bloody well going to do it now, to Willie and me.

I should have saved my breath. It was a futile polemic because to Mark, I suspect, the Hudson's Bay Company was not so much a company as a religion.

My last recollection of Willie is of him in the cookhouse, a day or so before we left Payne Bay and returned to the Tom's River camp. I had returned late from flying one evening and I went in for a solitary supper. The cook had covered my meal and left it on the stove for me. But I found Willie in the cookhouse, standing in contemplation of a calendar nude someone had hung on the wall. It was a large, coloured photograph of a girl sitting in the same position as the celebrated Copenhagen nymph, so that, although it was frontal nudity, nothing unmentionable was showing.

I walked up and stood beside him. "Good stuff, eh Willie?" I remarked. Willie nodded vaguely but he looked perplexed; he was obviously wrestling with an intellectual problem. This was in the days, you must remember, before it was socially permissible to publish photographs revealing that young women do indeed have pubic hair. In this particular case, the hair had been removed, either with a razor blade before the photograph was taken, or with an airbrush afterwards. And it was this deficiency that was puzzling Willie — as I understood when he tugged at his beard, then put his finger on the appropriate spot on the photograph and turned to look at me interrogatively.

I hesitated. To explain something so illogical was a challenge to my powers of communication. The first part wasn't too difficult. I went to fetch my razor and gave him a graphic demonstration. Willie chuckled incredulously, but he was satisfied that there had been hair and that that was how it had disappeared. But the next question was why? Why in the name of all that was muskeg would a young woman want to shave off her pubic hair? I wrestled with this one for awhile, then gave up and shrugged. Willie was far too intelligent to understand that curious taboo. He left me to my supper, still chuckling to himself and shaking his head.

CHAPTER 10

A Heart Attack

WE STAYED IN PAYNE BAY FOR ABOUT FIVE WEEKS, AND AFTER our third week there we had a change of pilots on the Norseman. Hartley went south for a break and he was replaced by Jim Aspinall. We were fortunate with our fixed-wing pilots that year: both were competent and both were excellent company. As a matter of interest, both also took helicopter training the following year and joined Spartan as helicopter pilots.

That is how I came to hear of Jim's incident; he didn't tell me about it at the time. One day, while we were still in Payne Bay, he set off from Chimo by himself to bring us a load of supplies. When he still had some 30 or 40 miles to go, the weather began to close in. There seemed to be more light to the east, so he swung that way, hoping to be able to pick up the coast and work his way round. Some five minutes later things were getting really murky and he was peering down anxiously, trying to see the ground, when all at once he caught sight of something moving astonishingly fast and coming straight at him. As an instinctive reflex he pulled back hard on the stick. The machine shuddered, which was to be expected in the circumstances, but then he became aware that it was continuing to vibrate. He was on the ground. He did not remember doing it, but obviously he must have pulled the throttle back because the next thing he did remember was that he had stopped moving and the engine was ticking over.

I doubt if it would be possible for anybody who has not actually flown an aircraft to appreciate just how traumatic an experience it would be to land purely inadvertently. Jim had touched down on the upslope, an angle of about 15 degrees, of one of the small hills in the area. The chances of doing this without an accident are so negligible as to be unreal. To have hit an area where there were no rocks or ridges of snow was astonishing. But the degree of mush when he pulled back on the stick had to be just right. Too much and he would have wiped off his skis and disintegrated. Too little and he would have bounced back into the air and stalled. The angle of his skis had to be perfect, too, or he would have cartwheeled.

He shut down and sat for a long time, too shaken to move out of his seat. As it happened, the worst of the weather was past and the sky began to brighten. He saw that he was near the crest of the hill. He climbed out and looked at his ski tracks. Because of the slope, he had travelled only about 200 feet. To the right of his tracks he could see the rocks which had seemed to come rushing at him out of nowhere, and made him pull back on the stick. He started the engine, turned around and took off down the hill, reaching Payne Bay without further incident.

I have only heard of one similar experience. It happened to a helicopter pilot when he was crossing the Frank MacKay glacier, flying out of Stewart, B.C., to the Iskut River. In this case, the pilot could see the mountains beyond, but the glacier was in white-out. He flew into the glacier, but bounced back into the air and managed to keep control. Although he damaged his machine, he was able to get back to base. If it had been a fixed-wing aircraft he would almost undoubtedly have stalled and crashed when he bounced.

At the beginning of May the first of the season's exploration crews arrived in the area. It was an advance party of five people who had come to reopen a drill camp some 15 miles to the north-west of the settlement. They were flown in on a DC-3 which left them, together with a big pile of equipment, on a lake about a mile and a half away from their camp. They were dropped around four o'clock, and after supper I decided to go over and meet them. They were glad that I did. The plan had been for them to walk into camp, start the Bombardier — a tracked vehicle — which had been left there the previous season, and then haul their gear into camp. Not surprisingly after the long winter, the Bombardier had failed to start.

They had packed the one and only live battery they had in from the lake on their backs. It was flat, and two of them were trying to start the generating plant so that they could recharge it, while the other three, when I arrived, were just setting off to fetch their sleeping bags and some food and personal gear from the lake. I did three or four trips, carrying their food and personal gear, and promised to look in on them from time to time. Reactivating a camp which has been lying dormant under the snow all winter is a dismal business, but I left them a good deal more cheerful than I found them.

Meanwhile, the weather had not relented. Unpredictable blizzards were still sweeping across the country with very little warning. One day we weren't able to fly early in the morning, but by eleven o'clock it began to clear up after a fashion. Eventually Nels and I decided to put out two ground survey crews, intending to pick them up around eight o'clock for a late supper. By six the weather began to close in again, and we performed our by now familiar scramble to retrieve them before it was too late.

We had six people out, some 18 miles to the north of us. This meant a trip for both helicopters and one more for one of them. We found our crews all right the first trip and I got back to base a minute or two before Nels, so I turned around and went straight back. By now the weather was getting really grisly, and two or three times I made up my mind to give up. In fact, I had begun to swing round for the last time when I spotted them. They were standing on a large, flat expanse of snow, perhaps a lake, and they were just about the only thing I could see. I had to land almost on top of them, using them as a marker.

When I got them into the helicopter I looked around and I could just make out the shadow of some rocks on an esker over to my right. Reaching the rocks, I found there was still enough visibility ahead for me to keep flying; but when I looked in the direction of camp, it was a blank. The best bet, it seemed to me, was to try to reach the drill camp. We nearly made it. I picked up two features on the ground which I was sure of; but then I started to run right out of visibility. It was very frustrating because I knew I was close to the camp, but in the end I had to land in the snow beside some rocks which were the only thing I could see by now.

My passengers were Pauli, the husband of Louisa, the young woman I had been fortunate enough to see taking her version of a bath, and a young Frenchman — not a French-Canadian, but a Frenchman. He came from Paris, and he was over on some sort of student exchange scheme. I think his name was Armand. He was a quiet, rather morose young man who seldom smiled at the things we found amusing. I suspected that, coming from Paris, he was inclined to regard us as a bunch of uncouth colonials. On the other hand, though, he may only have been suffering from homesickness; I had not had much conversation with him, so I couldn't really judge.

I told Pauli and Armand, who was sitting between us, that we would have to wait out the weather. Pauli shrugged and settled back as comfortably as he could — I have told you that three people in winter clothing were very cramped in the narrow bubble of the D model — but Armand started to say something. I couldn't make out what it was, so I asked him to wait until I had shut down. When the rotors stopped turning, I climbed out to put the tie-down on the blades. As I stepped back into the helicopter he demanded, with a curious intensity, that we start walking back to camp.

For once I thought Armand was being humorous, and I laughed. It was snowing hard by now and the wind was blowing about 30 miles an hour. The rocks I had used as a landing marker were only about 50 feet away; yet they were barely discernible. But he was obviously serious and began to insist with growing agitation that we start to walk. I explained to him, no doubt with a hint of impatience, that we weren't going to do anything of the sort. We were well protected in the bubble; the temperature was 20 degrees, but we were dressed for it and, although it might be uncomfortable, it certainly wasn't dangerous. I had emergency rations, together with a little primus stove, strapped to the cargo rack, which I would break out in the morning if we hadn't got away by then. We had nothing to worry about except a little discomfort and boredom.

But he merely shook his head and peremptorily repeated his demand that we start walking. I appealed to Pauli, making a gesture of walking with my fingers. Pauli laughed sardonically; he, too, shook his head and settled back in his seat. "There you are, then," I said to Armand. "He's lived in this country all his life, and if he won't walk there's no way I'm going to." But Armand still persisted and in the end I'm afraid I lost my temper and told him to stop being childish. I was the captain of the aircraft, I reminded him pompously, and I would call the shots until we got back to base.

It seemed to work, and we settled down to pass the night — a night that never got completely dark, but whose opaque grey gloom was even more depressing, I think, than total darkness. I found my feet getting cold, but I was able to doze for awhile. The trouble was, every two hours I had to get out in the wind and snow to take the tie-down off, so that I could run the engine up to operating temperatures; otherwise, we would not be able to start without a ground heater when the weather did clear.

I had done this for the third time, I think, at about one o'clock in the morning, and I had just got warm enough again to start dozing off when Armand sat up and said he had to get out to relieve himself. I cursed him for not doing it while I was running up, but he said he'd got to go and I let him out. I suppose it took me about five minutes to become anxious. I looked around and couldn't see him. I jumped out of the helicopter and called his name; soon I was shouting at the top of my voice. But it was as futile as I imagine it would be to shout at the top of your voice in a padded cell.

Eventually, I climbed back into the bubble and asked Pauli if he would go and try to find him. I had thought of going myself, but it seemed to me that Pauli would be much more likely to find him than I would. Pauli shrugged, but he unhesitatingly climbed out and went off in the direction Armand had taken.

Five minutes later I was horrified with myself. I should never have sent Pauli if I wasn't prepared to go myself. Dear God, I thought, now I've lost both of them. But after another five minutes Pauli suddenly materialized right beside me, and I nearly jumped out of my skin. He walked around to the passenger door, bashed the snow off his clothes and climbed in, shrugging and shaking his head.

There was nothing to be done now but sit back and hope that the weather would clear. I knew that if it didn't we had very little chance of ever seeing Armand again — of seeing him alive, that is. I had endless monologues with myself, by turns cursing Armand for his stupidity, and then blaming myself for not realizing that he had been a frightened young man. Who knew what visions of us all freezing to death he had suffered? Yet instead of reassuring him, as I should have done, I had snarled at him not to be childish.

It is difficult not to use clichés in such circumstances; but if that wasn't the longest night of my life, it was certainly one of the longer ones. The first ray of hope came at about seven o'clock in the morning, when it stopped snowing. Two hours later, the weather cleared so abruptly that I had difficulty persuading myself that it was true. I took the tie-down off, and I was just about to climb back into the helicopter again when I heard a vehicle starting up. It was an immense shock, because in my anxiety I had completely forgotten about the drill camp. When we looked towards the sound, we could see the camp plainly; it was scarcely half a mile away.

Coppermine, on the Arctic coast, looking its best in 1958.

A first encounter with the Barrens and the joys of navigation in the winter. Refuelling from cans carried on the racks en route from Fort Chimo to Tom's River, March 1955.

Bruce Craig beside the chimney, all that was left of Fort Confidence, near the northeast corner of Great Bear Lake, in 1958. This was the base from which John Franklin set out on his second expedition to the Arctic coast in 1826.

Nels Bentley (left) and the author at the Tom's River camp in northern Quebec, spring 1955. One float has been removed for repairs.

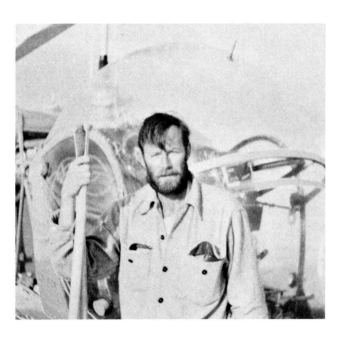

My first beard. The helicopter is a Bell 47-D. The joint running across the front of the bubble indicates that this is a modified B3, the first commercial helicopter to operate in Canada in 1947.

Nels Bentley carried an inflatable dinghy with him in the bush. I borrowed it frequently because it made a superb portable bath, though I found it somewhat tedious to empty afterwards.

A very different environment. The family tent on Shuswap Lake on the B.C. Forest Service inventory contract in 1964.

Wives of the Eskimo surveyors who worked with us out of Tom's River and Payne Bay.

In the early days of helicopter operations, people in the North invariably congregated, hoping for a ride. Yellowknife, 1958.

Max Ward's Bristol Freighter, which set out our camp and supplies on the Coppermine Geological Survey of Canada operation. Yellowknife, 1958.

A geological Survey of Canada camp south of Coppermine, 1958. This was a two-helicopter operation, supported by the Wardair Otter on skis before the break-up, and on floats after the ice had gone out.

The fish bite eagerly in the Barrens—as do the mosquitoes.

Some of the crew at Tom's River. The Lake Trout is not a particularly large one for that area.

The Eskimos always insisted on helping us to pump gas. Coppermine, 1958.

Port Radium, Great Bear Lake, the first Canadian uranium mine, which opened in the early 1940s. The tennis court can be seen at bottom left.

Two shy young women belonging to a small band of Eskimos on the Arctic coast, north of Chesterfield Inlet, 1960. They were still practising the cultural skills of the seal people; virtually none of their clothes or implements came from the white man.

Somewhere to the south of Baker Lake, 1960. "They looked for all the world as though they had been mushing along when the snow ran out; and now they were sitting waiting for it to come back again so that they could resume their journey."

The Wardair Otter that supported us during the Coppermine operation. Here, by the light of the midnight sun, the crew is preparing to convert the Otter from wheels to skis on Point Lake, spring 1958.

The Barrens can be very beautiful, particularly in a photograph when you can't see the mosquitoes.

A ship that didn't make it back to port. This was a Hudson's Bay Company supply vessel, the *Nichilin*. The Captain was forced to beach the vessel after it became trapped, and then damaged, by pack ice the previous fall. The crew was rescued by aircraft and the ship abandoned.

The urge for immortality. Building a cairn above one of our camp sites in the Barrens, 1960. *Left to right*: Geologists Bill Heywood, Jim Aitkin (wearing cap), Bruce Craig, pilot Claude Jolin and the apprentice helicopter engineer.

The helicopter that didn't quite make it to the airport at Churchill, 1960. We are tidying up the pieces before they were slung the last mile or two by a U.S. Air Force Vertol helicopter. *Left to right*: the author, pilot/engineer Garry Fields and a U.S.A.F. technician.

A remote band of Eskimos had lost all their dogs to disease. The R.C.M.P. flew out another team of huskies—not a popular task because the cabin invariably had to be hosed out afterwards.

I did a test flight on one of the profitable snowmobiles on the Penny Icecap, Baffin Island.

Summer fly-camp, Baffin Island, 1961.

Not a prayer, but a gravimeter reading on Baffin Island, 1961.

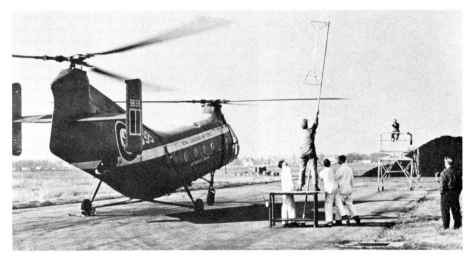

This was the task known as "tracking." The tips of each blade were marked with chalk of different colours; then the white flag was moved in until the blades flipped it. The resulting chalk marks would indicate which blades were high or low. Adjustments could then be made so that all three blades in each system flew the same "track." If they didn't, the helicopter would vibrate. Mid-Canada Line, Great Whale River, 1957.

We came across an Eskimo family butchering and drying caribou meat somewhere between Dismal Lake and Coppermine, 1958. The son was a little reluctant, but the mother was happy to pose for us. The whole family appeared to regard the arrival of the helicopter as a perfectly normal event.

Eskimo child—Tom's River.

Greg Lamb's Cessna 180—
our back-up in 1960.

G.S.C. geologists examining their collection of rock specimens at the end of the day.

A distinguished visitor on the Coppermine operation. *Right to left*: pilot Audley Black, A. Y. Jackson and a fellow artist whose name, alas, I have forgotten.

Three or four minutes later the Bombardier, driven by the foreman of the crew, drew up beside us. He was very apologetic. They had heard us land and they wanted to come and get us, but when they came out of their tents they just couldn't see anything. I brushed his apologies aside impatiently and asked if he had seen Armand. He shook his head. I explained what had happened. The foreman looked incredulous.

"No, we ain't seen him," he said, "but if we do, we'll throw a rope round him and keep him tied up until you get back."

I took off and began to search in a wide circle round our landing spot. But looking for someone in that country is much more difficult than it seems. It is true there are no trees, but there are a multitude of rocks which, from a distance, look like a person. Aften ten minutes I decided to whip back to camp, alert Nels Bentley and start an organized search with him.

We concluded that 15 miles was the most Armand could possibly have walked in the time available, and we set off on a square search of this area, flying parallel and about a hundred yards apart. Our first swing was at the northern limit of this area. We flew back about two miles south. We were on our fourth swing, I think, when I picked up what looked like footprints, some six or seven miles northwest of the drill camp. I went down to check them, but I couldn't tell which way they were heading. From where I was, they meandered all over the place; so Nels went one way and I the other. I lost mine after a mile or so, and when I swung back I saw Nels just settling into the hover to land. By the time I reached him, he was helping Armand into the helicopter.

I got back to base a few minutes before Nels landed, and when he did, Armand promptly stumbled across to embrace me. I had been standing, summoning up all the synonyms I could think of for ultimate stupidity, but I held my peace. He had lost his mitts and his fingers were mildly frostbitten; but it was his eyes we were worried about. Soon after he left the helicopter he had found himself stumbling and falling, so he had discarded his snow goggles. The light had been dangerously bright from about six o'clock on. From nine o'clock until we found him, some two hours later, the sun had been shining brightly — and even half an hour in bright sunshine on total snow means a severe attack of snow blindness. His eyes were already so swollen he could scarcely see out of them.

Jim Aspinall flew up from Fort Chimo to take him down for treatment. His blindness was so serious that the nurses shipped him down to Montreal and I never saw him again. He was a very fortunate young man. He had done just about everything that was foolish and inadvisable, but he got away with it. And because of this, I found it peculiarly sad and ironic when I heard, a year later, that Willie had been caught out in a prolonged spell of bad weather, while on a hunting trip the previous winter, and he had frozen to death in his igloo only a few miles from where we had spent our one night out. Willie had survived more than 50 winters in that country, and I am confident he did not do anything foolish or inadvisable; but in his case, the weather did not relent.

Late one night, a week or so later, I was sitting by myself in the cookhouse writing a letter, when Mark, the Hudson's Bay assistant, suddenly came through the door. He was in a state of considerable emotion, but it was difficult to tell just what kind of emotion. On the one hand, he looked excited and a trifle complacent; on the other, he seemed angry. He told me that Jimmy, the factor, had collapsed with a heart attack. I jumped up to go with him and provide what assistance I could, but he brushed this suggestion aside; he had done all that could be done, and he had called Fort Chimo on the company radio to ask for an emergency flight. Jim Aspinall wanted to speak to Nels or me, and this is what had made Mark angry. He had obviously wanted to deal with the emergency on his own; he did not want us involved.

It was after 11 o'clock. I looked out of the window. It was about as dark as it would get that night, and I had no thought that Jim would come until the following day. He probably wanted to set up an early morning radio sked for a weather report. I switched on the portable radio we had in one corner of the cookhouse, and while I was waiting for it to warm up I asked some questions about Jimmy's condition. He was unconscious, Mark said, and breathing with a sort of snoring noise. It sounded ominous.

When we got Jim on the radio, he wanted to know what the weather was like. I went out to check. It was pretty dark, but I could see some of the brighter stars, and there was very little wind. "Okay," said Jim, "I'll bring a nurse with me and give it a try. Can you guys round up some lights and put them out along the strip where I usually land,"

I assured him that we'd have some lights for him by the time he arrived. Mark went back to look after Jimmy, while I woke our crew up and we set about our preparations with some sense of drama. We had four Coleman lanterns, and we decided to use them, supplemented by flares made from empty soup cans full of fuel oil, with a strip of gunny sack for a wick. We tried one out; it worked well, but it was hard to light. We solved that by making torches with a handful of oil-soaked cotton waste tied to a stick.

We prepared about a dozen of these soup-can flares, then went down to the smooth patch of snow on the ice in front of the store, where Jim had been landing for the past three weeks. While we were setting them out, Ooma, Jimmy's Eskimo wife, came down to us. She was obviously excited and distressed. We tried to explain to her that we were doing all we could for her husband, that medical assistance was on the way, but she persisted and in the end we had to ask one of the other Eskimos, who were standing watching us, to take her back to the house. He did so, but then he, too, came back and began to jabber away. We grew impatient and sent him off. For heaven's sake, we were doing all we could. The Eskimos were all very well, I realized, but in an emergency they became excited and garrulous at a time when action is more important than words.

When we heard the Norseman approaching from the south, Ted Blanchet and I lit our torches and, starting from the middle, ran in opposite directions to the ends of our strip, lighting the flares. I was impressed with Jim's performance. It took some courage to fly over that country, virtually in the dark, in a single-engined aircraft. If he had had any trouble on the way, his chances of making a safe landing would have been very small. And there was some drama in the scene, I recall; the group of parka-clad figures standing in the smoky glare of the flares, while the Norseman, its exhaust stacks glowing cherry red, sank to a landing. This was the sort of thing I had anticipated in the north. People reacting promptly and courageously to an emergency.

Jim stopped at the end of the runway where I was standing. He decided to leave the aircraft where it was. I went to the back and opened the door, taking the nurse's bag and handing her down onto the ice. We hurried together up the bank to Jimmy's house, which was some 50 yards from the store. I had met the nurse several times in Chimo. Her attitude was briskly professional, almost severe, but I suspect some of this was deliberately cultivated in order to discourage men who had not seen a white woman for some time, and who tended to come on too strong. She asked me what Jimmy's condition was. I repeated what Mark had told me and said that none of us had seen Jimmy. Mark was looking after him.

As we went through the door into the kitchen, I saw that Ooma was sitting at the table. Jimmy's bedroom was off the kitchen, and Mark opened the bedroom door when he heard us come in. He was handling himself well, keeping cool in a crisis, but I noticed that after letting the nurse into the bedroom he closed the door rather pointedly to prevent me from following. I turned to look at Ooma. I had never seen an Eskimo experiencing grief before; they were always so cheerful. She had a grimace of misery on her face that looked almost like a smile. It was grotesque, and I felt awfully sorry for her. After all these years she would find it difficult to move back into an Eskimo tent if Jimmy died. I went and put my arm across her shoulder. I was embarrassed; I didn't know what to say. One can hardly murmur "there, there" to a woman more than 20 years one's senior. She put her face in her hands and let out a choking snort of distress.

I thought it best to leave her alone, and I was just moving towards a chair to sit down when the bedroom door opened and the nurse reappeared. She, too, had an odd expression on her face. She was breathing hard, almost panting. Then she uttered three or four words which, particularly in those days, you seldom heard from the lips of a respectable young woman.

"Do you know all that's wrong with that — that man in there?" she demanded.

I shook my head, bewildered.

"He's been into the sauce; that's what's wrong. I could smell it as soon as I went through the door. The son of a bitch is bombed out of his mind."

A snort of laughter escaped me before I could choke it off. I glanced at Mark, who was standing behind her in the doorway. There was a deep flush on his cheeks, but he did not meet my eye. I turned to see if Ooma had understood. As I did so, she finally lost control. A great, bubbling giggle burst from her.

Things came into focus for me rather quickly. I had heard from someone that Jimmy occasionally went on a solitary bender, drinking until his booze ran out or until he passed out, whichever came first. Mark, who had only been here a month or two, evidently didn't know this; Ooma, who had been married to Jimmy for years, just as obviously did. She had tried to warn us down on the ice, as had the other Eskimo, but we in our self-importance had patronizingly shushed them away. It was a bad scene. I knew that the nurse was very angry, but we had made such glorious fools of ourselves that it was almost impossible not to laugh.

I gritted my teeth and turned back to the nurse. In spite of everything, I made little blubbering noises. All at once she burst out laughing. We made so much noise the rest of our crew came bursting into the kitchen to find out what on earth was going on.

Young Mark had an interview with Jim Aspinall a little later that night. I cannot believe he found it a pleasant one.

CHAPTER 11

The Break-Up

WE MOVED BACK TO THE TOM'S RIVER CAMP AT THE END OF May. Things were beginning to improve: the days were warmer and the snow was melting at last. It was possible now to make out many of the lakes and we were hoping to get started on the barometer work. Once you had dug through the snow and established that you were on the ice of a lake, it did not matter where on the lake you took your reading; obviously it remained level. In practice, though, we still could not identify the smaller lakes, and the ice we found might often be covering a slough or connecting waterway. We could only guarantee the location of about three out of five readings; so we had to mark time for another two or three weeks yet.

Work started in earnest, I think, about the middle of June. By then the snow had gone off the lakes and the larger ones were breaking up. As is often the case in bush flying, we jumped right away from famine to feast. For months we had been sitting around getting bored; now we settled down to a regime of work, eat and sleep. In the next three weeks I doubled my flying time. We began at seven in the morning and usually got back at about nine o'clock in the evening. We would begin by putting out the two ground survey crews; then we put out the two barometer base-men, perhaps 15 miles apart. After taking our readings at half-mile intervals between them, we would leapfrog the first base-man another 15 miles and repeat the process. We became competitive. Paul, the lad flying with me, was determined to bring in more readings by the end of the day than Nels and his partner. On one or two occasions we exceeded a hundred readings a day — which is an awful lot of landings and take-offs.

For a little while, though, we established our supremacy and I felt smug about it — until a couple of incidents slowed me down considerably. We had developed a system which seemed to be working well. I would nod to Paul when we were down; he would jump out, his barometer slung over one shoulder, his clipboard in the other hand, and sprint about 50 yards away from the helicopter to avoid any pressure anomalies caused by the downwash from the rotor blades. Then he would wait impatiently for the two minutes he had to allow for his barometer to stabilize before he took his reading. On one occasion he jumped out before I nodded, and before I had settled right down on the ice. I had to compensate for the change in balance as he went out on the rack, and when he jumped I was still holding power. I shot up and sideways, straight at the bank of the lake some 50 feet away. I only just managed to regain control before hitting it. Paul had not looked back. He was unaware that anything untoward had occurred, and he was a little sulky because I insisted on slowing things down after that.

The next incident, which occurred perhaps ten days later, was a good deal more serious. In the first, I would probably have walked away from a wrecked machine; in the second, both of us came close to being wiped out. We had stopped to eat our sandwich lunch on the bank of a lake after taking a reading. Paul had laid his barometer on the cargo rack while we did so, and when we took off again he forgot to pick it up and bring it with him into the bubble. I had climbed to about a hundred feet, and I was looking ahead to pick up the next lake we were to land at, when all at once Paul let out an exclamation, unsnapped his seatbelt, opened the door and climbed out onto the rack to retrieve the barometer. He moved so quickly I had no time even to shout at him. In a D model, there was no way you could maintain control in this unbalanced condition. I had the Cyclic right against its left-hand stop, but we swung down and to the right in a steepening spiral. Fortunately, Paul was as quick and agile climbing back into the bubble as he had been in climbing out onto the rack. Another half a second and it would have been too late. As it was, we pulled out with everything shuddering ferociously and skimmed the ground before I could get things calmed down. After that, on threat of being grounded, Paul had to wait for my permission to unbuckle his seatbelt.

In general, though, we found that June is a pleasant month in the Barrens. Nowhere else have I experienced such an almost explosive coming to life. As the snow dissolved there were instant flowers everywhere. The flowers were so small that, individually, they were hard to see; but there was such a profusion of them that the gentle slopes glowed with colour: a sort of pastel glow — blue, mauve, pale-pink or yellow. And in amongst them, we suddenly found that the caribou moss was alive with lemmings. Then the birds came: every kind of bird imaginable, it seemed, and there were so many nests it literally became difficult to land without disturbing one. By now the ice was becoming too fractured for landing, and Paul would grow impatient when I put him down some distance from a lake to avoid these nests. But with all this came another form of life which gave us no pleasure at all.

When I'd heard people talking of mosquitoes in the north, I tended to scoff. I had been in Africa and I was sure I had seen as great a concentration of mosquitoes as anyone in Canada ever had. I learned that I was wrong. That year was a four-star one for mosquitoes in the Ungava area. I flew five seasons in the Arctic, and thank heavens I never saw anything like it again, because it was a scary feeling to shut down the helicopter after a landing on the caribou moss on a windless day. As the rotor blades slowed down, a grey cloud would rise up around you, and the noise was like distant hives of bees, innumerable bees, swarming. They were so thick they cut down the visibility; they were so thick they became a physical problem in flying. After two or three hours of landings and take-offs, the build-up of dead mosquitoes on the leading edges of the rotor blades began to affect the performance of the machine. For a period of about two weeks we had to return to camp every two or three hours, and take an hour off while the engineers scraped the blades.

In fact, it was the engineers and the barometer base-men who really suffered. Unless there was a strong breeze blowing, they had to wear headnets — and trying to do maintenance on a helicopter from behind a headnet is about as frustrating as anything I know. The rest of us doused ourselves in insect repellant and came to understand why, even on the hottest day, the Eskimos still wore their parkas with their hoods up. The insect repellant worked after a fashion, but it was messy stuff to use; it removed the paint off everything you touched. Our company colour was yellow, and gradually my clothes and my boots took on a pale yellow hue.

Jimmy, the Hudson's Bay manager, told me the story of how the most efficacious insect repellant had been discovered. During the construction of the DEW-Line, all the steel beams shipped up were coated with a special paint to inhibit rust. Apparently, this paint had to be removed before the steel was installed. For this purpose, the construction workers used 45-gallon drums of paint remover, and before long they noticed that every time they opened the drums the mosquitoes promptly vanished. The paint companies responded to this discovery with equal promptness: they marketed a watered-down version of the paint remover in small bottles at 50 times the price of the original.

My education, meanwhile, continued. I experienced two conditions which later became very familiar. First, I experienced friction with the party chief — later I was to learn that such friction is a 90 per cent probability — and second, I learned what is meant by the term, "getting bushed." The initial symptoms are an edginess and irritation, accompanied by a diminishing sense of the rational. The peculiarity of the malady is that it always happens to other people; never to oneself. Yves, our party chief, who had perhaps been under more pressure than any of us, started to become unreasonably demanding. We were working from seven in the morning until nine at night; yet still he was dissatisfied. We had to catch up for time lost, he kept insisting. I failed to see the logic of this; as far as I was concerned, I had not lost any time, but in any case, Nels and I pointed out to him that 14-hour days, on a seven-days-a-week basis, were more than enough, and that we'd probably have to cut back before long because it was dangerously tiring. Yves dropped the subject but then, ironically enough when we were working very hard, he decided that he had to economize on food.

I did not know it at the time, but the cook we had turned out to be one of the very best I ever encountered in the bush. He managed to provide enough variety to satisfy even the pickiest amongst us. Now abruptly he had the ordering of supplies taken out of his hands, and the small luxuries like pickled herring and chutney disappeared from the table; fresh vegetables were replaced by dehydrated ones. But worse was to come. Yves had discovered that by far the cheapest meat available was turkey. For the next month we had an unrelieved diet of turkey. It palled; it palled horribly, and the only alternative was canned meat — spam or spic or whatever it was called in those days. When I could no longer face another mouthful of turkey, I found myself on a regime of spam sandwiches and pickles. The whole crew began to react very strongly. We tried to reason with Yves, but he was adamant; we had to economize. More was to come. Yves now discovered that sausages, bought in bulk, were far cheaper than bacon. The next time the Norseman came in, we unloaded half a dozen cases of sausages with the now inevitable turkeys.

But the sausages must have been fairly mature before they were sent to us. After about five days and three cases of them, the remainder began to advertise their presence as soon as you stepped into the cookhouse. I complained to the cook, but he held out his hands in a gesture of Gallic resignation. It wasn't his fault. We'd never had bad sausages when he was ordering the food. What made this all the more irritating was that Yves had his wife and child with him. They lived in a separate unit, with their own propane stove, and we knew very well that they weren't subjecting themselves to a regime of turkey and tainted sausages. We knew, because when we were unloading the sausages we had come across a large carton marked with his name. It was full of joints of meat and thick, succulent steaks.

Things came to a head that night. I came in for supper in a bad temper; it had been a tedious day. I had lost a good deal of time with minor snags. I had to change plugs twice, and I'd thrown a fan belt. The cook, in a forlorn attempt to provide variety, had tried making a stew. Turkey stew was the last straw. I turned away from it and saw some of the breakfast sausages, sitting on a plate. They looked good. They were cold, of course, and when I picked one up and smelled it, it seemed all right. But when I bit into it, the sour, rancid flavour nearly made me gag. I sat sulkily eating bread and jam. After supper I tried writing a letter. But it was no good: the tone was unmistakably self-pitying. In the end I put on a head-net and went out to talk to Ted Blanchet, who was doing a daily inspection of my machine, FCK.

I never did understand how helicopter engineers could tolerate their existence. All day they sat around camp, doing nothing. Then, in the evening — when what little social life there is in a bush camp takes place, when the crew discusses what it has seen during the day — the engineer had to go out and work on the machine so that it would be ready to fly in the morning. And in the late evening, the wind almost invariably dies down so that the mosquitoes are at their most active. I used to try to make a point of going out to talk to Ted while he was working on the machine for at least half an hour every evening. On this occasion, not surprisingly, the subject turned to food. It was nearly 11 o'clock before Ted put his tools away. By that time everyone else had gone to bed, but our deliberations had borne fruit; we had come to a decision.

We made our way quietly to the shed attached to the back of the cookhouse, where the food was stored. We carried the three remaining cases of sausages to the back of another shed some 50 yards away. It was the shed in which the fuel oil and propane bottles were stored. Just beyond it were the two tents of the Eskimo families. And behind these were some 30 dogs, staked out on a long wire. The dogs were all asleep, noses tucked into their tails. One or two of them looked up at us indifferently before settling down again. Ted opened the first case. The sausages were in strings of about twelve each. He picked up a string and whirled it around his head once or twice, tentatively; then he warmed up, swung it around his head in earnest and let it go in a high, swirling arc up over the shed. The string of sausages landed more or less in the middle of the dogs, and it had a remarkably stimulating effect on them. One minute they were curled up, sound asleep; the next they were wide awake. Those within reach of the sausages fought ferociously and vociferously for them; those out of reach put back their heads and howled with deep emotion at the injustice of their lot.

It was a very considerable commotion. I shouldn't have been surprised to learn that they could hear it clear across in Payne Bay. And I'm afraid Ted and I got a little carried away. We began to dance around, whirling the strings of sausages round our heads and howling like the huskies before we sailed them up into the air. By this time the Eskimos were all out of their tents, watching us in fascination. When I looked round I saw that our entire crew, with the exception of Yves, was out cheering us on. It was something of a catharsis. We went to bed, if not exactly purged, at least very refreshed. I slept soundly.

But when I awoke, my mood had changed. I wasn't even sure that anyone had mentioned to Yves that the sausages were bad, and in the cold light of morning my behaviour the previous night seemed irresponsible and childish; a deliberate affront to the party chief. It even crossed my mind that I might be a little bushed — but that was absurd, of course, and breakfast helped to restore my confidence. We had hotcakes (there was nothing else); the crew praised us extravagantly for our gesture of defiance. The cook, who was still smarting over the insult of having the food orders taken away from him, was particularly generous in his praise. Nevertheless, when Nels and I went to see Yves to work out the day's program of flying, I was nervous. Surprisingly enough, nothing happened; the fierce recriminations I was expecting did not materialize. Yves was polite and business-like. He said nothing about the sausages.

I don't quite know what the psychology was, but I think it had something to do with the fact that it was our crew and not his who had reacted; thus he could back away from his mistake about the food without losing face. We learned that Yves had gone to the cook after we had taken off and told him to get on the radio and order whatever food he needed.

By that time, though, I was experiencing another problem. The long days of flying were beginning to tell on me. For the first time in my life I began to wake up in the morning still feeling physically tired. A light helicopter is, of course, a very tiring machine to fly. There is constant motion, noise and vibration — all of which bring fatigue. In addition, the bubble forms a natural greenhouse; the days were now hot and sunny. But what bothered me was that Nels didn't appear to be nearly as tired as I was. This was because I was still learning. I had to think about everything I was doing; I had not yet developed the reflexes which take much of the load off an experienced pilot. Then, too, experience teaches you that there are many ways in which to slow down the pace when it gets too hectic without overtly refusing to fly. It was known as customer management.

A week or so into July we heard, just as we going to bed, a noise that is familiar to people who live in the Arctic. The ice broke up on the rivers. There was a long groaning, grumbling sound, accompanied by sharp, explosive cracks. When we took off to fly the next morning we could see for the first time long, open stretches of water in both the Payne and the Tom's. That evening Nels called the crew together for a consult. He said that we had been working for nearly a month now without a break and that he was getting very tired — an admission that did a good deal for my morale. During that time we hadn't been able to take a bath, nor wash our clothes. It was unfair, he suggested, to expect the customer's crew to fly with pilots who smelled as we must. There was also the question of maintenance: the engineers needed a full day on the helicopters while the wind was blowing and the mosquitoes were down so that they could give them a good inspection. In addition to which, he added, he had heard somewhere that the best fishing was to be had right after the ice went out on the rivers.

Not surprisingly, there were no objections from our crew, but I was startled when we went to tell Yves and he appeared almost enthusiastic about the idea. I discovered why later. We had completed, in one month, the work he had planned for the entire season. He needed the aerial photographs of the adjacent area to start the next phase. He had sent an urgent message to his department for them more than a week ago, but they had not come yet. I could understand his reluctance to let us know this; only two weeks before he had been complaining that we weren't catching up on the time lost.

I remember that that day off seemed almost a sinful indulgence. Nels carried with him on bush operations a small inflatable rubber dinghy, which made a splendid bath. We heated buckets of water on the Coleman stoves and luxuriated in the hot water for a long time. Then we did our laundry and caught up with the other neglected domestic tasks. I was wearing an old pair of corduroy slacks — so old that they still had fly buttons. All the buttons had fallen off, and the Eskimos had begun to make ribald comments. After lunch the entire crew took what fishing gear we had and walked a mile or so across the tundra to the river.

Within a few seconds of the first cast, there were shouts and yells of excitement. I have only seen fishing like it in one other place: a small stream near Great Whale River, on the shores of James Bay; but then it was trout, none of which weighed much more than half a pound. Here we were catching char, which I believe qualify as a species of salmon. The smallest was about six pounds, the largest some twelve pounds; and if you did not get a strike within ten seconds of the lure hitting the water, you knew that you had lost the lure. They were clean run, in beautiful condition, but after the first half-hour of ecstasy it became boring. The charm of fishing lies in the patience required and the illusion of skill as you wait for a strike. If the anticipation is gone, if you know beyond any doubt that the strike is inevitable as soon as you cast, the only other thing is the skill with which you play the fish. Most of us had very heavy lines, and it soon became work rather than pleasure. Besides which, we soon had an absurd pile of fish on the bank.

It seemed to take hours to clean them, and when we staggered back to camp, each burdened with something like a hundred pounds of fish, our spirits were dampened considerably. A telegram had arrived from Spartan, advising us that the crew who were supposed to have relieved us nearly a month ago would not be coming up for at least another two weeks.

CHAPTER 12

Back South to Another Education

NELS BENTLEY WAS AMUSED BY MY INDIGNATION AT THE
failure of our promised relief crew to arrive. This was the third time
we had had word of a postponement. He advised me that I would
have to learn to live with broken promises in this business; in fact,
he wouldn't really be surprised if we were all still here at the end of
the contract in September. I was more than a little mutinous when
he told me this. I felt the company had been dishonest, and in any
case I was not prepared to be separated from my wife for seven
months at a time. In the end I persuaded Nels to send a telegram
hinting rather strongly that the operation might come to a grinding
halt if our reliefs didn't appear soon.

I don't know whether or not this made any difference, but at the
end of July a relief pilot and engineer did arrive. The pilot was
Carl Faulkner. I took him out in the helicopter to show him how
we had been operating. He had some two or three hundred more
hours of helicopter time than I did, and he made it clear that he
didn't need any coaching from me. I was eager to get away, and
there was nothing complex about what we were doing, so we went
back to camp. Carl went off to work, and I to finish my packing.
After lunch I went to tell Yves that we would be going out as soon
as Jim Aspinall was ready to take us. It wouldn't be until after
supper, anyway, because Yves had got him to put out the ground
survey crews and he would have to bring them in first.

Yves looked down at the aerial photographs he had been studying
when I came in. "No, I don't think so," he said. "I've decided to
keep the Norseman here for a week or so. Jim can look after the
ground crews while the helicopters get on with the barometer work."
He looked up at me. I can't really say he had a smirk on his face,

94

but he certainly looked complacent. He had not forgotten the sausages.

I went back to our quarters. Jim Aspinall was lying on the cot we had set up for him in our room, reading. He could put both ground survey crews out in one trip, after which he had nothing to do all day until he went to fetch them in the evening. He looked thoughtful when I told him with some bitterness what Yves had said. "You all packed?" he asked.

"Yes, of course I am."

"Well, let's figure on leaving after supper," he said with a grin. "I punctured one of my floats on a rock when I was putting those guys out this morning. It's leaking and I can't fix it here — I'll have to go down to Chimo. What time do we have supper?"

I told him around nine. He heaved himself off the bed. "I'll go see the cook. We'll eat around six, so we can get away by seven."

Yves' smile was unmistakably forced when I went to say good-bye to him. It was a pity; I had worked hard for him yet I left with a sour taste in my mouth.

Ted Blanchet and I flew down to Chimo in the Norseman that evening. We were expecting to have to wait in Chimo until one of the DEW-Line aircraft came through on its way to Montreal. But when we got there, we found an R.C.A.F. Boxcar parked off the end of the runway. The crew were staying overnight and then going on to Ottawa in the morning. They agreed to take us with them. The flying Boxcar was one of the aviation industry's mistakes. It was a very large machine which should have had four engines; instead, the designers had tried to make do with two. The result was that if one engine failed, it could not stay in the air for very long on the other, and there had been some notable mishaps. Even so, I felt it was less dangerous to fly in than one of the DEW-Line machines, and it was taking me direct to within a mile or so of my home.

For me the next few weeks turned out to be a period of discovery, disconcerting discovery for the most part, as I learned what an unstable business I was in, what a fractured existence I had committed myself to. After five straight months in the bush, I was confident I would be able to spend at least a month at home with my family. Instead, only a week after I got back, the phone rang. It was John Theilman, explaining apologetically that the company was having problems and that he wanted me to go out on another job — only for a week or so. I protested; perhaps squawked would be a better word, but he claimed it was an emergency: two weeks at the outside, and I would get my break afterwards. I didn't really have any option but to agree.

John certainly wasn't exaggerating when he said the company was having problems. They were bound to; they had expanded far too rapidly. I forget the exact numbers now, but when I joined Spartan they had 12 helicopters; three years later they had nearly 40, and they were challenging Okanagan as the largest helicopter operator in the world. Trying to find enough qualified pilots to fly these machines became an almost impossible task. In the rush to meet the demand during the boom of the 1950's, the company hired a lot of American pilots on the telephone. Some turned out to be competent; others did not.

One, whose name was Gabe, had been an army helicopter pilot in Korea. He came from Texas, and as soon as he arrived, before he had done any flying for the company, he was asked if he knew of any other pilots looking for a job. As a matter of fact, he did. His friend's name was Jed, and Jed was promptly summoned to join the company. They made a good pair. Between them, during the next four months, Gabe and Jed seriously damaged nine helicopters. But of the two, Jed was the more flamboyant disaster: there was a sort of total incompetence about his accidents that made you respect him for having the courage to step into a helicopter. His first flight for the company was in Quebec, from a place called La Tuque to Chibougamau. Approximately two hours after he had taken off he ran out of gas, tried to autorotate onto the road beneath him, and rolled the machine up into a ball. Some three mishaps later, I believe he was recalled to Ottawa for additional training, then sent back to La Tuque.

At the time, La Touque was our bread and butter operation. It was on the Pinetree Line, the southernmost of the three Canadian radar defence lines, and it was a year-round operation. We had a small hangar-cum-workshop there, and the flying was not demanding: all the sites had a prepared landing. Nevertheless, within three weeks Jed had missed one of the landing pads, smacked his tail into it and junked his tail boom. In the meantime, however, he had been making his name in other spheres. He was tall and handsome, with a romantic Texas accent. He owned a powder-pink Cadillac convertible which, fortuitously, ran very well on 80/87 octane, the fuel used in the new G2 models we were now flying on this operation (some calculations at head office revealed that that particular G2 had more than doubled its fuel consumption since Jed took over). According to all reports, the combination of his good looks, his accent and his car had bowled over the young maidenhood of La Tuque and, rugged Texan though he was, sometimes the demands made on him caused him to be late for flying when he was needed.

One day, the engineer wearily went the rounds of the motels until he found Jed, separated him from a reluctant young woman, and got him headed off for a day's work. Jed never came back. An hour or two after he left, he ran out of gas for the second time. On this occasion, he did it over a vast sandbar on the river. But that made no difference. Jed hit so hard that the crosstubes — the tubes which supported the floats — were bent up into an elegant bow, and the main blades cut the tail boom off on the first bounce.

Two supervisory engineers went up from Ottawa to help the base engineer salvage the machine and rebuild it, while the operations manager went up with the avowed and enthusiastic intention of firing Jed. He never enjoyed that satisfaction because, after the accident, Jed had waded ashore, walked to the nearest road, hitch-hiked back to town and then, pausing only long enough to pack his bags and load them into the powder-pink Cadillac, he had set off to return to the green fields of Texas. We never saw him again.

But I am getting ahead of myself. The problem I had to deal with on this occasion was caused by Gabe. Gabe was on his third machine by then. Two weeks before I returned from Ungava, he had started up with the rotor blades tied down. When a helicopter is left on the ground, a shaped block of wood is slipped over one blade and tied to the tail boom with strong canvas tapes to prevent the blades from thrashing around in the wind. Obviously, it has to be removed before the engine is started, and Gabe had neglected to do this. Bill McCarthy, the new operations manager, was philosophical about this mistake. He claimed there were two kinds of pilots: those who had started with the tie-down on, and those who were going to. Unfortunately, though, it is an expensive little error. When it happens, there is a strong smell of burning (so I'm told) as the clutch linings disintegrate. While this is going on, pieces of the clutch material drop into the transmission and later find their way into the engine. So the net result is that the engine, clutch and transmission all have to be replaced at a cost of several thousand dollars.

All this had been taken care of a week ago, and Gabe had returned to work in Chibougamau, where there was a mining exploration rush taking place. The night John phoned me, his engineer had just called to say that Gabe had poked his main rotor blades into the trees at the edge of a clearing, severely damaging them. In those days we had wooden rotor blades, and Gabe had insisted on taping them up and continuing to fly. Not surprisingly, the machine was vibrating badly, and the engineer was afraid the blades might let go altogether. We had to take Gabe a replacement machine.

The prevailing wisdom at that time was that one never flew a helicopter anywhere if one could transport it in any other way. The railways were tried, but we quickly discovered that no matter how carefully we tied the machine down in a railway boxcar it was invariably a wreck by the time it reached its destination. So after that, we loaded the helicopters onto a trailer specially made for the purpose, and towed them around the country behind a pickup truck. On that trip we towed the helicopter to La Touque; then we put the blades back on and flew it up to Chibougamau.

This was the first time I had flown the G2, the model which had superseded the D. There was no great difference, except that it was powered by a Lycoming engine, in place of the Franklin, which was slightly more powerful and used 80/87 octane gasoline, which was much easier to come by than the 6V4 mix we had to use on the D. The other big advantages were that the battery no longer had to be moved; and the fuel tanks were mounted fore and aft beside the rotor mast on the centre of gravity, so that there was no change in trim as they emptied. But when the G2 first came out, there was a limitation on the manifold pressure you could use. According to the book, you were not supposed to pull more than 24 inches of manifold pressure.

Two supervisory engineers were coming with me. We were not at all sure that the damaged machine could be flown out. It was their task to make an assessment when we reached the camp near Chibougamau. They were both large men, and by the time we had dumped our luggage on the racks, we had a hefty load. But then, of course, there were the tool boxes. When you are loading up a helicopter for a ferry flight with an engineer, he will inevitably say: "Oh, and there's my tool box — but that doesn't weigh much." Let me put it on record that I have never yet encountered an engineer's tool box that weighs less than a hundred pounds. This time we had two of them. Even at that, there would have been no problem if it hadn't been for the 24-inch manifold pressure limitation.

We had a nice long field from which to take off at La Tuque. But that didn't help. I made four attempts to get into the air. By the fourth failure, the faces of my passengers made an interesting study. I was still a new pilot, and their expressions suggested very clearly that they felt a more experienced pilot should have been assigned the job. I advised them, rather heatedly, that either someone was going to have to stay behind, or we were going to have to forget the 24-inch bit — which did they want to to be? This put them nicely on the spot. If they told me, as senior engineers, to ignore the limitation and something blew, they would obviously have to carry the can. On the other hand, both of them wanted to come so that each would have the support of the other when it came to assessing the damaged machine. In the end I told them to keep a sharp lookout for any wires on their side; then I pulled full power and took off without any difficulty. The manifold pressure limitation was removed by the manufacturer a few weeks later. It had been the product of an erroneous calculation, they said.

We reached the camp near Chibougamau without incident. But when I saw the other machine I became extremely nervous. For the moment, though, we decided to ignore it and concentrate on getting Gabe operational again. I remember we had to switch the floats from his machine to the new one, which was on skids, and this was a tedious business in the bush, where there are no hoists to lift the machine. We had to pump the floats up hard, then put gas drums under the machine, deflate the floats and remove them. Next we had to lift the new machine by hand onto another set of drums, remove the skid gear and make a swap. There are literally dozens of clamps and nuts and bolts and washers to be taken off and then reinstalled. It was getting dark before we were finished, but Gabe could now go to work in the morning. Not much was said about the other machine. We were all trying to postpone the moment of decision.

In the morning, however, we had to face facts. If we could fly the machine down to La Tuque and then trailer it back to Ottawa, instead of having to rebuild it here, we would save the company a great deal of money. But it was in sad shape. The caps had been bashed off the ends of both main rotor blades; both were split — one of them from the tip to within inches of the hub. They had been strapped with about half a pound of masking tape. I had read of the exploits of the early bush crews who had used bailing wire to make temporary repairs on their aircraft, but I felt inclined to draw the line at masking tape. In the end I fired up and reluctantly lifted into a hover. There was a horrendous lateral vibration. I put it down again and used strong language. The engineers spent some time trying to balance the weight of the tape on each blade. When I tried again, there was a marked improvement.

We came to the conclusion that as long as we didn't encounter any turbulence we could probably make it as far as La Tuque.

We tied our gear on the racks and took off before anyone had time to change his mind. I think it took about three hours, with a gas stop on the way, to reach La Tuque, and it was a very long three hours. Fortunately, the weather was calm and we had a slight tail wind. When we got there, we parked the machine outside the little hangar and promptly made our way to the nearest beer parlour to fortify ourselves.

The following morning, I flew the helicopter onto the trailer, we removed the battered blades, strapped the machine down and set off for home in high spirits. We felt we had been intrepid and in general that we had "done good." After driving for about an hour, we saw one of our helicopters parked in a field by the road, on the outskirts of a small town. We knew the pilot flying the machine was Shorty Ferguson. He had obviously gone into town for an early lunch. We stopped and debated going back to see if we could find him and have a chat with him. Shorty, who was a compact five and a half feet, made it clear from the outset that, because he was small, people should not make the mistake of thinking that he could be pushed around. There were stories of notable confrontations between Shorty and some of the party chiefs he had worked for.

As a general rule, Shorty did not mind working late into the evening, but he was unenthusiastic about early morning flying. On one occasion, when his crew were quartered in a motel, he returned from a celebration of some sort at three o'clock in the morning. Finding the thought of having to fly in another four or five hours distasteful, he cast around for some way of postponing this unpleasant necessity. His eye fell on the motel sprinkler, attached to the end of a long hose. He took it, climbed up onto the roof and somehow fixed it so that the sprinkler was playing on the party chief's window. Then he turned on the tap and went to bed. When the party chief woke up in the morning and saw that it was raining heavily, he turned over and went to sleep again. It wasn't until nearly ten o'clock that he discovered his error.

On another occasion Gordy Townsend, the manager of Spartan's helicopter division, was returning by car from a business trip and decided to call on Shorty, who was flying out of a resort camp on a lake just off the highway. As the manager approached the lake, he was gratified to hear, above the noise of his car, the sound of a helicopter in the air: Shorty was at work. But when he reached the lodge and climbed out of the car, he observed that Shorty was flying up and down the lake, towing two bikini-clad young women on water skis. Shorty claimed that it was a public relations gesture, one which was bound to benefit the company. I gather he didn't entirely succeed in carrying his point.

The story I liked best, though, about Shorty was of his first venture into mountain flying. He left Calgary in a D model, with his engineer and a good deal of gear on the racks, to fly to a diamond-drill camp in the mountains. The camp was at the 5,600-foot level, and when he found it Shorty saw that there was a reasonably flat and clear spot for him to land in front of the double tent, which he took to be the cook tent. His approach was a little hot, and he had to flare rather drastically to kill his forward speed. He was un-accustomed to the loss of lift at this altitude, and as a result he fell right through the flare and ploughed his tail rotor into the ground. One blade of the tail rotor broke off and went cartwheeling past the helicopter towards the cook tent, where the cook was standing watching him come in to land. At the last minute the cook dived out of the way of the spinning blade, and it went right through the open fly of the tent to create havoc as it ploughed into the pots and pans, the crockery and glassware in the cook's domain.

The tail rotor, of course, was replaced; it was as good as new. But the relationship between Shorty and the cook on that operation was permanently impaired.

But to return to the day when we found Shorty's machine parked by the road. We decided we couldn't spare the time to drive back into town and look for him; yet it seemed unfriendly, somehow, just to drive on without acknowledging him in any way. Then an idea occurred to one of us — I think it was Joe Sangemino. The field Shorty had left his machine in seemed to be part of an abandoned farm. Behind the helicopter, a few hundred yards away, there was a large, rather dilapidated barn. Why not, we agreed, cackling a good deal, fire up the helicopter and park it behind the barn?

It took only about five minutes to do this; then we drove on towards Ottawa in even higher spirits than before.

We arrived back at the hangar at about seven that evening and, just after we got there, Bill McCarthy, the operations manager, pulled up beside us. We had phoned in that morning to say that we were on our way, but I was surprised that anyone would bother to meet us. I didn't know Bill very well at that time, but he was an interesting character. He came from the American midwest, and he fitted perfectly my image of what a gangster should look like; he even had a scar on his cheekbone. "All right, you smart bastards," he greeted us amiably, "whose idea was it to hide Shorty's helicopter?"

We maintained expressions of startled innocence, tinged with sadness that anyone could consider us so irresponsible. But Bill was clearly not deceived and he told us that there had been quite a lively reaction. When Shorty found his machine missing, he had contacted the police. They in turn had advised a number of other agencies to be on the alert for a stolen helicopter. Fortunately, before things really got out of hand, the news had been broadcast by a local radio station and the farmer in the adjacent property had phoned in to say that he could see out of his window a helicopter parked behind the barn on the old Jurgen's farm. Apparently the police had been unreasonable about the incident; they had hinted rather strongly that Shorty had put the helicopter behind the barn for obvious security reasons, and then forgotten where he had parked it. Shorty had reacted to these allegations so vigorously that he had nearly been arrested for threatening a police officer.

We pointed out to Bill that the evidence against us was purely circumstantial and that it would be in everyone's interest if he kept his suspicions to himself. He contented himself with a warning that if we ever did anything like it again, he would have a part of our anatomy for bookends.

What happened next I still find hard to believe but, as I mentioned before, this was a period of discovery for me. As we walked into the hangar, the phone was ringing. Bill climbed the stairs to his office to answer it. The call was from Chibougamau. That afternoon, Gabe had landed on a makeshift landing pad on the side of a hill. The pad was a little skimpy and he had not landed quite far enough forward on it. He locked his controls and jumped out to help his passengers untie their load just as they alighted on the other side of the helicopter. Without their combined weight in front, the helicopter had tipped up and slid backwards off the pad, rolling down the hillside and chewing itself to pieces as it went.

Less than a week later I was on my way to repeat the trip. Gabe had finally been fired. A pilot who had been working on another job in the area, and who had just completed it, was to replace him. But the machine he was flying was time expired; it was due for an overhaul. By dint of considerable overtime, the base engineers had rebuilt the wreck we had brought out: they had installed a new engine, transmission, clutch, mast and rotors. I drove with one engineer to La Tuque, towing the helicopter. We put the blades back on and I flew back up to Chibougamau by myself. When I got there, yet another two engineers had just finished salvaging the latest wreck; it sat in a sad little heap on a flat-bed truck they had rented for the purpose. Bill McCarthy had come up with them to do some fence-mending with the customer. He decided to return with me in the time-expired machine.

For some reason which escapes me now, we went to Roberval for a couple of days before carrying on to La Tuque. I found Bill a very entertaining companion. He drank a great deal of liquor; but drunk or sober, he never seemed to change. And he was one of those fortunate people who had completely overcome his self-consciousness. I discovered this on our last night in Roberval. Bill had transacted some business with fixed-wing people, Nordair I think it was, and that evening several of them, accompanied by wives and girl friends, took us to the local night club. It wasn't a very exciting joint and Bill grew visibly bored. He was drinking rum and coke — large quantities of it. Our companions had all gone to dance, leaving Bill and I sitting alone at our table in the middle of the crowded room. He looked around with jaundiced eye, then abruptly sat up as an idea obviously occurred to him. He dug his wallet out of his pocket, extracted a condom from it and fitted it over the neck of the full bottle of coke sitting in front of him. Then, just as the dance ended and our companions were returning to the table, he shook the bottle vigorously and put it down again.

It made an admirable balloon, so supple that it swelled to majestic proportions; and it was intriguing to observe people's reactions. The men at our table would glance at it and look away quickly. The women sat gazing steadfastly at their hands. But our balloon was attracting a good deal of attention from other people in the room. They began to comment on it rather noisily. Finally, one of the women with us decided she had to visit the washroom. In a moment they were all on their feet and there was a minor stampede to get away from our table. Shortly after that a bouncer appeared.

He picked up the bottle and he was rash enough to pluck the unmentionable off its neck. It did what any balloon would do in the circumstances: it slipped from his fingers and took off across the room in an erratic, zig-zagging flight, squealing like a small, very apprehensive pig. The whole place erupted with an explosion of laughter, and I suspect the bouncer came very close to losing his composure. But he did offer us a choice: either we could walk out very quickly, or he would be happy to throw us out without bothering to open the doors.

CHAPTER 13

A Lookout and a Game Warden

I HAD BEEN BACK FROM THE SECOND TRIP TO CHIBOUGAMAU little more than a week when the phone rang again. John explained to me at some length that the pilot flying the contract for the Ontario Forest Service had had some sort of an altercation with them. He had been out since May, and he was getting a little bushed. Would I go up and relieve him? The contract ended on September 30, so it would only be for about six weeks — the company would make it up to me later. Once again I felt put upon, but there was nothing I could do about it — that was no time of the year to be looking for another flying job.

The machine was based in Cochrane, and as it turned out this was one of the more pleasant contracts I have been on. It had been a cool, damp summer, so there were very few fires — I think I only had to deal with one small one that year. For the rest, we serviced the fire lookout towers, and flew the material up for one new one. But servicing lookout towers turned out to be a more difficult task than I had anticipated. The people on them had been there, all by themselves, since early in May. Their only contact with other people was through the radio; as a result they enjoyed my company, and I found it very difficult to get away from them without hurting their feelings. I had perhaps three or four to do in a day, with other tasks thrown in, and if I spent too much time with them, the ranger would complain. It was an awkward situation. I remember, after drinking three cups of coffee with one old man, finding him grasping me by the shirtsleeve, physically restraining me as I tried to get back to the helicopter.

But there was one lookout person who posed a rather different kind of problem. The ranger explained the difficulty to me shortly after I had arrived. In a moment of what he described as dumb stupidity, he had been persuaded to hire a girl for the first time as a lookout operator. He didn't know what had come over him. He guessed there was no fool like an old fool — she was kinda cute. Now he was paying for it. She was an Australian, some 25 or 26 years old, who was hitch-hiking her way around the world. She had wanted the job so that she would have the opportunity to write a book about her experiences. But she soon discovered that total isolation was irksome. And it did not take her long to find a way of relieving the loneliness. When it came time for her evening report on the radio, there would be a silence; and the following day, since there was no road up to the lookout, the helicopter would have to take someone up to see what had happened. Usually this was the radio technician.

Some three or four days after I arrived on the job, one of these radio silences occurred. The ranger told me with some irritation that I would have to take the radio technician out there the following day. "But she can wait until the afternoon," he said. "We got others who need supplies — hit them first."

After lunch the following day I met the radio technician for the first time. He was a young, fair-haired Scotsman, and he seemed to be labouring under some sort of difficulty. "You know where we're going?" he asked.

"Yes, indeed," I replied with a leer. "We're going to see the celebrated 'Austraylian' girl — I can't wait to meet her."

He looked — well, embarrassed is the best word. But he stammered so badly I had trouble understanding him. And though I know that fair-haired people colour easily, there was no doubt that he was blushing. It was sometime before I was able to catch the gist of what he was trying to tell me.

I tied his tool box onto the rack and we took off. The tower we went to was situated on a pleasantly uncluttered hilltop. There was plenty of room to land and, fortunately for me, plenty of room to stroll around and admire the scenery — because that is what I had to do for the next three-quarters of an hour. Eventually, the technician came to the door of the cabin by the tower and invited me in for coffee.

I looked at the girl with a good deal of curiosity. She was much better looking than the ranger had led me to believe. Her hair was the colour of polished maple; she had the suspicion of a dimple in each cheek when she smiled. Both she and the technician had the soft flush, the faintly ethereal look of two people who had just done

106

we-all-know-what; a look which is profoundly irritating to someone who hasn't. Fixing the radio had obviously required very little of the technician's energy.

I thought it curious the ranger hadn't guessed what was going on but, from his conversation that evening, it was clear that he had. He liked to grumble, and give the impression that he was a hard-hearted, hard-driving taskmaster; in fact, he was a generous soul, and I am sure he got a good deal of vicarious pleasure from the expensive little romance taking place on one of his towers.

For me, however, the situation became a little more complicated. There were no more radio silences for awhile, but about ten days later I had to take a load of food and supplies up to the girl. I went once again in the afternoon. In the morning I had been lifting equipment up to the top of a hill on which a new lookout tower was to be installed. I flew up some 20 five-gallon drums of water, 20 bags of cement, and then what seemed like an endless succession of buckets of sand and gravel. It was a pleasant relief, after lunch, to take a light load and putter up to the tower. I had no more work planned for that day, so I had plenty of time; but in any case, I must confess that I felt far less reluctance to stay and talk to her than I did to other lookout men. She had worked her way from Australia to San Francisco as a stewardess on a freighter which carried about 20 passengers. Then she had hitch-hiked around the southern states before making her way up to Canada. When she had taken this job, she had thought it would be fun; and she really had intended to try to do some writing, but she found she couldn't settle down to it. Now she would like to quit; but she wasn't going to because she knew all the men would laugh at her.

It was undeniably pleasant, sitting talking to her, but after more than an hour had gone by I decided it was time to leave. She looked disappointed. I felt sorry for her — it must be lonely up here, all by herself. A number of other thoughts were going through my mind, but I put them aside firmly and told her we were pretty busy: I had another trip to do yet.

"Don't talk cock," she said. "These forestry blokes are never busy. Stick around for awhile; I'll make some more coffee. I get bored up here — and I get horny, too," she added.

I looked up at her in surprise; she did not look away.

Now I know how easy it is in these circumstances to harbour foolish fantasies, to make what turn out to be embarrassingly vain assumptions. But I'm convinced that wasn't so in this case, and I was faced with a cruel temptation. Everything was favourable. Unless, by some astonishing coincidence, another helicopter turned up, no one could possibly intrude on our privacy; no one but the girl and I could possibly know what took place on that deliciously isolated hilltop.

I suppose it's fortunate that life in the bush seldom exposes you to this sort of temptation. In the event, of course, I made the only decision possible.

Back at work I was getting my first taste of moving supplies and equipment in large quantities, and finding it tough sledding. The concept of loading everything into nets and slinging them under the helicopter on a cargo hook had not yet been developed; so everything had to be loaded onto the racks and tied down. We were moving all the building supplies necessary to construct a lookout tower and cabin up to the top of a hill — even the water with which to mix the concrete for the foundations. We were working off a make-shift pad by the end of an old logging road. The forestry people had cut a clearing in the trees, and then built the pad on the stumps. It was a good pad; the only disadvantage was that the ground rose gently for about a hundred yards, and I had to climb over this rise just after take-off.

I said it was hard work, but that's not really true. For me it was merely tedious. Paddy Reilly, the engineer with me, was supervising the tying-on of the loads at the pad; the forestry crew on top of the hill was doing the unloading. All I had to do, really, was to climb for about three minutes up the hill, land, wait while the forestry crew unloaded and then drop down, taking perhaps a minute to reach the pad again. But it was a monumental pile of equipment we had to shift; and every time we seemed to be making a dent in it, another truckload would arrive. I suppose it was this that made me suggest to Paddy that we try increasing our loads. We were moving 2-by-4 timber at the time — eight-foot studs. Paddy threw on another half-dozen on each rack. It was too much on that hot afternoon, with the summer breezes blowing first one way then the other. I had just got myself well committed to take-off, when I realized I wasn't going to make it; my revs were dropping.

I began to pump the Collective up and down to try to get the revs back up again, but it was really a futile exercise: a classic case of losing on the upswing what you gain on the down. By this time I was sinking into a tangle of stumps, and in desperation I propped the toe of one float on one of the larger ones. My tail went on sinking, and I sat in agony waiting for it to smash itself against one of the stumps behind me — but it didn't, and gradually I managed to get the revs up again and bring the tail up. Now, though, I couldn't make up my mind what to do. The gentle slope upward still extended for another 50 yards or so in front of me; the pad was about the same distance behind me. I moved up on the stump, so that I was balanced; then I sat there for some time, perspiring freely.

In the end, I took a hundred or so illicit extra revs, pulled up hard and swung sideways back to the pad. I had to prop myself on the edge of it for a moment or two to get my revs up again; then I swivelled round and put down safely. When I looked up, I saw that Paddy's face was as white as a sheet. He told me later I should have seen my own: it was like an Oxydol advertisement. We stuck to conservative loads after that.

The next stage of the operation was when the fun began for me. We were into September now; the hunting season had started and we went to work with the wildlife protection division. I am against hunting animals because it is too easy these days. Given four-wheel-drive vehicles, tracked vehicles, airplanes and helicopters to get them into the bush; and then high-powered rifles with telescopic sights when they get there, hunters have too many advantages over the animal for them to talk any longer about sport. I don't like hunting animals, but I found that I do like hunting people; and I learned that when the hunter for once found himself at a disadvantage — we had the mobility of the helicopter — he quickly and bitterly complained about injustice.

To begin with, two game wardens wanted to fly with me. I believe they had done a little sporadic protection work with the helicopter the previous fall, but this was the first consistent attempt to police hunters from the air. They needed to work in pairs, they told me, because there had been occasions in the past when a poacher had turned a gun on the warden; and this was less likely to happen if there were two wardens. But the essence of success in this sort of venture, it seemed to me, was to be able to land almost anywhere. Few people knew it at the time, but the helicopters we were flying could not rise vertically out of small clearings with two passengers. With one passenger we could.

After a week or so, I managed to persuade them that since I would accompany them whenever they confronted hunters, this would provide the two-person factor; besides which, the very fact that we were in a helicopter, with radio contact, would make even the most aggressive poacher think twice. They agreed to try it, and it paid off handsomely. I began to patrol with Sam Knodwell, and even when people were perfectly legal, armed with the necessary licences and tags, they seemed to become guilt-ridden when we suddenly dropped down on them in the wilderness.

American hunting parties, I recall, found it particularly disturbing. On one occasion we were working our way up a sizeable stream. We came around a corner to find two boats, full of hunters and their guides. There was a small, swampy clearing just beyond the boats and, since there was very little wind, I was able to drop the Collective, flare and land right then. Sam stepped out onto the bank of the creek. He looked very impressive in his khaki uniform, with its peaked cap, polished sam-brown belt and holstered revolver. There were no infractions in that case, but the Americans were bitter. They had come up to Canada for real wildrness; they felt that they had penetrated very nearly to the heart of that wilderness, and somehow Sam, in his uniform, had destroyed that illusion. "Jeez," complained one of them, "we don't even got helicopters with game wardens in 'em down stateside." I suspect it was this that really irked them: they regarded Canadians as a nation of hillbillies, and it infuriated them to see us employing such advanced technology.

On other occasions, when we suddenly dropped down on hunters, we found any number of infractions — from no licence at all, to one licence for about three guns. Sam was elated. They had never come close to detecting so many infractions before. But we had our disappointments as well. In one case, we came round the corner on a river to find three people portaging their boat around a small falls. When they spotted us they dumped the boat and we saw, a few seconds later, a gun go arcing through the air into the bush. "Got 'em!" said Sam with satisfaction; but he was wrong. They had only one licence between them, but by the time we got to them they only had one gun. If we could find the gun in the bush we had a case. We had seen almost exactly where it had fallen; but though we spent more than an hour searching for it, we never did find it. Even to this day, it still puzzles and frustrates me when I think about it.

But the most notable and satisfying bust we made was in the Abitibi game reserve. The game reserve occupied an area on the north bank of the river, and poachers would camp on the south bank, then sneak into the reserve early in the morning, ferrying their meat across to the south bank, where it was perfectly legal to have a dead animal. For several years the wardens had been trying to catch them; but this was difficult when you were in a boat because, unless you actually caught them on the north bank, they could claim they were merely carrying the meat along the river.

We made our preparations with some care. A forestry fixed-wing pilot had reported the location of several tents on the south bank of the river. Late in the evening, two parties of game wardens drove out in vehicles to the area. Each party of two was equipped with a boat, an outboard and a radio. They drove the last several miles without lights, hid their vehicles in the bush and carried their boats down to the river — one group on either side of the reported tents. Then they settled down as comfortably as they could to wait.

Shortly before five o'clock the next morning Sam and I took off. It was so dark I had to have the panel lights on to read the instruments. We had to fly for about half an hour to reach the area, and we had a walkie-talkie to communicate with the people on the ground. When we were a little more than halfway to our destination, one of the wardens on the ground reported that they had heard shots, a fusillade of shots, from the direction of the game reserve. "There are some more now," he said.

By the time we reached the area, the light was improving rapidly. There was a sort of tributary to the river on the north shore, more or less opposite the tents, which wound its way for two or three miles through swampy ground, and then petered out. I dropped down and began to fly up it, twisting and turning to follow it.

We both spotted the boat at the same time. It was a large one and it was coming our way at a good speed. Obviously the occupants had heard us and were making a run for the safety of the river. I pulled up into a hover over the creek, while Sam signalled to the people in the boat to go ashore and wait for us. They cut the motor and stopped all right; but then I saw one of them reach down into the boat and pick up his rifle. I hauled up and shot sideways to get behind the denser timber beyond the fringe of the swamp. We circled at a safe distance and saw that the forestry boats were just entering the tributary. We warned them about the threatening gun, so they found a log-jam which only left a few feet of channel on one side, and tied one of their boats across it before retreating to the shore. When the poachers saw the boat across their path, I thought for a moment they were going to try to ram their way through. But they cut the motor and came to a stop. We waited long enough to see that there wasn't going to be any more raising of guns, then went off to find what they had shot. It was a massacre. In a few minutes, we found four cow moose, three calves and a bull. Two of the animals weren't dead; they were trying to regain their feet. I had to land and wait while Sam sloshed across to them, put his revolver against their heads and dispatched them.

We went back and landed by the group on the bank of the creek, where the wardens had a conference. They added up the number of violations. I think it came to some 12 charges — with a total in fines of approximately $1,000, plus the confiscation of the poachers' boat, vehicle and all their equipment. I went to sit on a log and have a smoke while this was going on. One of the poachers came over to me. He was quite literally quivering with rage. "What kind of goddam dirty set-up is this?" he demanded. "Using a helicopter to catch a coupla guys just out to get a little meat for the winter."

After the gun-raising incident, and the slaughter I had just witnessed, I was hostile; but I merely shrugged and told him that I didn't make the laws.

"Yeah, and how much does it cost to run that thing?" he demanded. "How much's it costing the taxpayer just to catch a coupla poachers?"

"Oh, about two or three hundreds dollars," I replied. "But after all, the taxpayer won't be footing the bill — you will."

We left the people on the ground to bring the poachers in and look after the confiscation of their equipment, while we went to check the camps along the south shore. We had counted eight of them on the way in, all within a space of about half a mile. When we got back two had already disappeared; the others were empty — the occupants were obviously hiding out in the bush. When we returned the next day, there wasn't a tent to be seen.

The game reserve was only a mile or two from the Quebec border. Sam told me that in the past they had fought a constant battle with poachers who came across the border on Abitibi Lake, went into the game reserve for their meat, and then scuttled back across the border to safety. The boats were often large ones, some of them fully equipped as canneries. On our patrol to see if the poachers' camps were still on the south bank of the river, we carried on along the river to the lake. We found a 40-foot cabin cruiser tucked in under the trees, only a few hundred yards over the border. I landed and the three occupants were hostile. They demanded to know what an Ontario game warden was doing in Quebec. Sam was astonished. "Oh, are we across the border?" he said. "Well, we won't bother you then. But I hope you guys don't make the same mistake and come across our border. We nailed a couple of poachers yesterday. It's gonna cost them more than a thousand bucks, and," said Sam, looking at their boat appreciatively, "their boat."

In his next communication to our company, Paddy Reilly advised base that we were working hard to prevent Quebecers from kidnapping English-speaking moose.

The remark wasn't entirely facetious, because in some ways the border seemed more like an international one between two not very friendly nations. Sam said they got very little co-operation from the Quebec forestry people. As an example of what he meant, he took me into a lookout tower a mile or so on the Quebec side. It was vacant; the fire season was over, and when we climbed to the lookout I saw that the set-up was very similar to the Ontario towers: there was a large round table in the middle, covered by a map of the surrounding area. On it was a large compass rose, and a plastic scale rotated round the position of the tower on the map; thus the operator could simply line up his scale when he saw smoke and read off the location as a bearing and distance. But in this particular tower, the map had been cut off along the Ontario border; everything beyond the border was blank. I suppose that forest fires didn't belong to the Union Nationale and they were afraid to cross the border.

But it was the hunting ethic that dominated and at about this time I had a remarkable meeting with a hunter on my own. I was lying reading on my bed in the hotel one night after supper, when there was a knock on my door. I opened it to a man of about 50, who had the pink, fleshy look and self-assurance of considerable wealth.

"Are you the helicopter pilot?" he asked.

I agreed that I was, and he asked if he could come in and talk to me. When we sat down, he wanted to know if I had seen any moose while I was flying in the area. I said yes, there were quite a few of them around.

"Good," he said, and went on to tell me that he was from New York, an executive with a large corporation who had come to, as he put it, "get me a moose." He had his 19-year-old son with him. He could only afford five days away from the rat race. Tomorrow was the last day; their guide hadn't got them anywhere near a moose, and he didn't want to have to go back and admit to his associates that he had been skunked.

In brief, he wanted me to take his son with me, find a moose and put his son down to shoot it. All they needed was the head, so that he could have it mounted and show it to his friends in New York. He offered me $500. "Cash money!" he added, clearly implying that I could pocket the money myself.

I suggested that this didn't seem a very sporting way to hunt moose. He looked at me as I'm sure he must have looked at subordinates in his company who made smart-ass remarks. "What time can you get away tomorrow?" he asked.

I made another suggestion, proposing an alternative method by which he could dispose of his $500. He left, threatening to report to my company that I had refused a flying job. I was to hear a number of similar propositions in the years ahead; but never one quite so gross as this one.

After the excitement in the Abitibi game reserve, things quietened down almost completely. Northern Ontario is a gossipy place, and it very quickly became common knowledge that the game wardens were flying regular patrols, and that the helicopter was giving them an advantage which made the odds against the poacher unacceptable. I had enjoyed myself, but the exercise had damaged my social standing in the community. On several occasions I had to go to court to give evidence against people and, because of this, it no longer became safe for me to visit a beer parlour. Paddy continued to patronize them, and when people took him to task he cheerfully sold me down the river. If he had his way, he told people, the helicopter would never have a game warden in it; but it was the pilot who had the say and, like all pilots, I was a bastard who enjoyed chasing poachers.

One day, though, he blew his cover badly. He and I were going, for some reason I have forgotten now, to Swastika, a little town to the south of Cochrane. On the way we spotted a canoe out in the middle of a lake. The occupant was fishing. Paddy clucked disapprovingly. "We can't have this," he said. "The fishing season ended months ago — the man's breaking the law. We must do our duty."

As I swung towards the canoe and began to let down, we saw the occupant reeling in his line at high speed. He stowed his rod, picked up his paddle and began to paddle furiously for the shore. I was easily able to cut him off, and now we saw fish flying through the air as he threw his catch away. He had obviously done well: more than a dozen good-sized fish went over the side of the canoe. By this time I had settled down on the water, some 20 yards from him. He sat wtih his arms crossed, glaring at us defiantly. Paddy and I nodded approvingly and applauded, clapping our hands. Then I took off and we flew on to Swastika.

Two nights later Paddy suddenly decided to join me in my room for a beer instead of going to the beer parlour. After we had blunted the sharp edge of our thirst, I asked him why.

"You know that guy we saw fishing on the lake the other day? Well, he's a lot bigger than he looked from the air."

Paddy's replies tended to be oblique, but it was clear that the atmosphere in the beer parlour was now as unconvivial for him as it was for me.

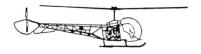
The North Shore

PADDY AND I FLEW BACK TO OTTAWA AT THE BEGINNING OF October in high spirits. We had suffered no calamities; we had enjoyed a good rapport with the customer; now we could look forward to a pleasant few months at home. Five days later I was on a commercial airliner, heading for Seven Islands, in Quebec.

I had something of a confrontation with the management over this one. I was tired; I wanted some time with my family, but they were adamant. The only thing I got out of it was an increase of $100 a month in my salary. The pilot who was on the job had threatened to walk out unless he was relieved. Once again, it would only be for a few weeks. The point was a difficult one for me to argue, of course: for some 18 months I had been badgering the company to hire me. Now I didn't want to fly; I wanted to stay at home. But this was a distortion. There had been a loose agreement that for every two months in the bush, I would get a month at home. I was obviously heading for a far higher ratio than this, and I was depressed about it. It seemed to me that if being a helicopter pilot meant that you could spend only a few weeks out of every year with your family, I would have to get out before long. All the effort and expense had been in vain.

But there was another reason why the company wanted me in particular to go on this job, and I suppose it had some merit. Two new iron-ore mines were being developed at Knob Lake and Labrador City. A railway had to be constructed to bring the ore down to tidewater at Seven Islands. Canadian Aero Services had the contract for the preliminary survey, and the party chief was Ed Anderson, who had been my supervisor in Ottawa. The rationale was that since I had specific expertise in this area, I would be able to do a better job than any other pilot. I was fond of Ed, but I

116

remember I had difficulty not transferring my resentment to him. There was a crew of five surveyors from Canadian Aero who were marking out the line, and another 12 or 14 Quebecers who were cutting it. They had all been out all summer and they were all, to some extent, bushed.

The living conditions were interesting. We had dropped back at least 20 years. The survey and helicopter crews had tents of a sort, with safari cots, and so did the cook; but the line-cutting crew had nothing but tarps which were used to make lean-to's at night. They cut spruce boughs for a mattress and slept on the ground. The cook had one collapsible card table to go with his wood-burning stove in the cook tent. Outside, he would have a log, roughly flattened along the top as a serving table. We would line up with our plates and he would slap the food onto them, the dessert with the main course all mixed together. Then we would repair to the nearest convenient log or rock to sit and eat it.

However, the French-Canadians on that job did much to destroy my prejudices. Cutting line is never an enjoyable task, but in that country, at that time of year, it was particularly unpleasant. Most of the time they worked in rain or sleet or snow, wading through swamp and muskeg, hacking their way through dense willow thickets all day — the sort of thing that would make most people discontented. But these were obviously throw-backs to their ancestors, the voyageurs, and in the evenings they would be so full of high spirits you had to keep a cautious eye on them.

Unfortunately, although the engineer with me was competent, he was totally unsuited to the bush; he was frightened of it. He visualized ferociously carnivorous animals lurking behind every tree or bush, and the Frenchmen capitalized on his nervousness. They would hide out in thickets, shake the branches and utter blood-curdling growls; whereupon, to everyone's huge delight, the engineer would break into a panicky run. But I was sharing a very small tent with him, and soon they began to transfer their attention to our tent. One night I awoke to hear rustlings and snickers. Before I had time to investigate, the tent suddenly collapsed on us. The engineer, I suppose convinced that a bear had jumped us, awoke with a scream of terror, and virtually the entire camp burst into a collective roar of laughter.

The following morning at breakfast I issued a solemn warning of retributions to come if there were any recurrences, but I could see from the bright, innocent looks I was getting that they regarded this as a worthwhile challenge. It was the kind of war they really appreciated. The camp was on the shore of a lake, and the helicopter was in a clearing some 50 or 60 yards from it. After supper the following evening, when the engineer was doing his daily inspection on the machine, I wandered over to keep him company. I knew that he suffered a good deal of anxiety, expecting some dangerous beast to emerge from the forest around him at any moment. I had been there about half an hour when I thought I noticed someone near our tent. I ducked into the trees and circled round towards it. All I found were a couple of the Frenchmen collecting windfall branches for kindling. They moved off, and I inspected the tent pegs and guy ropes carefully. I could see nothing wrong, so I returned to the helicopter.

When we went to our tent later that night, however, we found that there was a porcupine in it. Now a porcupine is a relatively harmless creature, but it has a strong aroma and, in a small tent, it is not easy to know how best to deal with one. The engineer retreated to a safe distance and I had to manage on my own. After some reflection, I went and cut two strong branches from a tree and used these to try to lift it out of the tent. The unfortunate animal was frightened; it made some curiously pig-like noises, which were followed almost immediately by muffled explosions of mirth from the direction of the line-cutting crew's lean-to's. I had just got it securely cradled in my two branches, and I was moving towards the entrance of the tent, when my foot slipped and I fell forward with one shin on the porcupine. It was painful and, before I could control myself, several expletives escaped me. This time the laughter from the lean-to's was not nearly so mufflled.

After I'd succeeded in evicting the porcupine, I had to limp across to Ed's tent for the first-aid kit to repair my shin. Ed offered a shallow pretence of solicitiousness, but he kept bursting into nasty little snickers, which he tried to disguise as fits of coughing. When at last I crawled into my sleeping bag for the night, I spent some time trying to think what to do. At least now I knew who was responsible. The two people collecting kindling by our tent had been Michel and Jean-Guy. On the other hand, though, even though I was still green, I knew enough to realize that this sort of warfare can quickly escalate to unmanageable proportions in a bush camp. If I was going to look for a retribution, it would have to be a final one.

In the morning, as we sat around on our logs and rocks, eating breakfast, I was asked a number of ingenuous questions. People had thought they heard some sort of activity around our tent — had anything happened? When I replied that I hadn't heard anything, some of them choked on their Red River Cereal, which isn't surprising because it is horrible stuff.

I put the survey crews out first; then I began to lift the linecutting crew. They had hacked out a little clearing at the end of their previous day's cut. It was on the edge of a lake-cum-swamp and, although it was tight, I could hang my tail boom out over the water, so it presented no difficulties. As luck would have it, Michel and Jean-Guy did not climb into the helicopter until about the fifth trip. When I reached our destination, instead of landing where I had before, I landed well out on the swamp, on a small round island of moss. The whole island quaked at I touched down, and it sank several inches when I lowered the Collective. Michel and Jean-Guy turned to remonstrate with me. They had cleared a landing for the helicopter. . . . I cut them off with the information that I had found it too small, they had left too much slash and debris lying around. I affected some surprise at their hesitation and hinted that their workmates had made no fuss about walking from here. If they had been thinking, they would have known this was not true because there was more than a skim of ice on the shallow water surrounding us and it was unbroken.

Eventually, after uttering a number of vehement *tabernac*'s and *colis*'s, they climbed reluctantly out onto the moss, sinking at once past their ankles in mud. It was the type of mud known in the vulgar idiom of the bush as loon shit. It is very black, very viscous and, I suppose because it is mainly composed of decaying vegetation, it smells very strongly. They had a good deal of equipment to carry with them: their packs, in which they had some tools and their lunches; two axes and two machetes; and a power saw, together with a can of gas and a plastic bottle of oil. As they broke through the ice and set off for shore, they sank up to their thighs in the mud. Michel stumbled and, in trying to keep the power saw out of the water, covered himself more or less up to his neck in mud. It wasn't an ideal way to start the day's work. I waited long enough to see that they got ashore before returning to fetch the rest of the crew.

That evening it became apparent that Michel and Jean-Guy had had an indifferent time of it. They received very little sympathy from the rest of the crew; in fact, their workmates obviously thought that what I had done was *une bonne blague*, and they had been digging away at them about it all day. But when I made it clear at supper that all of the crew might find themselves experiencing similar difficulties getting to and from their workplace if there were any more excitements in the helicopter crew's tent, their expressions for once were more thoughtful than challenging.

On the whole, though, apart from these no doubt childish diversions, that operation was a grim one. By November we were experiencing the sort of weather one expects at that time of the year: weather that makes flying very difficult. We had a good deal of sleet and snow, which cuts the visibility down to a few hundred feet. But we also had occasional spells of freezing rain, and to me this is the most dangerous weather condition you can encounter in a helicopter. Within a matter of 30 seconds the bubble can become completely obscured with ice. The only thing to do then is to open the door and stick your head out. Even then, it is not easy to see. The door is hinged at the front and it, too, is of plastic. With ice on it you can't see through it; you have to get your head far enough out to look over the top — where, of course, the freezing rain drives into your eyes while you desperately try to find somewhere to land.

Yet that is by no means all. The ice also forms very quickly on the leading edges of the rotor blades, and you begin to lose lift. The next stage in this progression is to have a piece of ice break off one rotor blade. This promptly puts the rotor system out of balance and sets up a horrendous vibration. I only experienced this once in my career, and it was on this operation. I had to fly for nearly a mile before I could find a clearing to land in, and the machine was shaking so badly I was sure it was going to disintegrate at any moment.

By now, too, we were running into difficulties starting the engine in the morning. I am not sure whether it was a peculiarity of the Franklin engine, or whether the Lycoming did it too, but when the temperature dropped to about 20 degrees, the engine would turn over and start. Then, after a brief and encouraging brrrrrrm, it would die, and that was it; after that, no amount of cranking it over would do any good. When you removed the spark plugs, there would be a small globule of ice on the electrodes. The only thing to do now was to remove the plugs, take them back to the tent and heat them on the stove. The engineer and I developed a routine. We would take out a row of plugs from each bank of cylinders, lay out a plug wrench on each rack; then when we had the plugs so hot that they burned our fingers, we would wrap them in a cloth, sprint to the helicopter and try to get them in and get the engine started before they had time to cool off. For several weeks I had permanently sore fingertips.

I sent a telegram to the company asking for a ground heater. Two weeks later it arrived and we breathed a sigh of relief. But when we came to start it, we discovered that someone had neglected to install a carburetor on it. Three weeks later, after I had sent a series of increasingly abusive telegrams to Ottawa, the carburetor arrived.

Another operational problem we encountered at this time was caused by defective fan belts. The fan is mounted on the front of the engine and it is surrounded by a canvas shroud to channel the air onto the cylinders. It sits only about six inches behind the pilot's back. There is a thin sheet of metal, euphemistically called a firewall, separating the passenger compartment from the engine, and when a fan belt lets go it invariably whacks into this resonant firewall. The noise is comparable to that of a high-powered rifle being discharged a foot or two away from your ear, and it is guaranteed to bring even the most stolid person right out of his seat.

When this happened, we had about two minutes to get down onto the ground and shut the engine off, or it would overheat severely enough to seize up. Apparently we were into a batch of fan belts which had been defectively manufactured, and we had at least one set a day let go for several weeks. It was a tedious business replacing them, and it was hard on the nerves.

Oh yes, there were many problems on that operation. I remember one day I was out doing a reconnaissance ahead of the line with Ed Anderson. We saw that there was a large lake lying across the route. Ed wanted to see if the ice was safe to walk on. It would save a lot of time if the survey crew could walk across it the following day, instead of having to go around it. I landed on the ice and thought I could detect a slight flexing. It looked shaky to me, and I told Ed I didn't think it would hold his weight. But Ed thought otherwise; he was confident, by its appearance, that the ice would be safe to walk on. He was a westerner, he reminded me, and every fall, since his earliest memories, he had been out assessing the strength of the ice to see if it was ready to skate on. If there was one thing he was strong on, it was ice.

Nevertheless, I kept a little power on because, if the floats did break through the ice, it was possible to gash them. Ed got out and walked carefully for a step or two. He was a large man, six feet five inches tall, in fact, and built to scale, so if he could walk on the ice, anyone could. He turned back towards me with a smile of satisfaction and did two little jumps to show me that it was safe. Descending from the second one, he kept going and vanished from sight.

I was alarmed, afraid that he might not be able to get back up through the ice again, and I was leaning as far forward and across as I could to see over the right float when two hands suddenly appeared along the top of it; then, a moment later, the top of Ed's head. His hair was plastered down over his eyes, so all I could see was his nose, a commanding organ, poking over the top of the float. It looked for all the world like one of those Kilroy drawings one saw so frequently during the war.

I thought it comical, but one does not laugh at party chiefs. And of course, when Ed had clambered back into the helicopter and I was flying him back to camp, soaked to the skin and shivering uncontrollably, I was as solicitous of his welfare as he had been of mine when I had my small mishap with the porcupine.

By the third week of November we reached what I think could justifiably be called the significant point of diminishing returns. There was enough snow on the ground to make travel through the bush very difficult, but not enough to allow the use of snowshoes. Both the survey and the line-cutting crews were making very little progress. And our living conditions were becoming intolerable. It was virtually impossible to wash our clothes because there was no way of drying them afterwards. Our tents were flimsy summer tents, and we were beginning to sleep cold much of the time. The Frenchmen would build a fire and then erect their lean-to's in a circle round it; but someone would have to keep getting up during the night to put more wood on the fire. In our tent we had one of the thin, metal wood-burning stoves called airtights, but it was not very satisfactory. We had to burn green wood, and it would either flare up until it was red hot, or fizzle out altogether.

Ed and I reported these facts to our respective companies. But in Ottawa, where people were alternating between comfortably heated homes and comfortably heated offices, our complaints did not strike a responsive chord. The philosophy was quite straightforward: if they pulled us out now, we would still be drawing our salaries and producing nothing. If we stayed, our progress might be painfully slow, but we were accomplishing something. Ed was in a difficult position. He had been instructed to keep us out as long as possible, and he was saddled with an increasingly mutinous crew.

Finally, at the end of the first week in December, the Canadian Aero surveyors declared that they had had enough: they were going out, whether they got fired or not. I remember it well, because Ed had to fly down to Seven Islands in a Cessna 180 the following day to make sure that all their instruments had been shipped safely back to Ottawa. The man behind the TCA counter asked him if that had been his crew who went out the previous day. When Ed admitted that it had, the man asked Ed if he could arrange to have them crated in future. After some refreshment, their behaviour had been so uninhibited that the stewardess had refused to board the aircraft with them.

The survey crew had marked the line far enough ahead to keep the line-cutting crew at work for some time at their present rate of progress; so we soldiered on for another ten days or so. But on the morning of December 17, we awoke to find everything, including the helicopter, coated in a thick sheath of ice. Then the ground heater chose this particular day to act up; we couldn't get it started. It took us more than two hours to repair it, at least another hour to get the ice off the helicopter. Finally, when the machine was warmed up and ready to go, the Frenchmen said eff it; they weren't going out at this time of day. I'd had enough, and I told the engineer I was going to take the machine down to Seven Islands, phone the company and tell them that if they wanted to continue this fiasco, they could send another pilot out. I was going home. When I went to tell Ed, his response was a fervent "Thank God!" He decided to move the whole crew out.

Since everyone had come out, I saw no point in phoning the company from Seven Islands that night; I could tell them what they needed to know when I got back to Ottawa. The weather was reasonable the following morning when we left. I followed the north shore of the St. Lawrence, but as we approached Montreal the clouds rolled in like marijuana smoke at a rock concert, and I had to go down to about a hundred feet in increasingly severe snow flurries. It was strictly going home weather, and in the end I had to fly under the bridges at Montreal, which horrified the engineer. Fortunately, there were no wires and we made it back to Ottawa just as it was getting dark. I landed behind a gas station on the outskirts long enough to phone Nina and ask her to pick me up, then flew on into Uplands, parked the helicopter in front of the hangar and went straight home before phoning John Theilman to tell him we were back.

He expressed surprise that we had come out, as he put it, without authorization. It was only a few days before Christmas; I had been away from home for nearly ten months of the year, and I had flown close to a thousand hours of revenue time. I was tempted to ask him if he wanted me to donate some blood to the company as well.

Later, when I had been home for a few weeks and I was in a more stable frame of mind, I realized how futile such recriminations would have been. None of the people running things in Ottawa at the time had any experience operating helicopters under winter conditions in the bush. Sitting in their warm offices, they could not possibly visualize the difficulties; so you had to make your own decisions and act accordingly. The temptation, if the customer could be persuaded that it was feasible, to stretch contracts into the winter was almost irresistible; and on two or three occasions during the next few years, I closed things down and came out. The company would be outraged, but I learned to live with it.

This time, though, I did manage to stay home for two full months. My first trip in the new year came late in February. It was to take delivery of a new helicopter from the Bell factory in Fort Worth, Texas. We were going to trailer it back, so I drove down with Claude Legault, one of the people in stores, in a pickup truck. The trailer was being constructed for us in Fort Worth. There was one complication. I was not considered sufficiently experienced to do the acceptance test flight; instead, Shorty Ferguson, who was on vacation in the States, would be there to do it.

It took us four days to reach Fort Worth. When we arrived the helicopter was waiting for us, but there was no sign of Shorty. I sent a telegram to the company advising them of this; they promptly wired back to wait. I waited for another four days; then, losing patience, I decided to go ahead with the test flight myself.

The machine we were picking up was a new model just introduced by Bell, a 47-J. I found it thoroughly unsuitable for our purposes. It had been designed to fill what Bell saw as a demand for an executive helicopter. The engine and transmission were now enclosed in metal panels, which may have made it look sleeker, but which all had to be removed for maintenance. And the tail boom was now of monocoque construction, totally enclosed, so that the old problem of the keel surface in a cross wind was back, and servicing the tail-rotor driveshaft and cables was much more difficult.

But, apart from appearance, what made it most attractive to executives was that they no longer had to sit next to the pilot. They sat, as in a limousine, behind him on a bench seat. Since a great deal of the work we did was in collaboration with our passengers, using maps or photographs, this could only be a disadvantage. From nearly all aspects, it seemed to me, the J was a disaster as a bush aircraft; and nobody I had spoken to in Spartan could fathom out why on earth we were buying one.

There were some other curious aspects of the transaction, too. As a down payment on the machine, I had been given a certified cheque for $10,000 to bring with me. I couldn't understand why this money hadn't been transferred through a bank. But the very first thing I was asked when I introduced myself to the Bell people was whether or not I had the cheque — I assumed there must have been problems with previous transferrals.

I was left in no doubt that their hope was to hustle me out to the machine, get the test flight done and the acceptance papers signed, and get rid of me. Instead, I suggested rather firmly that, since our company was buying an increasing number of their helicopters, and I might not get the opportunity again, I would appreciate a tour of the plant. They agreed with obvious reluctance.

The sales representative assigned to take me round was a gung-ho salesman, but it quickly became clear that he knew no more about helicopters than I did about Samoan fertility rites. I asked him two or three semi-technical questions and then gave up. But soon after we began the tour we came upon two of the new J models which were being worked on by a number of people. The sales rep told me in reverential tones that they were being prepared for the personal use of President Eisenhower. I suppose this was one subject he felt qualified to talk about, and he kept returning to it tirelessly. In the end I told him I didn't think the J was a very practical machine for the bush, but I guessed it would serve well enough to take Eisenhower to the golf course. He relapsed into a rather sulky silence for the rest of the tour and handed me over with obvious relief to the pilot who was to check me out before I did the test flight.

The attitude of the Bell people I met at that time was curiously insulting. They obviously regarded me as a hick from some place closely resembling Outer Slobovia. None of them, including the pilot, had any idea what it was like to fly a helicopter under operational bush conditions. As anyone in the industry knows, virtually every new model of any aircraft undergoes extensive modifications (at the expense of the customer) as design flaws reveal themselves under actual working conditions. Some of the new design improvements they were touting to us now were the product of our own experience and suggestions, and it was very irritating to be patronized by them.

As a matter of record, President Eisenhower never did fly in a 47-J. Some weeks after our return to Ottawa I heard that a design flaw had showed up. The straps securing the gas tanks to the frame were too light, and there had been at least two serious accidents when gas tanks had come adrift during flight and the machines had caught fire. The President, whose advisers were prudent men, changed his mind.

When I had test flown the machine and signed the necessary acceptance papers, we went to pick up our trailer. Claude climbed up onto it to check the fittings and one of the angle-irons of the frame let go under him. We found that the frame had only been tack-welded, and we had to wait another two days before a welder could be spared to complete the job.

As we were about to depart, Shorty suddenly turned up. We debated getting him to do another test flight, but decided it would be pointless. Shorty, however, insisted on seeing the sales rep I had dealt with. Bell at the time were giving out some rather attractive tie clips embossed with a neat little helicopter as a promotional gimmick. Shorty wanted one.

The sales rep, who was wearing one of the tie clips, was effusively apologetic. They had run out of them, but they were expecting a new order any day now, and he personally would make absolutely certain that one was sent up for Shorty.

"You really sure they're going to be here in a coupla days?" Shorty asked.

"One hundred per cent positive!"

"Well, in that case," said Shorty, plucking the clip from the sales rep's tie, "I'll take this one; you can get another for yourself when they do arrive."

I thought for a moment the sales rep was going to grab Shorty's hand and try to pry open his fingers to retrieve the clip. Instead, he turned and walked out of the office without a word.

The whole trip took us more than two weeks and, when I got back to Ottawa I found I was in trouble. First, I should have kept in touch — phoned or sent a telegram at least once a day. In future I was to make sure I did. And second, of course, they were upset because I had taken it upon myself to do the test flight.

But there was an interesting postscript to the purchase of our first J model. The company brass had bought it, curiously enough, without consulting any of the operational crews — the people who would have to fly and maintain it. Thus, when they tried to put it to work in the spring, they ran into massive resistance. Pilots did not like it and engineers were particularly incensed because it would require so much more work to maintain.

In the end the company successfully begged the issue by selling it. The D.O.T. was just beginning its spectacular expansion into the helicopter field and the J model would serve perfectly well for the gentle flying they were involved in. By this time the problem with the floating gas tanks had been remedied; but another equally dangerous one showed up a few months later. The main rotor blades were of laminated construction; some error occurred in the bonding process, and this particular machine threw a main rotor blade in flight. The pilot and his one passenger were killed. I am glad I only flew it for about ten minutes.

CHAPTER 15

Forest Fires

MY SEASON STARTED A LITTLE LATER THIS YEAR: THE LAST week in April. Unfortunately, this time there was another complication which made me unwilling to leave Ottawa. My reunions with Nina the previous year had been brief but affectionate ones, and now we were expecting our second child, Graham, at just about this time.

I was going out on the Ontario Forest Service contract, and I asked if someone could stand in for me for a week or two so that I could be on hand when our child was born. The answer was no; the forestry people had been impressed by my performance the previous year and they had asked for me in particular. At least two pilots whose contracts were to begin a month later volunteered to stand in for me, but the company refused and I found it a singularly ungenerous gesture.

As it turned out, it was an enjoyable season even though I had to work very hard. I was based, most of the time, in Sudbury; but, since that was a long hot summer, we moved around a good deal fighting forest fires. And I discovered that at that time people in the forestry service had only one real vocation: fighting forest fires. When there were no fires burning they would do other things, of course — a little timber cruising, silviculture, reforestation — but their real mission in life was obviously to fight fires, a task they approached with a sort of dedication I found alarming.

I have always been uneasy when I encounter anything resembling fanaticism, and the Ontario forestry people I met that summer, particularly the senior ones, had just such a tinge. They had invested the whole business of fire-fighting with an aura of wartime emergency. They even had their heroes: they spoke respectfully of one ranger, Lawless Cecile, who had worked such long hours directing activities on a celebrated fire two years previously that he had permanently impaired his health. I met Lawless a couple of months later. He was in excellent health and he was far too intelligent to do anything so silly.

I thought then, and I am convinced now, that fighting forest fires is very often a waste of time and money. In hot, dry weather, unless you reached a fire shortly after it started, the effect that large numbers of men with large quantities of equipment had on its course were at best marginal. As one conscripted firefighter put it, rather crudely I'm afraid, but I think accurately: "You might just as well piss up your leg and play with the steam." It was invariably the weather, steady rain, which brought the fire under control in the end.

But if I thought the forestry people's attitude to fire-fighting faintly absurd, I kept my views to myself. Fire-fighting is a very lucrative aspect of the business for helicopter operators. And I quickly discovered that the person who really was expected to be dedicated was the helicopter pilot.

In practice, most of the fires we fought would either work themselves into the loop of a river or a lake, and burn themselves out; or the weather would change and they would die down. In this case, the ranger directing activities would go home for a rest. The helicopter pilot, on the other hand, would be dispatched to a fire in another part of the province which had just got a good hold; and the crew on that fire, fresh and rested, were all set to do their heroic long hours for a few days.

The system was for the ranger in charge to fly the fire line at first light, so that he could plan his tactics for the day. This usually meant a first flight just before five o'clock in the morning. He would then issue his instructions for the movement of men and materials and retire to sit by the radio for the rest of the day, while the helicopter moved men, pumps, hoses, food, camping gear and all the other associated equipment — all of which had to be tied onto the racks, and untied at the other end. At last light, perhaps half-past ten at night, the ranger would once again fly the fire line to assess what had been accomplished by the day's activities.

When I suggested, after about ten consecutive days of this regime (and after the ranger in charge had been relieved by another) that working from five in the morning until eleven at night on a steady basis was becoming burdensome, the answer was, "Yes, but look at the money you're making." Since, at that time, I was earning $350 a month, I wasn't impressed by the cogency of this argument.

Fortunately though, as in any war, the generals often made mistakes. Their strategy might have been brilliant, but their tactical organization was often shaky, and you could sometimes take advantage of this to catch up on sleep. On one occasion I managed, not without some deviousness I'm afraid, to convince three rangers at three separate fires that I was working on one of the other two fires — while I slept peacefully in a motel room for most of the day.

But on other occasions these organizational lapses could be onerous. Les, the engineer with me for the first part of the season, was a lively young Englishman. He had been enthusiastic about the contract. It was hardly bush living; we would be in hotels and motels; we could go into towns and see real women. His favourite phrase was, "Let's live a little." Thus his disappointment was the sharper when the fire season kicked off with a bang early in May, and we spent the majority of our time during the next two months in makeshift fire camps, where living conditions were strictly basic.

One day, late in the evening, I was instructed to leave the fire we were working on, which had begun to die down, and go to another some 30 miles away, which had been spotted that afternoon. I was told which lake to go to; a crew had been dispatched to the fire. They would have the camp set up by the lake; I was to leave at first light in the morning.

Les and I threw our bags on the racks and took off at five in the morning without even the benefit of a cup of coffee. We could have breakfast when we got to the new camp. But when we arrived at the designated lake, there was no sign of any camp. The fire was about a mile away, on the other side of the lake. It covered an area of several acres and, in an hour or two when the wind started to blow, it would obviously take off. We flew round the fire and searched the surrounding countryside until we were convinced there was nobody around; then I landed by the lake to wait for the crew to turn up.

Les was not his usual ebullient self. He was hungry and discontented. The only thing I could find to eat, without breaking open the emergency rations, was a can of beans, accidentally left in the helicopter by some fire crew. Les cut his finger opening it with a screwdriver. He sat eating his cold beans off the end of the screwdriver and complaining bitterly. His comments about the forest service authorities would have done credit to a Billingsgate fishwife.

At about 7:30, when there was still no sign of the forestry crew, we decided to return to Sudbury, have some breakfast, sleep for awhile and then have a shower and a change of clothess. Shortly before two o'clock in the afternoon, I awoke feeling refreshed and phoned the district fire protection officer in Sudbury. He became very excited and accused me of going to the wrong lake. He had spent all the previous afternoon and most of the evening getting the crew organized and on its way, and if the helicopter had been there when it should they would have been able to control the fire. Now I had blown it by my incompetence. The fire would get away on them.

I asked him if he had been in touch with the crew by radio. This gave him pause for a moment, but then he brushed it aside. They probably hadn't had time to set up the radio; they were too busy trying to fight the fire without a helicopter. I pointed out to him that the lake we had gone to did in fact have a new fire by it, so there was little chance that we had made a mistake. He demanded my phone number and ordered me not to move from the phone until he called back.

Les and I went for a stroll to have a look at Sudbury. Although we were technically based there, we had had very little opportunity to see what the place was like. The fire protection officer eventually phoned me after supper, instructing me to return to the fire we had been working on previously. I asked him what had happened to the crew I was supposed to meet. He said, nothing; there had been a change in plans. I discovered later that the crew in question had just returned from another fire only two days before and they had no intention of going out again until they'd had at least a week at home.

As in war once again, when the going gets rough the dedication and sense of heroism tend to retreat from the front line, until in the end they reside only in the rarified atmosphere of command headquarters.

I think that year the weather broke in the middle of July. We had a spell of wet weather and it was very welcome. During the fires I had had to break away during the day and rush around trying to keep the lookout towers supplied. Now I could return to the more leisurely routine, and look after the other assorted jobs which had to be done.

The Ontario forestry people were very active at the time developing new methods of fire-fighting with aircraft. They had turned their de Havilland Otter floatplanes into water bombers and made some experiments with helicopters. Their experiments with helicopters had not been as successful as the ones with fixed-wing aircraft. One of the ideas had been to package water in one-gallon plastic bags. The plastic bags were laid on rollers fitted to the racks alongside the helicopter and, when the pilot reached the fire, he was to tilt the nose up and allow the bags to roll back off the racks onto the flames. On the first trial run, all the bags on one side rolled off; none on the other. The helicopter was so unbalanced the pilot had great difficulty keeping control; then, just as he was coming in to land in a clearing, the remaining bags had suddenly decided to roll off and the helicopter very nearly lurched into the trees.

That was the end of plastic-bag water bombing. But the promoters of the idea had had great confidence in it; so now the forestry people found themselves with a large inventory of one-gallon plastic bags. I had to fly the materials up to a hilltop for a new lookout tower. As had been the case when I did this job the previous year, I had to start by taking up the raw materials for the concrete foundations. It occurred to someone that the plastic bags could be used to carry up the water they would need.

I got the cement, sand and gravel up, but it was hard work. The forestry people had built a pad just below the sharp ridge on which the tower was to be constructed. The pad was about 20 feet down the sidehill. The wind was blowing from the other side of the ridge and the pad was right in the turbulence it created.

It was when I came to the water, however, that I discovered I had a real problem. In five-gallon cans, I could carry 50 gallons of water a trip. But trying to load 50 plastic bags on the racks nearly drove me crazy. It was like trying to handle jellyfish. I pleaded with the forestry people to throw them away and use cans. No good. We were in a bureaucracy; someone had found a way to justify the expense of the bags and they were determined to use them. In the end I had two more or less stable mounds of the bags on the racks. I used every bit of sashcord I had to make a sort of net over them, and then took off.

I had been climbing up above the level of the ridge to avoid the turbulence, then going down in a steep approach right onto the pad without any hover. This time I got caught in a particularly severe down-draft and found myself sinking much too fast. I pulled the nose up sharply and hauled in power; then abruptly, as I levelled off again, I lost control. The nose went down and I keeled over to my left at a 45-degree angle. I hit the edge of the pad a tremendous thump with the left float.

I was sure I was past the point of no return, and that I was going to roll down the hill. But somehow I must have sorted things out, because I finally got the machine on the pad. It looked a sorry sight. It was canted over to the left, its tail high in the air. I had ripped the bottom out of the two front compartments of the left float on the edge of the pad.

What had happened was that one or two of the plastic bags on my right rack had ruptured as the bags tried to slide backwards when I pulled the nose up. The rest of the bags had either ruptured or slipped out under the now-slack sashcord, and because none of the bags on my left rack had moved, I ended up in an almost hopelessly unbalanced condition.

That was the end of the water bags as far as I was concerned. Except for the floats, I couldn't find anything wrong with the helicopter. We decided to go back to base, get the floats repaired and return the following day with some cans. One of the youngsters on the crew wanted to ride back with me. The rest of the crew left in their vehicle and, just before we took off, I threw a couple of the water bags into the helicopter.

Considering it was his first attempt, the youngster did very well. I came up slowly from behind the forestry truck, which was winding its way along the dirt road. He opened the door, leaned out and planted the first water bag right on the hood of the vehicle; the truck very nearly went off the road. Then the crew were silly enough to get out of it and shake their fists at us. We damn nearly got them with the second one.

I think it was just after this incident that we had a change of engineers. For some reason Les was recalled to Ottawa and he was replaced by Dave. Dave was an Australian. He was tall, rugged and virile — very much a man's man. He was as forthright and outspoken as most of the Australians I have met; the sort of person you got on well with because it would have been very dangerous not to. I remember on one occasion getting stuck at a lookout tower with a flat battery. Dave packed a new battery on his back through four miles of rough bush and up the hill. When he arrived his breathing was hardly disturbed. And although he gave me the rough of his tongue for flattening the battery, he obviously wasn't in the least put out about having to pack another one up the hill.

One day we had to put out some timber-cruising crews. The crews — I think there were about eight people — were driven out to a lake in a van, and I was to put them out in the bush from there. The lake boasted a lodge and cabins; one of those expensive resorts which catered mainly to rich Americans. Dave had come with me for the ride, and after we had put the crews out he, the ranger driving the van and I decided to stay and have supper in the lodge before returning to Sudbury. We had just finished our meal when we heard an aircraft coming in to land. We wandered down to join a small group of people on the dock to see who it was.

The airplane, a very glossy American-registered Cessna 180 on floats, landed and turned towards us. The pilot, who was by himself, cut the engine as he approached the dock and climbed down onto the float. He made a striking figure. He was wearing a monogrammed white shirt, white shorts and tennis shoes. He had, for that time, a good deal of hair — curly blond hair — and penetrating blue eyes. He was an attractive youth. As a matter of fact, he looked very much as Pat Boone used to look in those days.

As the Cessna moved up to the dock, he leapt athletically ashore and paused to wave to us before turning to catch the strut and tie the aircraft to the dock. All at once, with a sort of inarticulate growl, Dave broke away from our group, ran along the dock and threw his arms around the young man, shouting, "He's mine — he's mine!"

The unfortunate youth struggled to free himself for a few seconds before Dave finally let him go. He stood for a few more seconds, looking stunned; then, with a cry of alarm, he remembered the aircraft and turned. But it was too late. The Cessna had passed the dock; slowly but inexorably it was sailing out towards the centre of the lake.

He turned back for a moment to the group on the dock, most of whom were having some difficulty keeping their composure by this time, gave a cry of frustration and ran two or three steps along the dock before diving gracefully into the water. He was a strong swimmer and he soon caught up with the Cessna, pulled himself up on the float and disappeared into the cockpit.

We stood waiting for him to taxi back to the dock — waiting with some interest to see how he would handle himself this time round. He didn't give us the opportunity. When he had started the engine, he turned into wind and took off. We never saw him again.

But I had other experiences that year which I found depressing.

I began to learn something of the way in which many people in the small communities of northern Ontario lived. One day I had to take the ranger into a largish lumber camp. It was a bleak place by any standards, built in amongst the trees, down in a rather swampy hollow. There was a large cookhouse, a sort of barn for equipment maintenance, two office shacks and two large bunkhouses. We visited it during a spell of rainy weather, and the area between the buildings was a sea of mud.

While the ranger was transacting his business with the camp manager, I took a stroll around the place. There was very little to see. The bunkhouses were just that: large, bare rooms, with rows of double-tiered steel beds, a row of washbasins with buckets of water at one end; they had the rancid smell of an ancient slum. The camp manager invited the ranger and me to stay for lunch. We stood talking for a few minutes outside his office shack, and at noon a veritable fleet of crummies — the vehicles used to transport loggers — began to arrive. The men in them walked straight into the cookhouse, still covered with the mud and grease of their workplace. I suppose there were about a hundred men living in the camp; there were no women. They trooped silently into the cookhouse and sat at rows of wooden tables on wooden benches. I noticed that the tables were heavily laden with pies and tarts and cakes and cookies, and that the men started to eat these as soon as they sat down. Five minutes later the cook shouted, "Come and get it," and they all left the tables to queue up for their meals.

It seemed a curious procedure to me, a reversal of the natural order of things: the dessert first, and then the meat course; but I learned later that this was not accidental. By far the cheapest commodities in the bush were flour and sugar; so, if the men could be persuaded to blunt their appetites with these, they would eat sparingly when it came to the expensive meat and vegetables. But what really surprised me was the absolute silence that prevailed. The only sound was the clinking of cutlery on plates. I asked the person next to me to pass the salt. Heads turned to look at me all round the room. A moment or two later I turned to the ranger, who was sitting next to me, and questioned him about the silence, remarking that they seemed a curiously unsociable bunch. He muttered out of the corner of his mouth that no one talked at meals. "What?" I said, genuinely shocked. The camp manager leaned forward on the other side of the ranger. "Stop talking," he said angrily. "No one talks in the cookhouse."

When the meal was over, less than 15 minutes later, the men went straight back to the crummies and were driven back to work. I tackled the manager about it, suggesting that it was downright uncivilized not to allow people to talk at meals. He replied, after some hesitation, that if you let these zombies talk at meals they would get into arguments and end up fighting. This was obviously a crude rationalization. I was convinced the real reason was to get them through their meal and back to work as quickly as possible. And as I looked around, it occurred to me that there was absolutely nothing in the way of recreation. There were no pool tables, for example; they didn't even have a projector so that they could watch a movie every now and again. They had nothing but the cookhouse, their bunkhouses and the logging show in which they worked. When I suggested to the manager that this was a pretty grim existence, his answer was terse: it was none of my goddam business.

I suppose he was right, but I found it depressing, nevertheless, and I had an experience a week or so later which I found even more disconcerting. I had to go to another lumber camp to pick up two forestry youngsters who were collecting cones for reseeding. The camp was almost identical to the previous one, though not quite so muddy. The two forestry people were not ready to come out — they needed another day or two. I was walking back to the helicopter when a small, wiry individual came running after me. Could I take him out, he asked, in a voice that was almost pleading. He'd been here for four months. He had intended to stay for six, but he'd got to get out before he went really squir'ly. I said sure, he could come out with me, and he was pathetically grateful, promising to be ready just as soon as he could get his cheque from the timekeeper.

When we arrived back at base, he pleaded with me once again; he wanted me to go with him to the beer parlour so that he could buy me a drink. I made some excuse and said I'd see him there later. After I had had a shower and something to eat, Dave and I went down to the beer parlour to have a drink with him. He was already well into his cups when we got there, and he was sitting with something like $200 lying amongst the beer bottles on the table in front of him. He was buying drinks for everyone in the place. The beer slinger would come to the table every now and again and pick up what appeared to be a random handful of money. Apparently our lumberjack had cashed his pay cheque for some $3,000 in the beer parlour.

A week later I was asked to take him back into the camp. His money was all gone. There was some talk of a hooker who had stolen most of it. He was gaunt and shaky, a thoroughly depressing spectacle. After a week of oblivion, he had to go back into that frightful camp and repeat the cycle. And there were so many more like him, enduring the same empty existences.

Towards the end of my stint with the forestry that year, I finally visited Wawa for a few days. I'm not quite sure why, but the name had caught my imagination and I was expecting to find something exciting and romantic when I got there. In the Indian language of the region, Wawa means wild goose, and it turned out to be a pleasant enough place — a mining town, set on the shore of an attractive lake which was surrounded by small but steep hills.

The name of the mining promoter who had discovered the ore and developed the mine was, I believe, Watts. Mr. Watts had made a determined effort to achieve immortality by having the name of what he obviously believed to be his town changed to Wattsville. I was encouraged to hear that the rough miners and their families would have none of it. They insisted on retaining the name Wawa, even though the pertinacious Mr. Watts had used his wealth and influence to obtain legislative sanction for the change.

Abiding by my instructions to keep the company constantly informed of my whereabouts, I sent them a telegram on the night I arrived. It said, "In Wawa stop Haha." I meant it of course as a facetious comment on the requirement to keep sending pointless messages to Ottawa when I was in constant radio contact with the forestry people while I was flying. But by this time Spartan had moved into a new phase of the big corporate image. They were publishing a monthly newsletter and the secretary, who thought my telegram amusing, merely advised my superiors that I was in Wawa and gave the text to the person editing the newsletter.

When it was published a week or two later, management did not think it was ha ha. I was sternly rebuked.

But it was a restful visit. There were no fires burning and no one was under any pressure. On the third day, I think it was, we went on a tour of the ranger's constituency. We called at three of the lookout towers, dropped in to a couple of logging camps, stopped to talk to some fisheries people who were doing some sort of trout study. We returned from this trip at about half-past four and the ranger invited Dave and me to join him for a drink in the cocktail lounge of the hotel. Three or four other forestry people joined us and we had just settled down with our first beer when a young woman came in. She looked brash, if not a little tarty to me, but the forestry people greeted her with some enthusiasm.

The ranger, who was sitting next to me, leaned across to murmur in my ear that she was one of the local you-know-what's, but that she was good fun and he hoped I didn't mind her joining us. I assured him that I had met such people before. When the girl, whose name was Maude, had been introduced to us, she sat down and turned to me.

"So you're the helicopter pilot?" she said, gazing at me speculatively.

I agreed that I was, smiling to myself because I thought Maude shared the popular illusion that helicopter pilots earned large salaries, and that she was making a professional assessment of her chances of sharing some of mine.

"There was a chopper pilot here last week," she said.

The forestry people uttered exclamations of surprise. They hadn't seen any helicopter.

"Me neither," Maude replied. "I just seen the pilot here," she pointed up at the ceiling, "in the corridor of this hotel. He was chasing a broad along it, and both of them was skinny naked."

"Oh come on," I smiled. "Helicopter pilots don't do that sort of thing. What was his name? I'm bound to know him."

"I dunno. I only seen him the once."

There was a cockiness about Maude that was irritating. She was beginning to get to me; I decided to put her down.

"Okay, let's get this straight," I said, leaning forward in my chair. "You say you only saw him once?"

"Yep."

"You didn't see him before or afterwards; you didn't see him in a chopper — and when you did see him he didn't have any clothes on at all?"

"Mother naked!"

"Well then, how on earth could you have known that he was a helicopter pilot?" I said, sitting back to rest my case.

"Oh, it was easy," said Maude brightly. "He had a great big wristwatch and a little tiny pecker."

I didn't think it was funny; rather coarse, in fact. But my companions thought it was vastly amusing. They began to shout and yell with laughter, pounding the table until finally the bartender came out from behind the bar and threatened to throw us all out.

CHAPTER 16

A Winter of Discontent

BY THE END OF AUGUST, MY RESENTMENT AGAINST THE company I was working for reached some sort of a peak. I was only two or three hundred miles from Ottawa; I had a son nearly four months old I hadn't even seen; yet still they couldn't get me home for a few days. Finally I told them that I was going to finish up the week, park the helicopter in Sudbury and catch a bus back to Ottawa. A relief pilot arrived two days later.

This time, though, I did not stay in Ottawa, waiting for the phone to ring. Nina and I bundled our children onto an airliner and flew down to visit some friends in New Jersey. We spent a pleasant two weeks with them, then stopped for another week with some friends on a farm in southern Ontario. There was much anger when I returned. There had been emergencies; I had no right to go anywhere without leaving my telephone number. I took very little notice of all this because I knew that by now crews all over the country were beginning to revolt against the ludicrous notion that they would have to forget all about their families and spend virtually the entire year out in the bush. The pilot who had relieved me on the forestry job had begun his season at the beginning of April. After five months in the bush, he had only been home for four days when he was sent out to relieve me — and he was just as ferociously resentful as I was.

I had been hoping at the end of my break to return to the forestry job in Ontario in time to bust some more poachers. Instead, I was sent off to do a three-week job in New Brunswick, followed by a series of relief jobs in Quebec. Some of these required me to leave the helicopter in villages and small towns overnight, and I was warned of a problem we had not encountered before. People had begun to steal things from the helicopter — such things as the axe, which we kept strapped to the frame for survival purposes, the emergency rations and the tool kit, which contained spark plugs and ignition points and other small spares which might make the difference between mobility and several nights stuck in the bush. There had also been some instances of vandalism.

In an attempt to forestall this, crews had taken to dropping round to tell the police where they had left the helicopter and asking them if they would keep an eye on it during their patrols. But this, in at least one case, had turned out to be a mistake. The police had suggested to Ben, the pilot in question, that he should provide them with $25, which they would give to a reliable person to guard the helicopter. Ben, objecting to the concept of protection money, refused. When he went out to the helicopter the following morning, he found that someone had taken an axe to it and done several thousand dollars worth of damage.

I don't know who came up with the solution in the end, but it turned out to be a very effective one. The first thing you would do after parking the helicopter for the night was to find the local priest and ask him if he thought it would be safe to leave the machine wherever you had parked it. The priest was invariably pleased by this recognition of his authority. He would phone the police for us and, in effect, tell them to let people know that he had given his blessing. I did not hear of any more incidents of theft or vandalism after we adopted this practice.

Things were getting a little better in the fall by this time. Many companies were beginning to hire students for the season; when the students went back to university, the job usually ended. Still, though, there were some die-hards, and it was in these jobs that I had to relieve pilots for a week or two at a time. One in particular was a gruesome scene. The people had been out since April without a break and they were so badly bushed they were dangerous. There were a couple of episodes of incipient violence during the two weeks I was with them, so I pulled out and told the company they would have to pay me a great deal more than my salary as danger money if they wanted me to go back in. The reaction was predictably hostile. I was told that I was becoming altogether too independent if I thought I could decide which jobs I would stay on and which ones I would not.

However, the fuss died down pretty quickly on this one. Only four days after I pulled out, another of our pilots who was flying in the area had to make an emergency flight into that camp. There had been an altercation of some sort, which had turned into a free-for-all. Several people had been injured, two of them seriously enough to be flown out to hospital. The police were called in and the camp closed down.

All in all this was a winter of discontent in the Canadian helicopter industry. For the truth is that most operators, and Spartan in particular, had rushed into helicopters without any real idea of the economics involved. It cost in the neighbourhood of $50,000 by the time a machine was fully equipped and insured to work in the bush. If you add another 30 per cent for back-up spares and then multiply by the 35-odd machines Spartan was operating that year, you will have some idea of the capital investment involved. And for all practical purposes, the season was from May to September. The crews who had tried it knew, and customers were beginning to learn, that any attempts to start early and finish later than this were futile. Thus the machines would be non-productive for seven months of the year.

To make matters worse, the operating costs for a helicopter were far higher than they were for a fixed-wing aircraft of comparable capacity. After 600 hours of flying, the engine and clutch had to be changed; after 1,200 hours, the helicopter had to be completely stripped and overhauled. Many of the parts had to be discarded and replaced with new ones. I think the main rotor blades, for example, had to be discarded after about six or seven hundred hours, and a new set cost some $1,500. In addition, there were a host of bearings, ball joints and couplings which had to be replaced, and the engine, clutch and transmission had to be completely overhauled. All of this was very, very expensive.

The nub of the problem in those days was this: It cost $120 an hour to rent a helicopter; it cost approximately $30 an hour to rent a fixed-wing machine of comparable capacity. And this disparity infuriated customers. It was a sheer waste of breath to point out to them the facts I have just given. It was equally futile to remind them that the helicopter had brought a whole new dimension to the field of raw-material exploitation. An exploration crew using a helicopter could now accomplish in one season what had previously taken at least five seasons with pack horses. The savings were enormous, but still customers insisted that helicopters were too expensive. Thus operators either had to increase their tariffs, and lose customers (as it was, a number of customers obstinately went back to their pack horses), or they had to function at a level which was barely self-supporting, let alone profitable.

By and large, helicopter crews were aware of these problems, but we were convinced we were being short-changed. The country was enjoying a very tangible wave of prosperity. It seemed to us that we were playing a very significant role in creating this prosperity — nearly all the new mineral, oil and gas discoveries had been made by helicopters — yet we were getting a very small slice of the prosperity pie. Disregarding the element of danger, we were living for the majority of the year in isolation and substandard conditions; we were separated from our families; and we were earning very mediocre salaries.

Even so, we might have been sympathetic to management if it had not been for other factors. The principals of Spartan were all fixed-wing people. From the beginning, they had regarded helicopters as a sideline to the real business — which was aerial photography. The SHORAN contract, in particular, had been so profitable that it nearly became a public scandal. The mandarins in Ottawa became nervous; so nervous that they revised future contracts drastically, and there were no more windfall profits. In any case, though, by the winter of 1956 the boom in aerial photography was over. Fixed-wing began to scratch for a living, and for the next two years the company survived only because of its helicopter operation, whose personnel were still clearly regarded as second-class citizens.

All these things made us resentful, but the biggest irritant was that the three or four years of prosperity had given the directors expansive visions. The company had blossomed into the big corporate image. We had a new hangar at Uplands and vast, luxurious office space downtown. All at once we found ourselves returning, after living for months in a damp tent, to find a host of assistants to the president, public relations officers and miscellaneous administrators occupying these luxurious offices. They were all earning far more money than we were, and they were all (in our no doubt prejudiced view) almost totally non-productive. It galled; and we were very cynical when, at the company's Christmas party that year, the executive assistant to the president gave out long-service pins. The most senior employee, I think, got a seven-year pin. They went right down to three years, so I missed by one year this most valuable symbol of corporate affection for its employees.

The temptation from this distance, of course, is to ask why the hell we didn't leave to find another job if things were so unsatisfactory? The answer, I suppose, would be a rationalization. Most of us had invested a great deal of time and energy, and our own money, getting into the business, and we kept hoping that things would improve. For myself, though, I was feeling increasingly guilty as time went on. Nina had been left for month after month with first one, and then two young children to look after. She had had to suffer all the inevitable anxieties of bringing up children on her own; she had had to make any number of decisions which should have been a shared responsibility. I was very fortunate that she had the personal resources to do all this; so many of my fellow pilots' marriages had broken down under the strain. And in any case, she had one attribute in particular which I treasured, one I had encountered in very few other people: she seemed to like me.

Then, too, there was another development at the time which made us hang on. The federal government had announced that it was going to hand over the support and maintenance flying on the Mid-Canada Line to commercial operators. Up to now, this had been done by the R.C.A.F. with heavy machines: Sikorsky S-58's. Okanagan Helicopters were awarded the contract for the western half of the Line, Spartan the eastern half, which stretched from James Bay to the Labrador coast. We were to use the large, twin-rotor Vertol 42's in the east. We looked forward to the bigger salaries we were bound to earn flying heavy helicopters, and to a much more stable life. Such is the silliness eternal optimism breeds.

When I returned to Ottawa in November that year, there was considerable excitement in the hangar. Conversion training onto the Vertol 42's for the Mid-Canada Line was about to begin. We were convinced it would mean the end of tent living and damp sleeping bags. We would be housed in comfortable R.C.A.F. bases at Knob Lake and Great Whale River. Most of us, I suspect, saw ourselves moving into supervisory positions after a year or two, because now the company would have the stability of a big, year-round government contract which was not subject to the exigencies of the free-enterprise system. In the initial phase, eight of us were to do our conversion training at Arnprior, some 30 miles west of Ottawa. I think I was about sixth in line, and my training would begin just after Christmas.

CHAPTER 17

The Mid-Canada Line

FOR THE NEXT 18 MONTHS I WAS INVOLVED WITH THE MID-Canada Line. It proved to be a period of high comedy. Only a country as wealthy as Canada could have afforded to persevere with such a fiasco. By the time the Mid-Canada Line was completed, it was utterly incapable of providing any worthwhile information. It could not detect an aircraft flying above 40,000 feet. Very obviously it had been built as a defence against the Russians, and the Russians had numerous aircraft by then which could comfortably exceed this altitude. In any case, as far as I could determine the radar only indicated a crossing of the Line; it could not plot the heading of the aircraft. Finally, at lower levels it was so undiscriminating that a flight of geese could not be distinguished from an aircraft.

However, I did not discover these things for some time. It took me more than three months to complete the mere 25 hours of conversion training I needed on the Vertol. On many occasions I had flown that number of hours in less than three days. Now my routine for the next three months was to drive the 30-odd miles to Arnprior, where the Vertol company had its Canadian plant. I would then sit around all morning, have some lunch and wait for the instructor to tell me, at about three o'clock usually, that the machine would not be ready to fly that day. I was at home all this time, so I didn't complain too much; but it was tedious, nevertheless, and I suspect much of the delay was deliberate: that once the training was completed somebody would be out of a job. In any event, it was March before I was ready to fly the Line. Because of the delay in training we had so far only taken over half of our part of the Line from the R.C.A.F. — the part that stretched eastward from Knob Lake to

Hopedale, on the Labrador coast. I had been assigned to work on the western part, based at Great Whale River.

Towards the end of March I was finally sent up to Knob Lake for an orientation with the crews who had been there for about three months. In the first week I made two full familiarization trips along the Line as co-pilot; then I had to make a short trip by myself to the second site along the Line, some 60 miles away. The machine I took was one which had just been ferried up from Arnprior after an overhaul. I travelled out to the site empty, picked up three people and about 400 pounds of equipment, and had great difficulty getting the machine back into the air. When I finally did succeed and settled down to fly back, I noticed that my gas gauge was going down at an alarming rate.

Feeling some anxiety because I was to take-off in the same machine for a full trip along the Line the following morning, I went to see the base engineer. He came for a test flight with me, but there were no objective manifestations of anything wrong. We were getting the maximum manifold pressure, around 40 inches I think it was, and he brushed off the fact that I had been using far too much fuel as a problem with the gauge. He would get someone to look at it. I was worried. I was only carrying a fraction of a load, yet that take-off had been a very difficult one. I went to look for Doc Demerah, the base manager, to suggest that we put a load on and get him to test the machine. Unfortunately, since he knew that I was taking the trip on the following day, and he would not have to fly, he was well embarked on a party in the officers' mess.

In the morning I fussed around the hangar for some time, wondering what to do. I was convinced there was something seriously wrong with the machine, but the engineers were unsympathetic. They were equally convinced that I was suffering from nerves because I had only just converted to the Vertol and this was my first solo trip along the Line. It was very silly of me, but in the end I decided that I had better go. I was empty leaving Knob Lake; it was a cool morning, with a stiff breeze blowing; even so, the machine was very sluggish getting into the air. I looked in vain for some sign of what the trouble might be, but all the temperatures and pressures gazed back at me with implacable rectitude.

I had Billy Auld with me, a young apprentice-engineer. He was red-haired, freckle-faced and very pleasant. He was also nervous, of course, because while the other engineers had brushed off my complaints about the machine, he was the one who actually had to fly in it. To him, though, the first take-off was reassuring: everything had seemed in order and he relaxed. I had to land at the first site out of Knob Lake (I have forgotten the site numbers now), pick up a maintenance crew of four men and their equipment and fly them to a site in the middle of the Line. They had five or six hundred pounds of equipment with them, so I had considerably less than half a full load. I should have been able to fly away without thinking about it.

The pad I had to take off from, too, was very nearly in an ideal location: it was on the top of a gently sloping hill. The trees had been cut down for a distance of about 200 yards, so that one could run gently down the hill before pulling up over the trees. Two factors govern a helicopter during take-off. They are called ground cushion and translational lift. The ground cushion is the extra lift you get as a result of the downwash, from the rotors, bouncing off the ground; the translational lift is the extra lift you get as a consequence of increasing forward speed. Thus the trick is, when you are heavily loaded, to get from the cushion into translational. A smooth but very positive movement is the ideal. In this case it should have been simplicity itself: I had a nice gentle run down the hill into wind. Instead, when I picked up and stuffed the nose down, I began to lose revs right away. I lost them so quickly that I couldn't stop and recover; I would have dropped into the jumble of tree stumps and inevitably tipped over. I was committed and I had to keep the nose down and try to pick up enough translational lift to get me over the trees.

When Billy and I discussed it afterwards, we found that we had both nearly strained our backs, forcing against the seat belts as we tried to lift the helicopter up physically. The last time I looked at the tachometer, the revs were well down in the red danger zone; the zone at which the blades were supposed to begin folding up. After that I had to watch the ground and the trees. We hit the tops of the trees, but we burst through them without damage and, blessedly, the ground dropped away sharply beyond them, so that I was able to stuff the nose right down. After a lot of shuddering, we finally got up enough speed to fly. When I looked at Billy, I burst out laughing. He looked like a very white, very speckled egg with a red cosy on top.

Even then, I had not learned my lesson. Instead of turning back right away, I decided to take the crew I had on board to their destination, and then go back to base. In normal circumstances, I would have been able to get to this destination with nearly an hour's fuel in reserve. Ten minutes before we got there, the red warning light came on, indicating that we were down to 20 minutes of fuel — 20 minutes at normal consumption, that is. When we gassed up at the site, we discovered that we had about six or seven gallons left in the tanks — enough for about two or three more minutes of flying.

Back at base, the engineers were still unconvinced. They dragged Doc Demerah out to do another test flight. We threw on about 2,000 pounds of assorted equipment and I sat back laughing while Doc, who had a ferocious hangover, made some five attempts to get into the air, flopping back ignominiously onto the tarmac every time. Eventually, they wheeled the machine back into the hangar and took the carburetor off. The diaphram which controls the mixture had ruptured, giving a mixture about twice as rich as it should have been. It was a valuable lesson to me. After that I didn't care what the temperatures and pressures said, or the engineers for that matter; if the machine was sluggish, I grounded it.

I think I stayed about three weeks on that first orientation trip at Knob Lake; enough to learn that operating a Vertol under winter conditions was even harder than a Bell. There was so much more of them to get covered with frost and ice. And none of the equipment on the sites had been adequately maintained. We flew maintenance crews up and down the Line, but they spent the vast majority of their time playing cards. Thus, if we had to stop the night at one of the sites, we usually had to spend the first few hours of the following day trying to get the Herman-Nelson heater working and the fuel pumps operating. Each site had avgas tanks, which we kept supplied, but the pumps were operated by Petter diesel engines; and since they, too, had received very little maintenance, starting them in cold weather presented a challenge. The form was to open a decompression valve, crank a very large and heavy flywheel until you ran out of steam, then drop the decompression valve and hope. In the end we took to carrying capsules of ether which we pumped into the cylinders as a primer. This usually worked, but you had to be careful to be moving towards the door of the little shack in which the engines were housed before dropping the valve. The resulting explosion was usually powerful enough to blow you through it.

I recall one pleasant experience, though, at the master site in the middle of that part of the Line. Doc Demerah and I were flying in opposite directions that day, and we both decided to give up and stay there because it was snowing so hard we couldn't see. The blizzard was an extended one; it was four days before we managed to get away again, and it so happened that one of the crew there, a Newfie with the delightful name of Merlin Jay, was in the process of preparing a batch of screech when we arrived. I was intrigued because I had never actually seen booze being distilled before. The process is not nearly so complex as I had imagined. The first part is very much like brewing beer. He put sugar, molasses and yeast into a crock and left it to ferment. When we got there, this process had just been completed. Now he dug out his still, which he kept hidden in a snowbank during the winter. It consisted of a ten-gallon gas drum with a hole in the bung, into which a union had been welded. When he had filled the drum with the fermented liquid, he screwed the bung on and attached a spiral coil of copper tubing to the union. Then he put the drum on the stove to heat and let the coil of copper tubing sit in a large tub filled with snow.

The condensed liquid which emerged from the copper tube was collected in bottles. He threw the first quart away, warning us always to do this because it was the first pint or so that so often poisoned people. After he had filled half a dozen bottles, he sat with a teaspoon and a box of matches, testing his product from time to time. When it would no longer ignite, he shut down and threw the rest of the mixture away.

The people on the site began to drink Merlin's screech right away. Our crews were cautious at first, but when we saw, on the following day, that no one had gone blind, we tried some. It was colourless and had a faintly sour flavour; apart from that, it was much like vodka, and since we had an ample supply of canned fruit juice as a mix, we were able to relax and enjoy the rest of our stay. Later I learned that at infrequent intervals, a Mountie used to fly along the Line to make sure no illicit stills were being operated. But that was one part of the warning system on the Mid-Canada Line which worked very effectively, and the stills were always well concealed by the time he arrived on the site.

Some six weeks later, I went up with Tim Schwenk to take over from the R.C.A.F. at Great Whale River. Like Knob Lake, it was a substantial base with an airstrip, a large heated hangar and ample accommodation. But the thing we were most gratified about at the time was that we had been equipped with, and flew up, two of the newest model of the Vertol, the 44. They were no larger nor more powerful than the 42's, but they had a sophisticated gyro-stabilizing system which made them quite the nicest handling helicopter I have flown. This gave us a boost, and to begin with everything was fresh and interesting. But then, as we began to discover what a fiasco the whole Mid-Canada Line was, it became increasingly difficult to maintain any enthusiasm for the job.

Tim Schwenk was the base manager and after he had looked around for a week or two, he came to a very sensible conclusion. Our main task was to keep the sites supplied with diesel fuel. Each site required some 300 drums of fuel to operate its generators for a year. During the summer months the fuel was flown in to the nearest lake to each site in an amphibious, twin-engined Canso, pumped into drums, and then moved up to the site in nets slung under the helicopter, eight to 12 drums at a time. In the past, helicopter slinging had been done all the year round, each site getting enough fuel to last it a month or so. This meant slinging operations in the winter, when things are always much harder, particularly for the engineers who had to stand in the downwash, signalling and hooking up, and who frequently suffered from frostbite. Tim and I decided that if we got stuck into it and worked hard during our three-month summer stint, we could supply all the sites for the entire year. Then, when things got tough in the winter, we would merely have to do supply runs twice a week.

The contractor at that time I think was Bell Telephone — later Marconi took over — and their representatives at Great Whale laughed when we told them what we planned to do. They were accustomed to a much more leisurely pace than Tim and I were, and they said we would be lucky to get a three-month supply into every site. Two and a half months later we had every site supplied with enough fuel to keep them going until the following summer. It was hard work, of course; we stayed out on the Line for two weeks at a time, working 12 and 14 hours a day. But we thought the effort worthwhile. Oddly enough, this did not seem to please any of the people running things. I think they liked having to monitor the fuel supply at each site, and keep sending out helicopters to supply them; it gave them a sense of purpose.

In fact, though, flying the Mid-Canada Line was a dull business. It was rather like driving a truck. You flew over the same country all the time, in and out of the same sites, and the only thing that really sticks in my mind about that first tour in Great Whale was my irritation with the visiting "firemen." We had a steady stream of middle-level mandarins from Ottawa who came up, ostensibly on an inspection tour, in reality to go fishing. There was a large stream — or a small river, whichever you prefer — some 40 miles away where trout could be caught by the hundreds, and we spent a great deal of time flying these fishing parties in and out of it. One day I had just got everything comfortably organized, hauling oil up to a site, when we received a message to return to base at once; there was some emergency. After I had picked up the crews, stowed all our equipment and nets and flown back to Great Whale, I found that the emergency was to take a group of five people, who had arrived that morning on a Nordair scheduled flight, out on a fishing trip. I made some sarcastic comments about their sense of priorities which did not go down at all well with the mandarins.

I kept a log of the flying we did purely on fishing trips that summer. Over a period of four months, it cost the taxpayer a little over $70,000. But it was really rather childish of me to worry about it. The Mid-Canada Line was such a massive pork barrel that this was an inconsequential sum.

My first tour on the Line was supposed to last three months; instead it stretched past five months. And two weeks after I got back to Ottawa, I was back out flying a Bell on the Ontario-Manitoba border. The dream of a stable existence — of three months on the Mid-Canada and then three months at home — quickly evaporated. To the company, the fact that the contract with the federal government provided funds for sufficient crews to allow a three-month rotation was immaterial. They saw it as a golden opportunity to keep crews out for the majority of the year. We resisted in our various ways, but by now it was clear that the company was in serious trouble: pay cheques were not always out on time; expense claims were often delayed for months. We had about ten chiefs for every Indian, and we began to hear stories of the monumental blunders this bureaucracy was making. In one case, as part of a foreign-aid program, Spartan had been awarded a large contract to fly aerial photography in Africa. After three weeks of steady flying, someone discovered that they were photographing the wrong area — an error which cost the company more than $100,000. We began to look around seriously for other employment.

I got home that year in October and, by refusing point blank to move, I managed to stay home until January, when I returned to Great Whale, this time as base manager. It was one of the coldest winters for several years in that part of the country and this gave us some problems. But the real problems we encountered had little to do with the elements; they were caused by people who were desperately bored. Since every site now had enough fuel to last it until summer, all we needed to do was to fly the Line twice a week, distributing food and mail. If we got away by 8:30 in the morning, we could be back at base before it got dark at about 3:30 in the afternoon. This saved an enormous amount of work because, as I mentioned before, none of the equipment on the sites had been properly maintained, and we had to rely on such things as the Herman-Nelson heaters to get us started after the helicopter had been sitting out on an exposed pad all night. We could, and often did, work from seven in the morning until early afternoon merely getting the helicopter started.

Such things, of course, were part and parcel of winter flying. But if the equipment had been adequately maintained we would have been able to start the machine in no more than two or three hours. And in any case, it was totally unnecessary for us to be out there in the first place. Our crews had worked very hard the previous summer with just this in mind, and as a result morale began to deteriorate rapidly. I went to the authorities on the spot and explained this to them with some care. The mail and hardware could be loaded onto the machines the previous night in the hangar; this left only the refrigerated meat and vegetables to be loaded in the morning. Surely it was not too much to ask that these be ready to load by eight o'clock in the morning? They told me it was up to us to fly the loads when they were ready; not to tell them when they should be ready.

I suppose they were right, but it was very irritating. The psychology of it was so obvious. In the past the local authorities had grown accustomed to a series of minor crises all through the winter as crews struggled to supply the sites with fuel as well as food, mail and equipment. Things would break down; blizzards would stop everything for days at a time; countless difficulties would keep cropping up and they, the supervisors, would sit at their command posts, in constant contact with the sites by telephone, offering advice and giving orders: it gave them an illusion of accomplishment. Now, with no fuel problems and the helicopters safely in a heated hangar every night, they had literally nothing to do. Parkinson's law had been reversed, and they felt insecure.

Things did not improve. Loads would never be ready before ten or eleven o'clock in the morning, and our crews were becoming increasingly hostile. I decided on a confrontation; I felt I had very little to lose. Nina and I had decided that we would have enough money saved by the end of the summer for me to give up flying, and for us to move to the west coast, which we had wanted to do for some time. If I got fired now, it wouldn't hurt us too much. So I wrote a report of the situation to our company, with copies to the civilian contractor, Marconi, and to the R.C.A.F. commanding officer. Then, the following morning, I postponed the supply trip until the next day because the load had not been available by eight o'clock.

There was much anger and recrimination, a flurry of long-distance phone calls. But my case was a strong one, and I had unanimous support from our crews. After that we only occasionally had to spend a night out on the Line when a genuine problem arose. But now some interesting difficulties began to occur with the machines. This was the first time the new Vertol 44's had operated under winter conditions, and although the Vertol people claimed that they had been extensively tested under Arctic conditions, we found some areas in which their simulations had obviously not been severe enough.

At approximately 20 degrees below zero (these were Fahrenheit days), we discovered that the bonding on the blades would begin to let go and the covering would literally start to peel off them. We contacted Vertol and their response was predictable. It couldn't possibly have anything to do with temperature; the blades had been tested in much lower temperatures than we were experiencing. We must, they said, have abused them in some way; perhaps flown in very severe turbulence. I pointed out that the weather was cold, clear and calm; there was virtually no turbulence. We changed the blades and went out two days later. The same thing happened. This time Vertol sent up two technical-engineering representatives.

The tech reps were fun. They had the implacable self-assurance of evangelists, and they produced some fascinatingly improbable hypotheses to explain why the blades had suddenly started to give way — all of them suggesting stupidity and gross incompetence by our pilots. I told them that the only way to sort it out was to put yet another set of blades on, and for them to come with me for a trip along the Line to see for themselves. They were clearly reluctant, but in the circumstances they couldn't very well refuse. I had satisfied myself that the problem began to occur at almost exactly 20 below, and we got a suitable day for our purposes. The temperature was about 23 or 24 below zero when we took off. It was a silk-smooth morning, and I flew with all the delicacy of which I am capable. At the third site I shut down to gas up. The two tech reps were up on top of the fuselage examining the blades almost before the blades had stopped turning. They had started to peel.

Now, all at once, the tech reps had very little to say (though I made up for that), and they hurried off to catch the first plane out of Great Whale when we got back. We were instructed to use up the two spare sets of blades we had on the spot; more would be sent up. The Vertol had a twin-rotor system, each with three sets of blades. At that time, each blade cost $1,200; thus it was costing $7,200 a trip just in blades for the next three weeks. I think we went through eight sets of blades before some new ones with a modified bonding system arrived.

However, by then, I was becoming accustomed to such expenditures. I had just experienced the ultimate in government spending. I did a supply run along the Line and found that the final site had nothing to be delivered but one letter. I suggested to the dispatcher that surely this letter could wait until the next run in two or three days time, when we would be taking a load of food and other supplies into the last site. The answer was no; it had to be taken on this trip. When we reached the site I looked at the letter before it was delivered to its recipient. It was a circulation-promotion letter from *Reader's Digest*. I doubt very much whether that magazine has ever been served better. It took 45 minutes of flying to reach that extra site. The operating costs of a Vertol were approximately $700 an hour. I prorated the cost of the new set of blades we had to install after the trip and worked out that the letter cost something in the neighbourhood of $1,350 to deliver. Such were the economics of the Mid-Canada Line.

The next mechanical problem we encountered was much more serious. We had a remarkably long spell of cold weather. For nearly a month the temperature seldom rose above 25 below zero — much of the time it was between 35 and 50 below — and we found that the heating system ceased to function when the temperature fell below −30 degrees. The engineers worked long hours trying to rectify the problem, but without success. I got on to Ottawa and told them we would have to shut down if the problem couldn't be corrected. They in turn contacted Vertol, who immediately suggested that we must be mishandling the equipment. The installation of the heater in the 44, they pointed out, was identical to that in the 42, and no one at Knob Lake, where of course they were experiencing similar temperatures, was having any problems.

Apart from the insult to our intelligence, it was fascinating to discover how little concerned people in Ottawa and Arnprior were about the failure of the heaters. I suspect none of them had ever been out in 45 below for more than a few minutes at a time. They had no conception of what it was like to be strapped into a helicopter, unable to move around to keep your blood circulating. In spite of constant rubbing, I had frostbite on my cheeks and nose from the last trip — and my feet were still swollen and painful. There was a suggestion that we should wear more clothes and I blew my cool, telling them that the machines were grounded until somebody came up and fixed the heaters. It was a matter of safety and, if they wanted to make an issue of it, I would call the D.O.T. in.

It all sounds very aggressive at this remove. But by this time I had discovered the folly of sweet reasonableness. When the forestry people had wanted me to fly their stupid plastic bags, I had gone along with them and nearly wiped out. The same thing happened with the machine at Knob Lake. And in this case, nobody appreciated that our problem was not merely a matter of discomfort: it was an extremely dangerous one. After some 30 minutes at the controls in these temperatures, I found not only that my co-ordination was failing, but that my faculties were impaired as well. It was a little like being drugged, I think. I began to lose interest in whether or not I was too close to a building or a guy-wire when I was landing; and if I dumped the Collective when I was still ten feet in the air and hammered into the ground, it didn't seem to matter.

Once the machines were actually grounded, we soon got action. The same two tech reps who had come up about the blades arrived the following day. They were no less confident but a little less hearty this time. They immediately went into a huddle with our engineers, emerging an hour or so later to say that the installation was, in fact, exactly the same as the one on the 42's; thus we must be mishandling the equipment in some way. The answer to that was easy. They could come with me on a trip tomorrow and operate the heater themselves. That wouldn't be necessary, they said; they had instructed our engineers on correct procedure. Like a fool I accepted this; I would try once more, but if the heater failed they would be coming with me next time.

The following morning was an ideal one to prove our point. It was clear and dead calm — and the temperature was 47 degrees below zero. We had some R.C.A.F. Arctic gear in one of the lockers, and the engineer and I climbed into thermal trousers and boots, as well as our parkas. There was a good deal of hilarity from the tech reps; they talked of Arctic explorers setting out on a dog-team trip.

When it was as cold as this, we would open the hangar doors, get into the helicopter, tow it out onto the tarmac, and I would start the engine as soon as the tractor tow-bar had been disconnected. The engineer sat in the co-pilot's seat and operated the heater control switches. Seven or eight minutes after we took off, the heater failed. When this happened, you became aware of it remarkably quickly.

I was furious with myself for not making the tech reps come too; but there were two sites getting short of food because of the trouble we had been having with the heaters. It would only take about 15 minutes to get to the first one; another 20 to the second. I decided to keep going. When we finally got back to Great Whale an hour and a half later, and were towed back into the hangar, we both had difficulty walking because we had lost all sensation in our feet and legs. The tech reps suddenly realized that this was serious. There were no more jokes about Arctic explorers as we sat and suffered the pain one does when frozen feet and hands begin to thaw out.

The tech reps were motivated at last. They phoned Arnprior to demand that heater-installation drawings for the two different models be examined. It became obvious that no one had actually done this up to now; they had simply assumed that they were. By that evening they had discovered that there was in fact a significant difference between the two installations. The fuel line on the 42 was routed to the inside of the heater; on the 44 it was routed on the outside, where it got so cold that the fuel gelled. Rerouting the line was a relatively simple matter, and after that we had no more trouble with the heaters.

By the end of that tour, I realized that my days on the Line were probably over. I had done what I had to do to resolve our problems, but done it, I think, a little too aggressively, and I felt sure that even if I had wanted to, I would not be able to go back. One memory of the Mid-Canada Line lingers in my memory. It is hard to re-create on paper, but I'll try. On Christmas Day we decided to fly a supply run — there was a good deal of Christmas mail to deliver. Ben Arnold, the other pilot, went one way, and I the other.

The sites were identified by three figures, the aircraft by three letters. As Ben was approaching his first site I heard him on the radio, singing "224, 224, this is JJS" to the tune of jingle bells. It was a perfect summary of the comedy that was the Mid-Canada Line. The cost was $220 million. Only six years after construction was completed, the entire Line was abandoned.

CHAPTER 18

Back to the Barrengrounds

MY SECOND TOUR ON THE MID-CANADA LINE, LIKE THE FIRST, lasted for closer to five months than the three it should have, and when I returned to Ottawa it was apparent that the company was now in serious trouble. People who were out flying were receiving their pay cheques on time, but people back in Ottawa were having trouble collecting them — and expense cheques were hopelessly in arrears. The company said it was just a temporary cash-flow problem, but we knew better. And in any case, Nina and I had made our decision that the helicopter business was not going anywhere and it was time to abandon it. I would fly one more contract for Spartan in the summer, and then we would pack up and drive across to the west coast to look for another job.

Meanwhile, though, there had been an interesting development in the helicopter business. The Coast Guard division of the Department of Transport was expanding and in many ways it was a very attractive proposition. They did not do any rescue flying: that was done by the R.C.A.F. Instead, they flew supply and maintenance for the lighthouses, and provided reconnaissance for icebreakers. Working on the icebreakers meant being away from home for three or four months in the summer — a burden that was rotated among the pilots, so that it only fell on you once every two or three years; otherwise, they were never really away from home for more than two or three days at a time. The salaries in the late 1950's were comparable to the best in commercial aviation. It was all very tempting. By 1958, I think seven or eight of Spartan's pilots had already gone to the Coast Guard, and at least as many engineers.

We used to claim sardonically that people who had joined the D.O.T. had retired — they had joined the Department of Tranquillity. In retrospect, I know this was very unfair — it was the government that decided the Coast Guard were going to do the maintenance, the R.C.A.F. the rescue work — but it's always nice to have a whipping boy.

It so happened that there was a competition for another pilot that spring. I decided to apply for it. I had good experience by now: some 2,500 hours and an endorsement for heavy helicopters. There was, however, a small snag: one had to have five years of residence in Canada to join the Coast Guard. By the closing date of the competition, I was a month short of this magic figure. My application came back in record time, pointing this out to me.

So I was denied tranquillity, but my feelings were ambivalent. Commercial flying didn't seem to be going anywhere, and I hadn't really wanted to join the D.O.T. — but at the same time, the thought of giving up flying altogether was a wrench. There had been much pleasure in it during those early days. A helicopter pilot was a somebody; wherever one landed, a crowd would assemble, and this was satisfying to the ego. But in any case, the characteristics of a helicopter afforded you a great sense of power and independence. Quite simply, it was fun and I knew I would miss it.

However, the decision to give up flying and look for something else had been made, and when I returned to Ottawa from Great Whale River that spring, I asked to be taken off the Mid-Canada Line and sent on a Bell operation for the summer. The suggestion was accepted with such alacrity that I'm sure other people had already made it. In any event, I was given a plum Bell contract: an operation with the Geological Survey of Canada in the Arctic, up above Yellowknife, in the Coppermine River area.

For the past 18 months Spartan had run a western helicopter division, based in Calgary. Ours was to be a two-machine operation and we flew commair to Calgary to pick up our helicopter. It was fun to meet crews again who I had not seen for nearly two years. Besides which, there was none of the phoney executive affluence about the Calgary division. It was being run purely as a helicopter operation, and it was run as a helicopter operation must be run — with a minimum of overhead: just a manager and a secretary.

As a result we set off from Calgary with two machines in beautiful condition, and with everything we needed. This was to be the happiest operation in my experience, and it proved so right from the start. We had a long and interesting ferry flight up past Edmonton and Lesser Slave Lake to Peace River; after which we followed the Mackenzie Highway to Hay River on the south shore of Great Slave

Lake. From there we cut across to the western shore of the lake and followed it round to Yellowknife. Arriving towards the end of May, we found that the break-up was late that year. There was still so much snow on the ground that the geologists could not do any work yet. So, without too much dismay, we settled down to wait for two or three weeks in Yellowknife. I looked on it as a sort of unexpected holiday.

But this was the awkward season in fixed-wing flying. The break-up had just begun. It was too early for floats; yet ice conditions were treacherous on skis. Only a day or two after we arrived, I had to go out on an attempt to salvage two aircraft which had gone through the ice of a lake some 15 miles away. They belonged to a small operator, one of the many who were struggling for an existence at the time. One of his machines had broken through, and he had gone out in another machine to see what he could do about it; he, too, had broken through the ice. So I took him out to the lake to see if we could help him. In the end we decided that the only solution was to fly out some empty 45-gallon drums, tie these to the bottom of the wings so that the planes would not sink when the ice went out, and he would have to try to get them ashore somehow and convert them to floats after the break-up. I don't know whether or not anybody ever did salvage those two aircraft. If so, it was not the operator. He gave up a week later and hitched a ride south (ironically, on a Spartan fixed-wing), leaving a lot of disgruntled creditors — including Spartan, of course.

Two days later, to my surprise because there was so much snow on the ground, I was called out on a forest fire. The forestry people at Fort Rae, on the northwest tip of Great Slave Lake, called for me late in the evening. I arrived at the settlement early the following morning and found what seemed to me a very casual attitude towards the fire, which an Indian had reported was burning some miles to the north of them. They gave me a splendid breakfast, I remember. The choice ranged from hot cakes to bacon, sausages or ham, with eggs cooked however I liked them. The meal lasted for well over an hour, and after it we sat for some time, drinking coffee and chatting. Finally, I mentioned that perhaps we had better go and look at the fire. "Yeah, I guess so," the ranger agreed.

I had used about a third of the fuel in my tanks on the trip up from Yellowknife, and I suggested that it would be wise to gas up now, so that we would have plenty of time to locate and assess the fire. The ranger thought we shouldn't bother; he didn't expect to see much in the way of a fire at this time of the year; they just needed to be able to advise their superiors that they had checked the report. We flew north for about 15 minutes and then the ranger said, "Okay, there's nothing there; let's head back. These Indians are always imagining things." It all seemed very odd to me, but it was revenue flying and I shrugged and turned back for Rae.

I was intending to gas up and return to Yellowknife right away, but they insisted that we go back and attack the coffee pot again before I left. Inside I found a young R.C.M.P. constable. He looked very nervous, and I grew increasingly puzzled because I had never encountered a nervous Mountie before. After some small talk, the ranger asked me if I would mind taking the Mountie back to Yellowknife with me. He had some business to transact there. I agreed readily enough — there was no reason why I shouldn't — and the Mountie positively leapt to his feet and shot out of the room to get his suitcase.

I studied the ranger's face for a moment. He was avoiding my eye. "Come on," I said eventually, "what the hell goes on — there was no fire, was there?"

After some hedging, he admitted that what I said was true. They had found themselves in a bind. The Mountie, who was about 24 years old, was to be married in a few days, in his home town in Alberta. The ceremony had been planned for some time and it was to be a sizeable affair. Elaborate catering arrangements had been made; relatives and friends were travelling considerable distances to attend. Normally, by this time, floatplanes would have been landing at Fort Rae several weeks ago, but because of the unusually late break-up, the Mountie found himself trapped. He had talked of trying to walk out to Yellowknife and they were concerned because walking at this stage of the break-up was very dangerous. Finally, the ranger had the brain wave that resulted in the report of a fire and the necessity for a helicopter to be called in.

He had just finished telling me all this when the Mountie returned, looking quite remarkably elated. I told him that I was very sorry, but now that I had heard the real reason for this trip, I couldn't possibly take the responsibility of transporting him to what I had discovered from personal experience to be an intolerable bondage. The biggest favour I could do him, I said very seriously, was not to take him, and thus give him time to reconsider the dreadful mistake he was making in getting married. I never for a moment expected him to buy it, but I suppose he'd been under a considerable strain for the past week or two and he flew into a dramatic rage. I started to laugh, which didn't help much, but in the end I managed to calm him down and got him to Yellowknife in time to catch an earlier plane than he had anticipated. He was a very happy young man when I last saw him. I hope my predictions turned out to be false ones.

The next excursion, too, was back to Fort Rae, but this time it was not an amusing one. It was also the only time I ever flew an aircraft without being entirely sober. We had gone to a party, I think thrown by the resident geologist of the G.S.C. in Yellowknife, and the party was just breaking up at two o'clock in the morning when the phone rang. The call was from the R.C.M.P. A young Hudson's Bay assistant at Fort Rae had disappeared in his kayak. At that time of the year, of course, it was light enough to fly all night, and obviously they wanted me to get over there as soon as possible. I drank a lot of black coffee and had a shower, but I was still glowing a little when I took off at about a quarter past three.

We began the search just after four in the morning. An R.C.M.P. constable came with me and told me what had happened. The youngster had built a kayak during the winter. Eager to try it out, he had set off on the river which runs into the northwest arm of Great Slave Lake only a day or so after the ice had gone out. He had not told anyone he was going, but when they discovered that both he and his kayak were missing, and they began to question people, an Indian remembered seeing him carrying his kayak towards the river. Unfortunately, as we began our search, the wind chose to blow — it was gusting up to 45 miles an hour, and I felt unwell. Half an hour later the Mountie got sick. I gave him ten minutes on the ground; then tried again. He got sick again, so I took him back and the Hudson's Bay manager came with me. He was sick, too, and in the end I went off by myself.

After the first hour it was clear that we weren't going to find the youngster. The river was flowing so fast that even someone really experienced in a kayak would have little chance of surviving. We had hoped, to begin with, that he had somehow managed to get ashore; and if he had in that country, he would not be difficult to spot. Now we assumed that he must have been swept out into the lake and under the ice — which had not yet begun to move out. I found his paddle, a woollen cap and his tobacco pouch at different places along the river bank. I put in about eight hours of flying before we abandoned the search.

We eventually moved out of Yellowknife on or about June 10. There was still a good deal of snow around, but the geologists decided that by the time we had our camp set up we would be able to do some work. The fixed-wing support was to be provided by a small bush operator in Yellowknife: Wardair. Max Ward had a couple of Otters and two or three Beavers, I think. But he had also just bought a much larger machine — a Bristol Freighter. It was an excellent aircraft for the bush: big and rugged; but a number of operators had tried it and had run into trouble with the Hercules radial engines. Mechanics claimed they were unsuitable for cold-weather flying. Max had taken the trouble to send two of his mechanics over to the Bristol factory in England for a maintenance course, and as a result he had great success with the machine. In fact, I think Max would probably agree that the Bristol Freighter did much to move him in his rapid progress from bush flying into the jet charter business which has made Wardair a familiar name.

The first two camps that spring were wet and mucky. The ice was still sound enough for the Bristol to land on, but there was a foot of slush on it, and a perimeter of open water all around the shore. We had to load everything onto an inflatable rubber dinghy and slosh ashore with it. But once we had our camp set up, it was a good one. We slept, two of us, in a conical Logan tent, which is comfortable enough but a little cramped. In addition, though, we had a 14-foot aluminum-frame tent for our equipment — a luxury very few customers were thoughtful enough to provide — and we were able to set up one end of the tent as a sort of lounge, where we could sit and talk or write letters.

I think there were two reasons why I enjoyed that season so much. First, it was like a very large breath of fresh air after the futility and seedy antagonisms of the Mid-Canada Line; second, that was the first time I had been out with people who regarded the land not as a simple money-making resource, but as something that was valuable in many other ways. The discovery of an unusual geological formation gave them just as much satisfaction as the discovery of a significant mineral deposit. In any case, though, they weren't narrow specialists. They had read virtually everything ever written about this country, and there was always something of historical interest to look at. A lake where some exploration party had nearly starved to death; an Eskimo-Indian battlefield; the remains of a fort from which some celebrated explorer had set off. They were interesting and knowledgeable about every aspect of the country, including the beasts and the birds, and this made them great fun to work with.

And, since this was a systematic survey, we covered all of the country. On a typical traverse, we would travel ten miles north of camp, then turn east for 50 miles — stopping whenever the geologist wanted to examine rock formations in detail — turn north for ten miles and then fly back the 50 miles to the west, which would bring us back to our base line. The following day we would repeat the pattern to the west, or ten miles further north. If the weather remained fine, the Wardair Otter would move our camp some 50 miles, and we would begin the next area.

We worked as far west as Great Bear Lake and Darnley Bay, and as far east as Contwoyto Lake and Bathurst Inlet. To the west, we were on the fringe of the tree line; to the east, very much in the Barrens — I think perhaps the most beautiful part of them. There were a multitude of lakes, of course, but a good deal of rolling moss and grass country; whereas to the east of Contwoyto lies the endless, or seemingly endless, expanse of broken granite — which really is lifeless and forbidding. And of course, this was the most interesting part of the Barrens historically. Samuel Hearne was the first white man, not only to explore it, but to describe it in detail. He was a Hudson's Bay Company employee who, in the early 1770's, walked from Prince of Wales Fort, in Churchill, to pick up the Coppermine River north of Yellowknife and then follow it down to its estuary in Coronation Gulf. What makes Hearne stand out among the early explorers of Canada is that he, like the geologists I was with that year, was interested in every aspect of the country he was passing through. And fortunately he was a gifted writer, both perceptive and witty in his observations. His *A Journey from Prince of Wales's Fort to the Northern Ocean,* published in 1776, remains one of the gems of exploration literature. Hearne's written objectives from the Company were to examine the possibility of a northwest passage and try to seek out the source of the copper with which both Indians and Eskimos used to fashion their tools (the Yellowknife Indians were so named because of their copper knives). There had been boulders of pure copper as big as a whale, so the legend went. But Samuel Hearne was interested in many things besides the commercial value of copper and trade routes.

He had some difficulty persuading the Indians to guide him on such a long journey. The first two attempts were abortive; they turned back after a week or two. Matonabee, the minor chief who led him on his successful expedition, explained to him that the earlier parties had turned back because they stupidly neglected to take women with them. Matonabee then went on to formulate his often published thesis of the value of women as beasts of burden. In fact, the Indians emerged as rather ugly people from Hearne's observations. They thought little of indulging in a rape and torture session with some unfortunate squaw when they were bored. And the only reason they finally agreed to undertake such an arduous journey was the hope that they might find some Eskimos to kill. The Indians and the Eskimos were traditional enemies; there was a long legacy of retribution and bloodshed. They came upon their first Eskimos at a falls some ten miles from the Arctic coast, which John Franklin later called Bloody Falls.

Hearne gives a horrifyingly graphic description of the episode. The Indians waited until the Eskimos were asleep in their caribou-skin tents, then crept up on them and slaughtered "Men[,] women and children, numbering upwards of twenty...." They impaled their victims to the ground with their spears; then stood, laughing and joking, as they watched them writhe in agony. The attack was completely unprovoked, but Hearne could do nothing to prevent it; if he had tried to interfere, the Indians might easily have turned on him.

Before they became accessible by aircraft, the Barrens had attracted many explorers. There were three motivations: the search for a northwest passage to the Pacific Ocean, harvesting furs — particularly the valuable white fox — and the hope of religious domination over the Eskimos. And there were two principal routes into this difficult country. Starting from Edmonton, people travelled down the Athabasca River to Lake Athabasca, and then down the Slave River to Fort Resolution on the south shore of Great Slave Lake. From there they either travelled northeast across the lake to Fort Reliance — which led to Artillery Lake and the Thelon River country, where Jack Hornby and his two young companions starved to death in 1927; or they turned west and travelled down the Mackenzie to Fort Norman, and then up the Bear River to Great Bear Lake, from the northeast corner of which they could reach the Coppermine with, speaking very relatively, no great difficulty.

A host of people followed this last route. Franklin, Back, Simpson, Dease, Douglas, Melville, Hornby, and finally, the unfortunate Roman Catholic priests, Fathers Rouvière and LeRoux, who fell out with the Eskimos on the coast and were murdered shortly after they set off to return up the Coppermine River.

Nearly all of them had left some trace of their presence behind, and we visited many of these sites. We spent an hour or so at Fort Confidence, I remember, where Sir John Franklin had wintered before setting off on his second expedition in 1826. The foundation could still be seen, and the fireplace and chimney were still standing. The whole building had been about the size of a two-car garage, but apparently all cabins built by white men in those days were automatically called forts.

All this historical retracing was fascinating, and the only thing that marred our pleasure that year was the weather. We hit a really bad season. It stayed cold and damp for virtually the entire three months we were up there. We got periods of snow throughout July and August. Apart from the fact that it was uncomfortably cold most of the time, flying in these conditions was extremely difficult. It wasn't so much the fact that we couldn't fly over that flat country, as the fact that we could very quickly get lost in quarter-mile visibility. Even with aerial photographs, it was all too easy to become confused by the multitude of lakes.

One day, towards the end of July, both machines started out for a traverse to the west of our camp. We were both going up into the foothills of the Richardson Range, the highest of which reached perhaps 2,500 feet in this area. Ten minutes out of camp, snow began to fall. I chickened out and turned back, but Audley Black, the other pilot, was intrepid; he decided to press on, and another four days were to pass before we saw him, or Lloyd Davison, the geologist with him, again. They were trapped in white-out conditions, up in the clouds and snow on top of the hills.

Another day, I was flying a traverse in relatively decent weather when the geologist asked me to land by an outcrop of rock. We were over a large, flat, more or less featureless plain, and I landed without thinking anything of it. But when I came to take off again, some 40 minutes later, I found I had forgotten in which direction we had been flying. The magnetic compass at this latitude is useless; it wanders erratically around in its cage; and there was no sun, so we had to circle around for nearly ten minutes before we finally managed to re-establish our orientation. It was a very disconcerting experience, and I made sure it never happened to me again.

Apart from Coppermine, the only other settlement we visited that year was Port Radium, on Great Bear Lake. This was Canada's first uranium mine and it was still producing at the time. The area had also, as I was to discover later, played a very important part in the history of bush flying. Port Radium was an intriguing place, the buildings all set on a spine of rock jutting out into the lake, with a series of wooden ladderways leading down to the water. There was even a tennis court, surfaced with mine tailings, on the spine, and we could see two women playing tennis as we circled before landing.

On our way there from our camp, some 60 miles to the east, I did a traverse with Al Frazer, the party chief, breaking off some 30 miles from Port Radium and flying directly to it. We intended to cut straight back to camp after Al had spent an hour or two with the geologists on the mine. But when we came to leave, we found that our map, which had some of Al's geological notations on it, had disappeared. Presumably someone had stolen it in the hope that it would contain information about mineral deposits. We did not discover that the map was missing until we had been in the air for about five minutes. I began to turn back to see if we could borrow a map from somebody when Al suddenly told me with great confidence that he could get us back to camp without a map.

He did, too. He knew the co-ordinates of our camp and he made some calculations; then he fixed up a sun-compass by taping a piece of string with a weight on the end of it to the roof of the bubble with masking tape. I had to keep the shadow from the string lying diagonally across a blank sheet of paper he held on the clipboard on his knees. Every five minutes or so he would alter the position of the paper to allow for the movement of the sun. I was very nervous about flying over that country without a map for nearly an hour. But fortunately that was one of our brighter days; I was able to climb up to about 3,000 feet and we could see the tents of our camp when we were still some 15 miles away. We were heading straight for them. It was a remarkable feat of navigation.

We did not meet many Eskimos on this tour, but the ones we did were just as pleasant and friendly as the ones I had known in the Ungava area. When we reached the settlement of Coppermine River, the Eskimos immediately came to help me. We had a stock of avgas there which had been brought in by ship the previous summer and, as soon as I started to roll a drum across to the helicopter, two or three of them promptly moved me aside and took over. And when I had put the filter in the tank and started to pump gas with the hand pump, the pump was gently but firmly removed from my hands. This sort of behaviour, when it happened to me in

Africa, invariably meant that I would have to distribute largesse — a "dash," or whatever a gratuity was called in the local dialect. But the Eskimos never seemed to expect anything; they just did it because they were friendly people, I think.

Apart from the Eskimos at Coppermine, the only other meeting we had with them occurred way out in what seemed to be the middle of nowhere. We were flying along on a traverse one day when we suddenly saw figures sitting on top of a low, rocky hill — little more than a mound, really. It was a single family: father, mother and two children. They had killed several caribou, and they were dressing the meat before laying it out on the rocks to dry. The woman was using one of the traditional half-moon shaped knives. She smiled at us pleasantly, but carried on working as though the arrival of a helicopter was the most natural thing in the world. We smoked a cigarette with the father, who indicated that the caribou had been reasonably plentiful this year, and then went on our way, feeling somehow reassured by the sense of continuity of the scene.

A few days later we were flying along the coast when we suddenly came upon a largish ship — largish for the size of ships which ply the settlements on the Arctic coast, anyway — and it was sitting up on the shore, high and dry. It was a Hudson's Bay vessel, we learned later, which had been trapped in the ice late the previous season. It had suffered some damage in the ice and the crew had to beach it, after which they were flown out by a fixed-wing aircraft on skis. There were still the remains of a meal on the table, and quantities of expensive tools and equipment lying around. I wish now I had helped myself to some of them bcause I heard later that it was never salvaged.

On another occasion, at the estuary of one of the many rivers that flow into Coronation Gulf, we came upon a substantial cabin. The estuary was completely flat and remarkably desolate. Nobody had read of a cabin here in their exploration literature and we were intrigued. The cabin was unoccupied, but furnished and clean; it had obviously not been empty for too long. One of the furnishings in the main room was a large and quite sophisticated liquor still — an essential piece of apparatus for survival in that bleak and lonely place, I would think. We learned afterwards that the cabin had been built and occupied by an Anglican minister for some three years, but that he had fallen ill a few months previously and had to be taken out. I could only admire the strength of faith which had led him to live so long in such remarkable isolation — because I have a strong suspicion that the missionaries, particularly the Catholic ones, made very little progress in their attempts to convert the Eskimos.

In August, the cook had a toothache. It is not uncommon for cooks to have this problem in the middle of the season and, as a rule, immediately they get within reach of a dentist, they are also within reach of a liquor store and they seem to be able to alleviate the pain without any assistance from the dentist. In this case, there was a complication. By the beginning of August, none of us had had a drink since leaving Yellowknife, so we each gave the Otter pilot ten dollars and asked him to bring us a jug when he returned with the cook. The pilot, a young American, was very pleasant but still naïve. When he reached Yellowknife, the cook offered to relieve him of the burden of buying our booze for us. The pilot agreed and handed over our money. So, not surprisingly, when it came time for him to bring the cook back to camp two days later, he couldn't find him. The pilot seemed astonished at our indignation when he came back empty-handed and told us what had happened. A trusting soul, he had yet to learn that almost any bush cook who gets his hands on a hundred dollars worth of booze will disappear for at least a week. Al Frazer had to go down to Yellowknife with the pilot, find the cook, get him sobered up and bring him back to camp.

Although there weren't many people in that country, there was an abundance of wildlife, and we had lots of fun with the animals. We came across several herds of musk-oxen. They would form their celebrated defensive circle as we flew towards them — the cows and calves on the inside, the bulls on guard outside — and I was hoping to get a photograph; but the helicopter was too much for them and they would always break and stampede before we got close enough. One day when I was out with the young graduate geologist, we saw a solitary bull a couple of hundred yards from a pingo. A pingo is simply a very large frost heave. This one was about 10 or 12 feet high and some 30 feet in diameter. We landed behind it and stalked the musk-ox, the geologist with his rock hammer in his hand, and I with my camera in mine. I am sure the geologist was just as nervous as I was, but neither of us wanted the other to perceive this. The official advice we had been given by conservation biologists who had studied the behaviour of musk-oxen was that if you stood your ground when one of them charged, and shouted as loudly as possible, it would veer off at the last moment. Theoretically, I found this interesting, but I had no real inclination to put it to the test. And when we climbed up onto the pingo and peered cautiously over the top, the musk-ox suddenly began to canter towards us. He stopped only about 30 feet away and began to paw the ground. What looked remarkably like smoke was coming out of his nostrils. I was terrified, but after an imposing display of aggressiveness, he turned and went peacefully back to his grazing. The only photograph I got was a blurred and shaky one of the top of his head.

We saw large numbers of caribou but never, on this trip, in a migratory herd. They seemed to be scattered haphazardly all over the country. They were so numerous, and so tame, that we came to regard them much as one does domestic cattle. I found that if I stood more or less perfectly still, fluttering my handkerchief every 30 seconds or so, after much puzzled zig-zagging and snorting, one would approach within a few feet of me, peering myopically to see what sort of a creature I was. Then, almost invariably, it would stretch out its neck and let out a majestic belch.

But it was the smaller animals, particularly the ground squirrels, which were the most fun. The Eskimos call them zic-zics, which is an almost exact replica of the peremptory call they utter. We usually stayed about three weeks in a camp before moving to the next area. And after a week or so, we would have several very tame zic-zics wandering around among us. One morning I awoke to find one sitting up on his hind legs on my chest, cleaning his whiskers. He dropped down to all fours as I stirred, but when I saw him and lay still, he resumed his toilet. We had another who used to appear in the cook tent every morning and demand breakfast. If we didn't serve him immediately, he remonstrated with a deafening staccato of indignation. His favourite food was a cake of shredded wheat, which he would rotate in his paws like a corn cob until he had got it all packed away in his chubby little cheek pouches. Then he would disappear for a few minutes to empty them somewhere before returning for another one.

The birds, too, were fun. I did a sort of survey to determine what speeds different birds could achieve. I would fly just above and behind them, cutting them off if they tried to swerve away. Swans, I learned, flew at about 30 m.p.h., flat out; Canada Geese at 35 to 40; and eagles were the slowest at a little over 20 m.p.h. The fastest bird I came across was a duck. I never did succeed in identifying which particular kind of duck it was, but I clocked it several times at over 65 miles an hour. One bird I learned to keep away from, though, was the Arctic owl. All other birds would keep down, trying to swerve away if they could, and I used to break off after a minute or so to be sure I didn't exhaust them. The owls had a different pattern. They would accelerate up to full speed which, because they are large birds, is only about 25 m.p.h., and then they would abruptly pull straight up into the air. On two or three occasions I very nearly collided with one, so I left them alone after that.

All the birds at this time of the year were extremely tame and you could walk right up to most of them. This was particularly true with ptarmigan. One day, after a camp move which had lasted well into the previous night, I did an abbreviated traverse, returning to camp in the middle of the afternoon. When I had shut the machine down, I stood chatting for awhile to two or three of the geologists. Bill Heywood wasn't around, and I asked idly where he was. I received the stock answer: he was resting his eyes. In the Geological Survey of Canada people might sometimes rest their eyes, but they never slept during the day. It so happened that at this moment a family of ptarmigan strolled through the camp in a neat procession. There were two adult birds and six or seven young ones, and it occurred to me that it might be amusing to let them stroll into Bill's tent.

I nipped over and quietly unzipped the fly of his tent. He was indeed resting his eyes, and it took us only a minute or two to herd the dignified little procession of birds into his tent and zip up the fly again. There was silence for a little while; then all at once Bill let out an oath and a ptarmigan squawked with alarm. Soon they were all squawking vociferously, and we could see the bulges as they thudded into the canvas walls of the tent in their attempts to fly to safety. Eventually Bill got the tent fly unzipped and the ptarmigan regrouped into their procession, clucking as indignantly as old women who had just discovered the movie they went to see turned out to be a dirty one. Bill was stuffy about the incident, too.

The early explorers failed to discover any of the giant boulders of native copper that were supposed to exist in this area, and I am sure our geologists were hoping to be the first to do so. When we reached the area, near the estuary of the Coppermine River, we spent a good deal of time looking for them, but we only found one specimen worth mentioning. This was on the river bank, some miles upstream from Bloody Falls and the geologist with me searched diligently amongst the boulders for a long time. It was a miserably cold day; I soon lost interest and retreated to sit and wait for him in the helicopter. While I was doing so, my eye fell on something that looked odd just by the left float. I got down and picked it up. It was about the size of a child's fist and it was pure copper — no boulder, to be sure, but it was the only piece we found, and I made much capital out of my ability to come up with what half a dozen highly qualified geologists had failed to find.

Towards the end of the season we had a most interesting, in fact a most most distinguished, visitor. A. Y. Jackson, one of the celebrated Group of Seven, came to stay with us for a few days. Silvery-haired and spry, with a hawk nose and very bright blue eyes, he had the kind of wit I've always envied: he could mock people without incurring any resentment because it was an affectionate mockery. He had come to paint, of course, and we would take him out in the helicopter in the morning, find him a scene to his liking a few miles from camp, and leave him painting happily for most of the day. When you went to pick him up in the late afternoon, there was something oddly moving about the sight of him, sitting on a little collapsible canvas stool in front of his easel, totally absorbed in what he was doing.

One night he gave us a sort of combination exhibition-art lecture. It was a setting of some little drama. His paintings hung on the walls of the cook tent in the bright white glare of two Coleman lanterns hooked to the ridge pole, while he talked of his early days in Paris, northern Ontario and Quebec, and the furious condemnations he and his group provoked from the art critics. He was 74 then, I think, and still very much in control of his faculties. He had a host of fascinating anecdotes and he could talk interestingly on almost any topic. It has been said that he was too poor to marry until it was too late. Success had not come easily to him and I think now he was enjoying a sense of fulfilment few of us are talented enough to experience.

The weather, which had improved for the last couple of weeks of the operation, turned sour again when it came time to leave. We flew back to Yellowknife from our last camp of the season through almost continuous showers of snow and sleet. Fortunately, by now we knew the country and were able to pick our route, following the larger and more easily recognizable lakes and drainages. We left at five in the morning and arrived at Yellowknife about seven that evening. We were to fly the helicopters directly back to Calgary. Normally, we would have travelled round Great

Slave Lake, heading west from Yellowknife to cut across the north arm and follow the western shore down to Hay River.

But when we got down to Yellowknife, I heard some disquieting news about the situation in our company, and I was in a hurry to get back to base and find out what was going on. Thus I was up early on the morning of our departure, with some hopes of making Calgary in one day. There was a very low overcast, but it wasn't raining and the wind, which was blowing steadily from the northeast, would be partly behind me. After some hesitation, I decided I could save myself at least two hours if I cut straight across to Gypsum Point, a peninsula jutting out on the west shore, and then more or less directly south across the lake to Hay River. If the wind changed I would have to stop for gas at the cache just to the south of Gypsum Point; if not, I could keep going and save myself even more time.

Since the compass was useless, I lined myself up on the shore of the lake as I left Yellowknife and then used the angle of the waves for direction. I made my landfall some two or three miles northwest of Gypsum, and by this time I was down to about 200 feet, just below the clouds. I hesitated again, then decided to press on across the lake without stopping for fuel. It was a little more than an hour before I saw land again — sheer stupidity. I had no radio contact. If I had gone down on the lake, the helicopter would have capsized very quickly in the six-foot waves which were sweeping across it. The wind might easily have veered or backed, putting me miles off course. And the real trouble was that I could not climb to see where I was when I reached the shore; nor did I have more than 15 minutes of reserve fuel to follow the shore until I had found myself.

In fact I had drifted about five or six miles to the west and, just as real anxiety was setting in, I saw a pale ray of sunshine on my left, the only one on that gloomy day. In it I caught the silvery gleam of the oil-storage tanks in Hay River. It was reassuringly providential — I felt that the Great Chief Pilot up there was watching over me.

The rumours I had heard in Yellowknife proved true. I returned to Ottawa in the middle of September, and a week or so later Spartan Air Services went into receivership. Some 18 months previously, in response to our complaints about low salaries, the company had instituted what they called a bush bonus — three dollars a day for every day spent away from home base. It was a good idea, but they never paid it and I was down some $1,200 when the company folded. Most of us were in the same boat, and we talked of renting a barn somewhere on the outskirts of Ottawa, taking a helicopter and hiding it there as our form of mechanic's lien. Our resentment was increased by the knowledge that the helicopter division was doing well, and that mismanagement and a redundant fixed-wing operation was responsible for the company's breakdown.

In the long run the collapse of Spartan improved things for many of us. Several groups of ex-employees went into partnerships to form helicopter companies of their own, and many of these new companies prospered. For myself, I followed my plan and set off with my family to drive across the country to Vancouver in October. It is an old myth, of course, that going west will solve all one's problems. It turned out to be true for me in the end, but there were to be some lean years ahead before then.

CHAPTER 19

More Arctic Time

THE FEELING THAT EVERYTHING WOULD SORT ITSELF OUT once we reached the west coast wasn't borne out. We arrived late in October and spent the winter in Richmond in a very old, very drafty house — while I searched for a job. The trouble was, I didn't know what kind of a job. I thought vaguely of broadcasting, or earning my living as a writer. I remember answering an advertisement for a publisher's assistant. The job turned out to be a sales job: selling magazine subscriptions door-to-door.

Early in the spring, the phone began to ring. I got several offers, but they were all for flying jobs. At the time there were few helicopter pilots with Arctic experience, and all the job offers were for operations in the far north. It was gratifying to know that I had become an expert in something; so in the end I accepted a summer contract with Spartan, who by now had been taken over by the Bristol Aeroplane Company, and I went off cheerfully enough.

This was to be another two-machine operation, working for the Geodetic Survey of Canada. Doug Dunlop, a young and relatively inexperienced helicopter pilot, was to fly the other machine. He and another pilot flew the two G2's to Edmonton, where I met them. The engineers had to strip the helicopters and put them into a Pacific Western Airlines DC-4 to be flown up to Cambridge Bay, where the operation was to start.

The two pilots of the DC-4, I recall, were remarkably superior people. They scarcely deigned to speak to us. Since the initials of Pacific Western Airlines were at that time generally translated to mean "Please Wait Awhile," and since they were flying a beat-up old DC-4, I didn't really appreciate what they had to be superior about. But it was an uneventful trip; they got us to Cambridge Bay without any difficulties.

Several days passed while we assembled the machines. The weather was pleasant, so was the accommodation. Cambridge Bay was a well-equipped DEW-Line site. Our party chief was a delightful person to work with. He used to drive us to and from the airstrip in a Jeep. He drove as fast as Stirling Moss. I couldn't help wondering if he was as skilful.

When we had the helicopters working satisfactorily, we were faced with another couple of those pleasant weeks of relative idleness. I can't remember exactly why the snow was a factor — something to do with reflections and the tellurometers, the instruments for measuring distances — but there was still too much snow on the ground to allow us to start the survey.

In fact, though, we weren't reduced to idleness. A party from the Hydrographic Survey of Canada was up there to take soundings and revise the nautical charts of Queen Maude Gulf. The party chief was going to have to rely on the goodwill of the R.C.M.P., whose launch he would be using. He was delighted to see us. In four or five days we did for him what would have taken at least a month in the launch. He put out all the triangular markers from which cross bearings would be taken and positions plotted for the soundings. Tom was fun to work with. He became a friend and I was to see a good deal of him in Victoria, on the west coast, before promotion exacted its penalty and took him to Ontario.

While this was going on, I was called out for another emergency flight. An Eskimo child had contracted diphtheria in Spence Bay, a settlement some 550 miles to the north of us. It would have been a relatively simple trip for a fixed-wing aircraft, but the break-up had started, so it had to be done by helicopter.

I could gas up at every other DEW-Line site, and then fly north up the Boothia Peninsula to Spence Bay, where they had some drums of 80/87 octane avgas used by the fixed-wing aircraft which normally flew in and out of there on floats or skis. I took off with Shag O'Shaughnessy, the apprentice engineer, less than an hour after we had been asked to go.

The DEW-Line sites are spaced irregularly, so I decided to gas up at the first one to the east, then to take the long jump over the ice and water to King William Island. For some reason, though, we had neglected to warn the DEW-Line people of our plans, and we promptly set off a mild panic. The operators had never picked up a helicopter flying at 200 feet and 65 m.p.h. on their radar screens before. At first they speculated that we might be an errant weather balloon. But the course was too steady and there was very little wind; a balloon couldn't possibly be travelling at that speed. Thus we became a UFO, tripping alarms all the way down to NORAD headquarters in Colorado Springs. When I landed at the first site, half a dozen rather sheepish-looking people came out to glare at us.

The rest of the trip was uneventful. When we reached Spence Bay, we found that our patient was a seven-year-old boy. He was clearly very sick. Pausing only long enough to gas up and drink a cup of coffee, we wrapped him in a blanket, sat him between us and set off. When we reached the first site on the way back, we paused to administer medical treatment. The nurse at Cambridge Bay had given us a hypodermic syringe and some ampoules. She had explained to us very carefully how to administer the shots, but we were squeamish and very nervous. We managed to persuade ourselves that the shots we gave him every two hours or so did some good.

This happened early in June, so we had continual daylight. The trip took us more than 18 hours and, when we arrived back in Cambridge Bay, a fixed-wing aircraft was waiting to fly the sick child down to hospital in Edmonton. I wish I could report a happy ending. Unfortunately, he died two days after reaching the hospital.

Once the snow had thinned enough to let us get to work, we had a pleasant and productive season. Crews of two surveyors with their camping gear, food and survey equipment were put out on preselected high points, and we moved them to new sites every three or four days. The biggest problem we encountered during the first month happened when I was moving camp and we spotted a Barrenlands grizzly bear with two cubs some five miles from our intended site. The Barrenlands grizzly is much lighter in colour than its forest relative, and it's a very rare creature. The two surveyors wanted to return to camp for a rifle to shoot it. Instead, I dropped them at their site and then spent more than an hour herding it miles across the country away from them.

Our first main-camp move was from Cambridge Bay to Bathurst Inlet, a Hudson's Bay post, which had a settlement of about two dozen Eskimos. They were as cheerful and pleasant as ever. If we had to move drums, carry supplies, pump gas, they invariably offered to help. I had one problem while I was there that I couldn't have solved without them. A few days after we moved in, Doug Dunlop spotted something that looked interesting on one of his trips. He landed to see what it was and found a large soapstone cooking bowl. It was sitting on a rock in the middle of nowhere, and he decided to bring it back to camp with him. The bowl was carved in the shape of a large D, with bevelled edges, and weighed just over 25 pounds. Seal blubber was poured into the bowl; then tufts of caribou moss were laid along the bevelled edges to act as a wick, and the resulting stove was used for heating snow houses and tents, as well as for cooking. It was a very smelly object. Something like an inch of seal blubber had been baked into the bottom and sides. Doug didn't want it; I most certainly did. Cleaned up and polished, it would make a very attractive ornament and conversation piece.

But first I thought it wise to find out if any of the Eskimos wanted to claim it; so I took it to one of the elders and asked his advice. He told me his people hadn't used soapstone bowls for many, many years — and speculated that some family on a hunting trip must have found themselves short of food and decided to lighten their load on the way back to the settlement. I was welcome to it. The next problem was to get rid of the seal blubber, which had been baked almost to the consistency of porcelain. I tried chiselling it off with a screwdriver, but I was afraid of cracking the bowl. I tried heating it on the primus stove to see if it would melt; I tried scrubbing it with sand; I even tried putting it into the sea, hoping the tide would scrub it out. Nothing worked, and finally an Eskimo quietly took it away from me and went back to his tent. The following morning he gave it back to me, clean, polished and gleaming. I never did find out how he did it.

For the rest, it was a very well-organized operation, and as a consequence I remember few of the details. The party chief was one of those rare and sensible people who explained to us what had to be done, and then left us to work out the best way of doing it. The survey crews could be moved from one site to the next in two loads. Doug and I worked as a team most of the time, arriving together, tying on half the load each and then, each with a passenger, flying to the next site. It wasn't a demanding job and that summer the weather treated us kindly.

It didn't do my bank balance any harm, either. On that operation, I worked for a flying bonus rather than a straight salary for the first time. The deal was $850 a month for a base of 75 hours; then $10 an hour for each additional hour in any one month. Since I logged an average of 120 hours a month, I made good money. On top of which, a friend of mine had become Spartan's operations manager, and I discovered that my base salary cheques kept arriving right up to Christmas, even though I went home in the middle of September. I recovered all the bush hours I had been owed when the company went bankrupt the previous year.

When we had evacuated the surveyors from each site after they had taken and recorded their readings, they would place a large sheet of white canvas squarely over the top of the survey bench mark they had established, pinning it down with heavy rocks. I would then fly back with one of the base crew to photograph this marker from the air. The points had to be transferred to aerial photographs when the crew returned to Ottawa and the task of map-making began. There had to be some identifiable feature in our photographs — a lake, usually — and sometimes I had to climb to four or five thousand feet to get one into the frame.

When Doug and I had flown the last crew out — we had occupied something like 25 sites — I took the photographer back. "That's it!" he said after he had clicked the shutter. It was a pleasantly symbolic gesture, and he sat back to wind the film back in his camera. But when he opened the camera, there was no film in it. We didn't have a photograph of a single site.

Fortunately, there was enough avgas left in our caches for me to re-fly the whole area. It took two days and some 12 hours of flying. I was well past my 75 hours for that month, so I got another bonus. But the biggest bonus of all that year was the knowledge that I wouldn't hear the phone ring a week after I got home; I wouldn't hear the operations manager's apologetic voice explaining that the company had a problem and that I would have to go out again — only for two or three weeks. . . . I knew I would be with my family for at least six months. It was bliss.

The only flaw was that we were still living in the wastelands of Richmond. In the spring we decided to move to Victoria. I would either be out in the bush or home for the winter. We might as well live in the most attractive climate and surroundings this country has to offer. We found a very old but suitable bungalow on the waterfront in Oak Bay. I was now being paid a retainer of $100 a month by Spartan and I didn't have to go through the unpleasant motions of dickering for a job in the spring.

Towards the end of May I flew by commercial airline to Churchill, Manitoba, to take charge of another two-machine operation for the Geological Survey of Canada. Bill Heywood, who had been with us two years before, was the party chief. Bruce Craig and

Lloyd Davison were repeaters, and they brought with them Moose Tremblay, a big and very charming French-Canadian. Moose had been in Tanganyka, working for the eccentric diamond magnate, Williamson. His experiences in that colony had turned him into a royalist. I remember that he was deeply affronted because Princess Margaret had married Anthony Armstrong-Jones, whom he described as a bum.

I was to have not one, but two pilots with me this year, both of them relatively inexperienced. Claude Jolin, who had just come out of the Navy, and thus had no bush experience, and Gary Fields, an engineer who had learned to fly the previous winter. Garry would fly only occasionally and at my discretion; his main task was to maintain the two helicopters.

Garry and Claude were to fly the two machines to Churchill from Ottawa. It was a very long cross-country trip, and on the phone I tried to persuade the operations manager to let me come to Ottawa and lead the way. But he wouldn't have it, so I flew to Winnipeg on TCA, then up to Churchill on Transair to meet them there.

Churchill was an interesting experience. We lived for the three weeks we were there in the military base. It was a curiously sterile place, but comfortable enough. All the buildings were connected by tunnels, so that you could live a subterranean existence, never emerging into the fresh air. But the food was good and the officers' mess was a model of what such an establishment should be. Furnished with large leather armchairs, the walls panelled in wood, it was far superior to anything I had seen in Ottawa. And this was one of the very few rooms on the base with windows — large windows looking out over the snow, which was glazed by the daytime thaws. In the evenings, superb sunsets turned the snow into a blaze of colour.

The town of Churchill was another story. The buildings were unpainted and invariably dilapidated, and they were surrounded by debris: everything from junked machinery to plain, ordinary garbage, through which the dogs, and an occasional polar bear, roamed, foraging for food. The situation was so bad that the Manitoba government put out tenders that summer for the removal of garbage from the township of Churchill. One sensible entrepreneur put in a bid to move the township, on the very logical grounds that it would cost less to move the township than it would to move the garbage.

This wasn't a superficial irony. In fact, the township had been moved three times in the last century for just that reason.

Two or three days after I had joined the geologists in Churchill, I learned from one of the tower operators that our fixed-wing support had arrived, a Norseman from Lamb Airways, based in The Pas. The crew were staying at the hotel, so I got hold of a vehicle and drove down to meet them, intending to invite them up for a drink in the mess, where I could introduce them to the rest of the party.

Somebody at the reception desk gave me their room number and I walked up the stairs. Their door was open and I was about to knock and step inside when I paused. One young man lay stretched out on his bed right in front of me, reading a book. The other bed presented a far more intriguing spectacle. Another young man was lying face down on it, talking to someone — someone lying on the floor in the space between the bed and the wall. All I could see of this person was two bare knees, sticking up above the edge of the bed.

The conversation in progress was clearly an intimate one, and I had begun to back away when the book-reader looked up. "Oh hi!" he greeted me cheerfully. "Come on in."

"I, er — well, perhaps I'd better drop back later." I glanced at the other bed. The knees had disappeared, and the young man had rolled over. He was looking at me without enthusiasm.

"I'm one of the helicopter pilots with Spartan," I told him. "Thought you might like to come up to the mess — have a drink, meet the G.S.C. crew?"

"You bet," he replied, perking up right away. "Be with you in a . . ." He paused and glanced down beside his bed. "In about ten minutes, eh?"

The person reading the book was Ron, the engineer; the other was the pilot, one of the Lamb boys. Ron rolled off his bed with a chuckle. "We'll wait for you down in the lobby," he told his companion, and we went back down the stairs together. This was my first encounter with the Lamb boys, one of the most enjoyable associations I had in the bush.

There were five of them, or perhaps it was six, all sons of Tom Lamb, a bush pilot who had worked out of The Pas since the late 1920's. They were an irreverent and ribald bunch who all worked hard and played hard. Tom Lamb doesn't seem to find much of a place in the histories of aviation I have read, even though his company became very prosperous in the 1960's and 1970's. I'm not sure why he has been overlooked.

Of all the stories I heard of his early experiences, though, the one I liked best was of the day he got lost in grungy weather in the winter. He turned to follow a creek bed, hoping it would lead him to some recognizable feature. A few minutes later he spotted someone with a dog team and sled, also following the creek bed. The man on the ground had stopped his dog team and was waving vigorously. There was nowhere to land, so Tom shut off the engine of his plane, opened the window as he glided down and shouted to the figure below, "Where the hell are we?"

"Son of a bitch," the figure on the ground shouted back, "that's just what I wanted to ask you."

When I met them, the Lamb boys were still operating very much in the tradition of the early bush pilots. They were a tough bunch and it didn't bother them at all if they had to sit down on a lake for two or three days to wait out the weather. I never saw people who could fillet a fish or skin a goose more expertly. The same thing applied with their aircraft. They were perfectly willing to fix things with baling wire if necessary, and they did it very effectively.

But in one respect, the Lambs had a huge advantage over the rest of us. They always remained fresh and cheerful; they never got bushed. This was because, as soon as one of them began to feel some tension on an operation, he would discover that his aircraft needed servicing back in The Pas. A few days later one of the other Lambs would appear with a replacement aircraft, and the first one would return home for what they called an oil change. The problem for the rest of us was that they were always crisp; they always had their tails up, and since they all possessed sharp tongues it was hard to keep abreast of them.

Most of their repartee is unprintable, but one example will show how careful you had to be if you wanted to avoid ridicule. We were in the officers' mess at Churchill. The place was fairly full and during a lull in the conversations, Greg Lamb shouted along the bar to me, "Hey, did you hear that the Limeys've found a new cure for piles?"

"Yeah," I replied, my mind on something else.

"Yeah, they're exporting all their ars'oles to Canada."

Everyone found this hilariously funny, and I had countless solicitous inquiries about the condition of my haemorrhoids for the rest of my stay there.

In fact, it turned out to be an eventful pause. Some two days before I had arrived, a group of five single-engined, fixed-wing aircraft had gone through Churchill on their way north. They were a group of some significance for us, because they were there to try to prove that fixed-wing aircraft could be as versatile as helicopters in the Barrens — at, of course, a fraction of the cost. The idea had been pioneered by Weldy Phipps, one of the founders of Spartan Air Services. He had fitted huge balloon tires to Piper Cubs, making it possible, so he claimed, to land almost at will on the eskers and muskeg.

The idea had seemed so promising that six aircraft had been converted, and six pilots trained to fly them during the winter. Unfortunately, the fields around Ottawa are no substitute for the Barrens, and even though the pilots had been given extensive training in short take-off and landing techniques in soft snow, they were unprepared for the reality. All six of them had set off together that spring. One of them came to grief at North Bay. The remaining five had reached Churchill and split up to join their respective exploration parties to the north and west of us.

Now, a few days after my arrival, we heard that two of them had crashed within an hour of each other in white-out conditions, killing the two people in each aircraft. Some accident investigation people from the D.O.T. came through on their way to the scene, and cast a chill on all of us.

Our two helicopters had been delayed for several days by bad weather, but finally one lunch time, the tower phoned to tell me they had left Wabowden and should reach Churchill in about three hours. When the time came, I drove down with two of the geologists to meet them at the airstrip. It was a chilly afternoon, with a stiff breeze blowing, so we retreated into the lee of the hangar, peering around the corner, along the railway line, to see if they were coming. Eventually, the two black dots appeared on the horizon and we went back into the hangar, knowing that another ten minutes or so would elapse before they reach us.

When we emerged again to check, five minutes later, they had disappeared. We were standing, gazing in surprise along the railway line, when all at once a siren went off. I dashed back into the hangar, trying to persuade myself that a fixed-wing must have crashed and that our two helicopters had gone to give assistance. It took me a minute or two to find a telephone. When the person in the tower picked up his receiver, he was speaking to someone else. "Can you see any smoke," he asked. I couldn't hear the reply. "Sorry, Mac," he said to me, "we got a helicopter down. Phone me later." He rang off.

The next few minutes were bad ones. I tried climbing a wooden ladder fixed to the side of the hangar, but there was nothing to be seen. At least there was no smoke. I went back down and tried phoning again without success. The tower man didn't answer the phone. In the end, a car came racing across the field to the hangar. The U.S. Air Force had two helicopters there which they used to retrieve rockets from the missile range just outside Churchill. They wheeled the Vertol out of the hangar and the pilot, who knew who I was, let me go with them.

We found our helicopters about five or six miles down the railway line. One was standing beside the line, undamaged; the other sat, canted over, with its tail boom sitting in the middle of the tracks right beside the bubble. I met Claude Jolin for the first time. He was a small man and he looked surprisingly unconcerned. His engine had cut. "Must 'ave been a fuel blockage," he told me.

He was unhurt, and once this had sunk in I couldn't help observing that he should have been able to make a relatively easy auto-rotation, either on or beside the railway line, and that he had been flying directly into a good stiff breeze, which would make it even more simple. But there was no point in saying anything then. We lifted the tail boom off the railway line and flew back to the airstrip to sort things out.

By any token, it was a discouraging start to the season. It was also very silly. I had arranged for two drums of avgas to be put out along the railway, approximately halfway between Wabowden and Churchill. Claude had decided he could make it without stopping to top up at this cache. In the circumstances, there could be no possible excuse for running out of gas. I was particularly angry because Claude had been leading and we were very lucky both machines hadn't gone down. We drained the tanks on Garry's machine and found about half a gallon in them.

The company left it to me to decide whether or not to can him. I decided not; I could be reasonably sure that he didn't run himself out of gas again now that we were together. Besides which, he was a first-year dental student in a Montreal university. The loss of his summer job would really have set him back. In the event, he gave us no more anxiety for the rest of the season.

Spartan reacted remarkably quickly to this accident. They had a replacement machine up in Churchill within four or five days. In the meantime, the U.S. Air Force had used the Vertol to sling the wrecked machine back to the airstrip. We loaded it into a railway boxcar and shipped it out. I was relieved when we finally moved out, heading north through Eskimo Point to Baker Lake. We were in the land of Duke Schiller, Punch Dickens and the McAlpine party. One little accident wouldn't have deterred them.

The most interesting part of that operation was that we were to undertake yet another in the series of searches for Franklin remains. The loss of Sir John Franklin's third expedition in 1845-48 still intrigues people, principally because it is so difficult to believe that more than a hundred men could disappear with so little trace. At the same time, it is a difficult subject to write about; first, because the topography of the Arctic is so complicated; second, because the terminology is so confusing. What is the difference, for instance, between a "gulf" and a "sound," or between a "bay" and an "inlet," or a "cape" and a "peninsula" — and what on earth is a "bight"? The same sort of thing applies to "channels" and "straits" and "narrows." When I first saw the strait named after Bellot, which separates the Boothia Peninsula from Somerset Island, it was filled with chunks of ice and the tide was swirling through it like a white-water river. The ideal name for it should surely have been a narrows; instead, they called it a strait.

Franklin's expedition, like all other Arctic expeditions in the nineteenth century, was to seek out the Northwest Passage — the quick and profitable route to the east that everyone hoped to find. His two ships, the *Erebus* and the *Terror*, with a combined crew of 139 officers and men sailed from Chatham on May 19, 1845. They sailed up Davis Strait and turned west into Lancaster Sound. Passing Devon Island, they turned north and sailed as far as 77° north — a little beyond the northernmost end of Devon, before the ice stopped him. Now they headed south again, along the west coast of Cornwallis Island. By then the short Arctic summer was over, and they retreated into winter quarters behind Beechey Island, on the southwestern corner of Devon Island.

The following summer, when the ice moved out, they turned south and sailed between Somerset and Prince of Wales Islands. From here on, nearly all is speculation. Most Arctic experts think that, had Franklin sailed to the east of King William Island, through Ross Strait, he would have made the Northwest Passage. Instead,

Bentinck Arm, 1963. The helicopter operated off this scow, towed behind the Forestry launch, *Forest Surveyor.*

The dream camp at Kluayaz Lake, 1966. Geologist Will Tompson and his partner (seen here) comprised the entire crew, so the three of us spent most of every day in the helicopter.

The cook tent in Will Tompson's dream camp was a little Spartan, but we lived like kings.

By the 1960s it was often possible for the family to join the helicopter crews in the field. Here, the author's family load up to fly from Alice Arm to Prince Rupert at the end of the season. Donny, our Shetland sheepdog, would curl up and fall asleep; but Crackles, our cat (in a box behind the dog), was never able to reconcile herself to helicopter flying. *Left to right*: Graham, now completing his Ph.D. in marine biology at Simon Fraser University; Nina; Gerald, now base manager for Highland Helicopters in Fort McMurray; and the author.

The ideal combination for a bush operation in the late 1950s: A de Havilland Beaver and a Bell 47-G2.

The dog days at the end of a summer's operation, Knight Inlet, British Columbia.

A large Pingo, or frost heave, near Dismal Lake, 1958. In the spring, at that time, you would see numerous, though somewhat smaller, examples of this phenomenon on city streets in Ottawa.

Will Tompson's partner and myself interrupted while we argued over the map about where we were. Since Will was the photographer, I never did get a photograph of him on that operation.

WILL TOMPSON
PHOTO

At the headwaters of the Skeena River, during the Groundhog Coalfield survey, 1967. Geologist Mick Roper and the author at "Wolf Meadows."

WILL TOMPSON
PHOTO

Taking a breather after lunch on a Skeena River gravel bar. *Left to right*: Dave Jenkins, the author, Cal Graeber and Will Tompson Jr.

WILL TOMPSON PHOTO

The delights of fly-camping were more evident in fine weather.

The Resurrection of FZX

An account of this project is in the Epilogue.

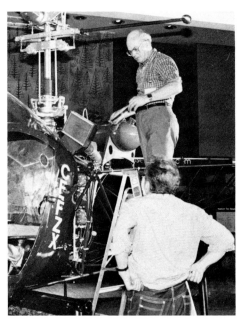

Eric Cowden installing the air intake.

DAVE PARKER
PHOTO

After three years of hard work, the reconstructed Bell 47-D1, Okanagan Helicopter's original CF-FZX, on display at the Royal British Columbia Museum in 1988. We acquired parts from all over North America, and enlisted the necessary skills from veteran helicopter engineers for this project. At right, Ian Duncan works on the rotor head.

ROYAL B.C. MUSEUM,
ANDREW NIEMANN PHOTO

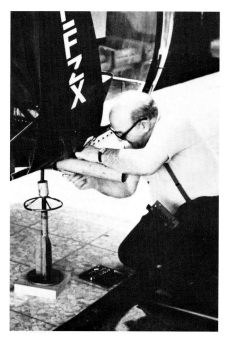

Art Johnson bolting on one of the cross tubes, to which the skid-gear would later be attached.

DAVE PARKER PHOTO

Taking off for another futile attempt to produce some barometer elevations, Tom's River. The snow was too thick in April and May to allow us to pinpoint our locations accurately enough to provide data for a contour map.

British Columbia Forest Service inventory work up Bentinck Arm, 1963.

Two of the original miners standing at the entrance to a sample adit, driven into a hillside during the survey of the Groundhog Coalfield in 1911.

Geologist Cal Graeber stands in front of one of the cabins erected by Campbell-Johnson's crew in 1911. We found a large selection of blacksmith's tools under the floorboards, left behind when the last crew left. The tools were all carefully greased and wrapped in cloth for future use.

There were benefits to working among the trees. In this case, the boom of a log-loading rig provides a convenient hoist to remove the complete rotor-head system and mast for a clutch change.

No trees in this country. Looking across the strait to the settlement of Pond Inlet, Baffin Island, from Bylot Island, 1961. The icebergs moved with disconcerting alacrity.

he tried going through to the west of it and was trapped in the ice just off the northwest tip of the island.

We know from messages found in a cairn at Victory Point, on King William Island, that Franklin died on June 11, 1847. Apparently the ice didn't move out in 1846 and the two ships spent their third winter in the ice. After that, there is very little evidence of what happened to the crews. Skeletons of several of them, together with the sad relics of wood and cloth and metal of their attempts to survive were found around the shores of King William Island, as well as on Montreal Island in Chantrey Inlet. This is what intrigues people — the fact that so little has been found, because the disappearance of the Franklin expedition set off one of the biggest search and rescue attempts in history. There is a suspicion that the British government was as much motivated to find a quick passage from the Atlantic to the Pacific as they were to find Franklin and his crews. But in any case, it is still astonishing to most people that no message describing what went wrong has ever been found.

To anyone who gets into the enormous literature on this subject, though, one thing is bound to become apparent. The Eskimos who lived in the area were surprisingly reticent, curiously unwilling to talk about the subject. To me it seems obvious what happened. When the McAlpine party — a bush-flying expedition — disappeared in that country in the early 1930's, there is no possible doubt that they owed their survival to the Eskimos. But theirs was a party of eight men. In Franklin's case there were 139 men — a number quite large enough to upset the delicate balance of nature which governs the Eskimos' lives. The Eskimos, in short, couldn't provide for them; they had to let them die and, because they are such generous people, the Eskimos felt guilty and defensive about this unavoidable decision.

Still, even though so many people had looked in vain before us, we had high hopes of finding something. We would be flying the area for a period of months in helicopters. We felt sure that if there was anything left in one of these cairns, we would find it. And privately I had visions of fame as the discoverer at long last of Sir John Franklin's grave.

In fact, we found nothing more than our predecessors had: a few sad pieces of cloth and wood on the shores of King William Island. We could add nothing to the solution of the mystery. In our attempts, though, we pulled down an enormous number of cairns — always hoping for a bottle or a can with an historic message in it.

For the most part they turned out to be cairns marking an Eskimo grave, but there were one or two interesting exceptions. One cairn, much larger than most we had come across, had something buried in the middle of its base. We could see a gleam in the dark shadows and with growing excitement we began to dismantle the cairn. The rocks were large ones; it required a good deal of effort to remove them, but after ten minutes we could see that there actually was a bottle in the base — a corked bottle with a message in it.

We tried to persuade ourselves that this was it; we were going to make history. But it didn't really add up. The bottle was a chutney jar and the note inside it was remarkably well preserved. When we finally came to read the message, it was a terse one: "What were you expecting — a case of Molson's?"

For the most part, that operation was too similar to the previous one I had flown for the G.S.C. to warrant much description. Soon after we had set up our first camp at Baker Lake, a Catholic priest came in on foot to tell us that a group of some 14 Eskimos were starving. They were camped some 60 miles to the west of us and, since they weren't camped on a lake, I had to go out and move them to the nearest lake so that Jack Lamb could fly them out in the Norseman. I never did discover what had gone wrong, but they were in bad shape — I think in another few days they would have starved to death. It was a touching scene. In spite of their condition, they all insisted on struggling to their feet and shaking hands with me when I arrived. I bundled them into the helicopter and flew them to the lake. Jack had to make two trips to get them back to Baker Lake — but we heard later that they all recovered and returned to their camp on foot less than a month later.

Another interesting group we came across, about seven or eight of them this time, were camped on a rocky headland on the shores of the ocean. These were seal people and there was practically no hint of the white man's technology about them. They were dressed in sealskin parkas and mukluks, and they were still using a soapstone stove for cooking and heating. They were the shyest Eskimos I ever came across and I had great difficulty persuading them to pose for a photograph. Everything about them was greasy, including their hair, but they looked healthy and were in excellent spirits. Once again, they all smoked — even a young girl who looked to be no more than ten years old. They cleaned out my supply of cigarettes before we left.

But it was a group of only two Eskimos that intrigued me most of all. We came across them about 20 miles inland, in the middle of nowhere. They were sitting on an upturned komatik, their dog team staked out among the rocks. They were well dressed, healthy, in the best of spirits, but as far as we knew there wasn't another Eskimo within 50 miles of them. What on earth were they doing there? They didn't speak any English, so we couldn't ask them. They looked for all the world as though they had been mushing along when the snow ran out. And now they were sitting waiting for it to come back again so that they could resume their journey. It's one of those puzzles that still irritates me whenever I think of it.

I should have asked Greg Lamb. He always had an answer ready. I remember standing with him once in an Eskimo burial ground at Bathurst Inlet. I was looking at a wooden grave marker, carved in Eskimo script. "Well, you're the Arctic expert," I said, turning to him. "What does it say?"

He studied it for a moment. "It's the grave of an Eskimo jazz player," he replied soberly. "It says, 'Don't dig me, Dad — this time I'm really gone.'"

CHAPTER 20

Baffin Island

THE NEXT YEAR, 1961, BROUGHT A CALL TO FLY IN THE FIRST week of March. It was to be another two-machine operation, this time on Baffin Island. I hesitated for a day or two before accepting; first, because I knew it was much too early in the season to fly that country, and second, because there had been a significant change in the company. Bristol Aero had sold out to a group of Toronto promoters. I should have turned the job down, but by then Nina and I had decided to build a new house for ourselves and the long season sounded attractive financially.

When I arrived in Ottawa, I soon began to discover what I'd let myself in for. To begin with, we were going to use the Bell 47-J, a machine totally unsuitable for bush flying. But the customer, a government department, was adamant; they wanted J's. Next I found out that a company in Montreal had also bid on the contract. An agreement had been reached that, if the Montreal company won the contract, Spartan would lease them their J, and vice versa. As a result, neither company had prepared the machines in case the other won the contract. A frantic, last-minute push was going on to make the machines even vaguely serviceable.

But it was when I went to see the government people that I knew I was in for a real fiasco. They had planned the operation on the pattern of a nineteenth-century expedition. The only difference was that we were to use helicopters instead of dog teams and sleds. In short, two of us were going to set off with all our camping gear for two-week treks. We wouldn't need a tent. That's why they'd asked for the J model — two people could sleep in it. They looked puzzled when I was sarcastic about the prospect of working, cooking, eating and sleeping in the bubble of a small helicopter for two weeks at a time.

All this was so preposterous I didn't really know where to start. We would be flying in the mountains, which meant a smaller payload. Going out for two weeks at a time, we would have to take an engineer with us to do the maintenance, and we would have to take ground-heating equipment with us to start the engine in the mornings. There was no way the J could carry three people with all the food and equipment required. On top of which we were to have no fixed-wing back up for the first two-and-a-half months of the operation. Now it was the customer's turn to be sarcastic. They had discussed all this with the executives in my company, and agreement was reached that it was perfectly feasible. The executives in my company now were Bay Street promoters; they knew virtually nothing about how to operate helicopters — and absolutely nothing about conditions in the Arctic.

I should have packed it in right then and gone to look for another job. The customer went back to our company and demanded a replacement pilot — somebody who, as they put it, was willing to co-operate. This was a laugh, because our company hadn't been able to find another pilot. The mountains of Baffin Island in winter are not an attractive proposition. Half-a-dozen experienced pilots had refused the job, and they had turned reluctantly to me — reluctantly because they objected to having to pay my air fare from the west coast and back again. In the end, they had to hire the second pilot for the operation from the States. No one knew what his qualifications were, nor what experience he had.

It was a no-win situation and I'm still not sure why I didn't back away. I suppose it had something to do with vanity; a conviction that once we got up there I could sort things out and make a reasonable success of the operation. I knew, too, that the Lamb boys were going to do the fixed-wing flying. Things couldn't be all bad with them there. In any event, I wrung an agreement out of the customer that for the moment we would work locally out of the DEW-Line sites. I also delayed the operation for more than a week, insisting that the engineers put the machines into some sort of shape.

It was interesting to learn that the operation was actually funded by the United States, not by the Canadian government. The Americans wanted information about gravity fields for their space exploration program. Thus we would be repeating the sort of thing I'd done on my first operation in Ungava, except that this time we would be using gravimeters instead of barometers. With the major expense paid for, and the economies realized by the fly-camp system, the Canadian government could afford to do some of their own research — mainly glacialogical work on the two major icecaps on Baffin Island.

All in all, it was about an inauspicious a start to a season as one could imagine. My own company were angry because they couldn't replace me; the customer was furious because I was making the decisions about what was safe or feasible. The fact that they had virtually no experience in the Arctic, and I had a good deal, made no difference. They were unmistakably hostile right from the start. The chief pilot, Bill Loftus, and I flew the machines to Montreal in the middle of March and we went through the now familiar exercise of stripping them down and loading them into a DC-6 to be flown to Frobisher Bay. The other pilot hadn't arrived yet. He was to be flown up as soon as he did.

For the first week or two, things worked out fairly well. The other pilot had no snow time, but he claimed some mountain experience in Korea. I could only hope for the best. I found that the equipment on the DEW-Line sites was well maintained. Ground heaters actually worked, and we were able to fly local traverses when the weather allowed. The temperatures were still well below zero most of the time, but that didn't bother us because, with the gravimeters, the operator didn't even have to get out of the helicopter to take his readings.

Then the inevitable happened. They wanted to do a swing of 150 miles — which was just about the limit of our range — refuel at a gas cache, and then cover another 150 miles of traverse on the way back. There were four drums of avgas in the cache.

"When was it put out?" I asked.

"Last summer. Lambs put it out in a Norseman."

"Was he on skis or floats?"

"Floats."

I looked at the map they had spread out on the table. The cache was on a lake — a lake more or less in the middle of a fairly extensive plateau at about the 3,000-foot level. A large pencilled cross, which at the scale of the map covered about half-a-mile, marked the position of the cache.

"You realize, of course," I told them, "that those drums might easily be under a 20- or 30-foot snowdrift by now?"

They looked incredulous. I really don't believe it had occurred to any of them that the drums wouldn't be sitting up in full view on a sandy beach. They were convinced it would only take a matter of minutes to find the drums once they got there.

"We'll find them all right," said the party chief confidently.

"Yes, but what happens if we can't?" I insisted. "The other helicopter could only bring enough gas to get one machine back. The Lambs aren't due up for another two months yet. So we'll have to leave one helicopter out there for two months."

They wouldn't have it. They were sure the gas drums could easily be located. I had no intention of putting it to the test; I ended the conversation with a blank no. Later that evening I saw them all huddled over the map in serious consultation. I wondered what would come of it, but I wasn't to find out until the next day — and when I did, I had to give them credit for determination.

What they did was to charter a DC-3 that had just dropped a load in Frobisher and was heading back for Fort Chimo the next day. Eight of them went off at half-past four in the morning. They intended to be back before breakfast — in time to tell me that the drums were now sitting up in full view.

Other people on the base told me what was happening, because when I got up all eight of the crew had gone, taking shovels and a long metal rod for a probe. There was nobody left to fly with, so I settled down with a book after breakfast. It turned out to be a leisurely day. They didn't return until after dark, about seven o'clock that night. They were all exhausted, having spent something like 15 hours probing and digging in the snow. They had finally located the cache, but they hadn't been able to get a single drum out into the open, where it could be pumped.

It is pleasant, of course, to have your judgement so clearly vindicated; but at the same time it makes for a difficult atmosphere. Short fuses prevailed for several days, and it was hard to get a smile out of anyone.

Soon after that we ran into a peculiar problem with one of our helicopters — peculiar because both were identical models, yet only one gave us the problem. At anything more than 20° below zero, the throttle on this particular machine would freeze up. It first happened to the other pilot when he had come out over the mountains at about 6,000 feet and began to let down towards the sea ice. Fortunately, when he got down to about 1,000 feet, it thawed out. But the experience shook him up and, not unreasonably I suppose, he refused to fly the machine after that. So we swapped, and I got the engineers to strip the throttle system and check it before I would fly again.

Two or three days later, it happened to me. I came out over the coast at about 4,000 feet, turned towards base and throttled back to let down over the ice. When I got down to about 700 feet, I began to feed in power again. Nothing happened; the twist-grip was rigid. After dithering for a moment or two, I switched off the ignition, turned into wind and did a full autorotation onto the ice. Fortunately, the throttle was frozen in the idle position. As soon as I'd settled, I started the engine again and about a minute later the throttle came free.

It was hard on the nerves, and this time the engineers really went at it. They spent two days stripping the cam box and the cable system, drying it out and lubricating it with graphite. Time and again, they went to the other machine to check that the cable was routed the same way. Both systems were identical; we never did discover why only one of them froze up. It was a miserable experience for the engineers, who had to lie under the machine in the open in below zero temperatures, struggling to find some reason for it.

When they finished, I took off for a test flight, climbing up to 7,000 feet and flying around for ten minutes before I throttled back to come down. The same thing happened. I had to autorotate onto the ice.

By now we were in a classic bush situation. There was no logic to the fact that one machine could be made to work, and not the other. The customer became increasingly critical. Our masters in Ottawa began to hint that it was an imaginary problem — that we didn't want to fly. If that had been the case, the obvious thing would have been to ground both machines. But logic seldom prevails in these circumstances, and the unfortunate engineers had to go back to work again in an atmosphere of increasing acrimony.

A few days later the weather warmed up considerably and I flew for two days on traverses that didn't require me to go very high in the mountains. The third day was a little crisper, but by then I had begun to think that the engineers had cured the problem. We came out of the mountains to a ridge above a fiord. A cliff rose vertically from the sea ice to a height of about 1,500 feet; then it sloped upward, climbing at an angle of 50° for another seven or eight hundred feet to the ridge. The slope from the cliff was an unbroken mass of rubble and boulders.

My passenger asked for a landing on top of the ridge. There was an offshore wind blowing. I picked a landing and turned into the wind. I made a steepish approach to avoid the inevitable turbulence from the ridge. At about a hundred feet, I began to feed in power for the landing. Nothing happened. I kicked on right rudder and set off down the slope to try to get over the cliff-edge. It was almost a carbon copy of the near miss I had on the Mid-Canada Line. My revs were dropping; my body was arched up against the seat belt as I tried physically to keep the machine in the air. On this occasion, though, I bounced gently off a rock, and my passenger was yelling blue murder before I got over the edge of the cliff and poked the nose down.

There was a distinct pause and a jelly-like shudder before the rotor blades began to pick up speed again, and for the third time in as many weeks I made an autorotation onto the sea ice. It took several minutes to free the throttle after I'd started the engine, and it was still stiff and ratchety as I followed the coast back to base. The engineers found that I had twisted the frozen throttle so hard I had bent a metal arm in the cam box.

It was a dreary situation. I phoned Ottawa and the microwaves crackled with recriminations. My suggestion was to get a G2 up to me; otherwise, we were going to have one machine grounded for at least another six weeks while we waited for the temperatures to rise. I think they actually made some arrangements to do this; but it never came about, and for the next month we were down to one machine.

This was a bad scene. One helicopter, without fixed-wing support, meant no back up if that one machine went down for any reason. We had to be very sure of our weather before we flew; consequently, we didn't do much flying for the next month. And then another complication arose. A friend of mine working for another company in Montreal phoned and left a message for me to call him that night. When I did, he advised me that Bell had issued a mandatory modification bulletin for the 47-J. Did we know about it?

The elevators, which are mounted on the tail boom, had revealed a design fault. The main spars in them were cracking, and there had been two or three serious accidents during the last few months when elevators had broken off in flight. We had been flying for nearly six weeks without knowing about it. We pulled the elevators off our machines. Both the spars were cracked — one heavily, the other still only a hairline crack. When we phoned our company to tell them, they were more concerned to know how we'd found out about the problem than they were about remedying it.

We were grounded for about ten days, waiting for the replacement spars to arrive. By this time we had settled in to the rhythm of life on a DEW-Line site. It was very much like being in prison; a very comfortable one, but a prison, nevertheless. Most of the sites were perched on the edge of a cliff, so even if the temperatures weren't too low, there was nowhere you could go for a walk. The people there signed on for an eighteen-month tour. We came to the conclusion in our own crew that you might as well rob a bank. Then at least you had a chance of not going to prison. And if you did, the money would be waiting for you — just as it was when you came out of the DEW Line.

People living in such conditions quickly became eccentric. As an example, on one site water had to be fetched from a lake some two miles away. The man who was responsible for keeping the tanks filled had worked out a routine. He had a tractor in a shed, with a large tank mounted on a sled. He would tow the sled down to the lake, where there was another little shed containing the pump. A metal pipe ran down through the ice. He would start the gasoline-driven pump, fill the tank, return to the site, start another pump mounted on the sled, and fill the inside tanks.

All this took him about four hours. It was his sole responsibility; he did nothing else, and he did it once every two weeks. But when our crew of seven arrived, he found that he would now have to do it every ten days. He complained bitterly that we were taking too many showers and generally using water unnecessarily. Since we were only operating one machine, we had plenty of time on our hands. I offered to go down with one of our engineers and fill the tanks for him. He wouldn't hear of it. I think he only had to make one extra trip because of us, but he hated us with a bitter passion, constantly snarling at us about the number of showers we were taking.

By now it was nearly time for Greg Lamb to arrive with his Beaver, and for us to move off the DEW Line into another phase of the operation. A week before he was due, I flew with our party chief to the last site we were going to operate from to make the necessary arrangements with the man in charge. On the way, we took a swing through the mountains, landing every two or three miles to take gravity readings. It was tedious work because the pilot, sitting in his front seat, had to look over his shoulder all the time, while the passenger crouched forward to hold out the map and photographs. The J model was absurdly unsuited for the work we were doing, and if I flew for any length of time, I'd end up with a stiff neck.

Towards the end of the traverse, when the site we were heading for was only a couple of drainages away, the wind started to thump us about. Coming in for a landing, it became almost unmanageable, so I called off the traverse and climbed up to head over the two ridges between us and the site. It was only about six or seven miles away, but it took us a good 15 minutes to get there. By now the wind was gusting up to 50 m.p.h.

This site, too, was perched up on a cliff, some 400 feet above the sea ice. The only place I could land was in a tight clearing between two buildings. It was a horrible landing because the wind was breaking up over the edge of the cliff, but I managed to hammer the machine onto the ground without damaging anything. The next problem was to get the rotor blades stopped. The wind was coming over the cliff at just the right angle to keep them autorotating. I nearly had an arm wrenched off before I got them tied down.

It was an ominously cold wind. We took our sleeping bags and carry-alls and hurried gratefully into the main building. We didn't come out of it again for three days. Each site was equipped as a weather reporting station, and that night the anemometer on the roof broke off while recording a gust of 117 m.p.h. Such winds weren't uncommon on that coast — it has something to do with a cold air mass rolling down off the Greenland icecap. But when it finally died down on the third day, and I went out to get the helicopter running, I found a most discouraging sight. Only the top of the bubble and the main rotor blades were visible. The rest of the machine was buried in a huge snowdrift.

It took us a day and a half to dig out. The snow had sifted into the bubble through the door joints; even the tool compartment in the tail boom had to be shovelled out. The DEW-Line people came out and gave us a hand for some of the time, and I finally got the engine started by about five o'clock in the evening of the second day. Everything was in order, so we loaded our bags and took off to return to our base. I had to back out over the edge of the clearing, and then swing around into wind. I took enough weight off to slew the floats sideways with the rudder to make sure they weren't frozen in. The tail seemed to be low, but I assumed this was because the wind was pushing it down. I should have pulled right up into the hover to check, but that was a tight landing, made even tighter by the drifted snow. So I picked up and backed out in one motion, turned into wind and pushed the nose down.

Trouble was, the nose wouldn't go down; in fact, even with the stick right forward against the stops, the nose was still rising. After a moment or two of panic, I rolled over to the right and brought the nose down with rudder. As soon as I straightened out, the nose went up again. I yelled to the passenger to flip his seat belt and move right up to the front of the bubble. He looked confused, as well he might because we were wallowing around the sky like a bird which has been into the fermented berries. Luckily for me, he didn't lose his head; he moved right up by my feet, pulling all our equipment with him. Now I found I could just keep the nose down if I had enough forward speed to make the elevator on the tail boom effective.

I let down slowly towards the ice, wondering how to land without smashing my tail rotor. As soon as the speed dropped below 40 m.p.h., up would go the nose. In the end, I chose a smooth stretch of ice and made a fixed-wing landing, running her in at about 50 m.p.h. It worked. Then I sat for a moment or two trying to conceive what on earth had gone wrong.

"What the hell happened?" my passenger demanded.

"——ed if I know. I guess we must have hooked our tail into something heavy." I lit a cigarette with fingers that really were quivering, shut the engine off and climbed out to see what I had managed to hook with my tail-rotor guard. There was nothing there. Nearly five minutes passed before the obvious dawned on me. The tool compartment had been full of snow; the whole tail cone behind it must be full of snow.

I took a screwdriver out and opened the hinged inspection panels. Then I spent the next twenty minutes scooping snow out of the tail cone. It was packed tight. Heaven knows what it weighed. But, of course, I had nobody to blame but myself. In spite of this, the incident only reinforced my conviction that no one who isn't mentally handicapped should ever fly the mountains of Baffin Island in the winter in a 47-J.

In June we moved out of the DEW Line into one of our own camps for the first time. The camp was put in by Denny Lamb (Denny had come instead of Greg) in a ski-equipped Beaver. It was in a location no pilot would ever choose as a flying base, but we didn't have a choice; it was smack on top of the Penny Icecap. We were based there for a month, and it wasn't a dull month because icecaps present some problems which don't occur anywhere else, except perhaps on the largest of glaciers.

In the evenings when the air cools, it rolls down off the ice. Thus when we returned from a traverse, we would often have to battle our way back against a 50-m.p.h. headwind. Another difficulty, of course, was with white-outs. Our camp was about 20 miles from the edge of the ice; but it might as well have been 200 when the weather socked in, because there just wasn't any visibility. We were always worrying about whether or not we'd be able to get back at the end of the day.

Apart from that, the camp was well equipped, so that life on the ice wasn't too bad. But one night we awoke to what felt like a minor earthquake. When we emerged from our tents to investigate, we found one of the helicopters straddling a crevasse which had just opened up. The crevasse was about three feet wide and, even though the sun was shining, we couldn't see the bottom of it. We hastily fired up and moved the helicopter.

From the Penny Icecap we moved to a settlement called Clyde River for a few days, before moving up onto the Barnes Icecap. Clyde River consisted of a two-man Mountie detachment and several D.O.T. people running a weather and radio station. I remember that everyone there was horribly bushed, and I was glad to leave, even though we were going back onto the ice. On this camp, which we occupied until early August, a new problem arose. We were flying our gravimeter traverses across the low country to the south of the icecap, and the other pilot, who had coped reasonably well in the mountains, suddenly started to have trouble with his navigation. He got lost twice. Both times we managed to find him within a day or two, and I flew out more gas so that he could get back to camp.

The glaciologists were having their problems, too. They were using seismic equipment to measure the depth of the ice, but the equipment didn't work. They had brought with them one of the very early versions of the snowmobile. The idea had been to do traverses across the ice in the snowmobile, stopping every 200 yards to set off charges and take seismic readings. But the snowmobile broke down with monotonous regularity, and when they weren't fiddling with the snowmobile, they were tinkering with the seismic equipment. I don't think very much was accomplished.

From the Barnes Icecap we moved to our final camp for the season, the settlement of Pond Inlet. This was a much more interesting place than either the DEW-Line sites or Clyde River because there was a largish group of Eskimos here. I went seal hunting with them, and on one frightening occasion I went out after narwhal with them. The seal hunting was done in the open water, which was still full of ice floes. I sat in the back of the boat, operating the outboard motor. The Eskimo knelt in the bow, giving me signals as we moved very slowly towards a seal. Then, when he'd shot the seal, I'd have to twist on full throttle and, to the accompaniment of a series of "Quvik ... Quvik" from the Eskimo, try to reach it before it sank.

The whale hunt was a much more rugged affair. On this occasion I was in the boat, merely as a spectator, with three Eskimos. When we spotted the school of narwhals sounding, I thought it was going to be a relatively simple matter to harpoon one. In fact, it was nearly an hour before one finally surfaced in the right place. And then all hell broke loose. They drove the boat right up onto its back; and not unnaturally, when the harpoon sank in, the whale lunged, flipping us into the air. Miraculously, we didn't capsize. The boat hit the water with a resounding smack, and one of the Eskimos went over the side. While we were hauling him back in, we nearly lost sight of the ten-gallon drum tied to the end of the harpoon rope. It was only a half-grown male, but even so it took us four hours to get it back to the beach, where the entire Eskimo encampment came down to help us drag it ashore. I came away with the delicately fluted ivory tusk as a souvenir.

From Pond Inlet we finally did some long traverses, fly-camping for three or four nights before returning to base. In the summer weather we could manage with a pup-tent and we didn't need a heater to get started in the morning. I still wasn't very enthusiastic about the idea, but I did one trip without incident. Now it was the other pilot's turn. He had rather cleverly given the impression that if he'd been in charge, we would have been fly-camping right from the beginning of the operation. Now he suddenly began to find all sorts of reasons for not going. I insisted, and finally, looking very sulky, he took off.

He was to camp out for two nights, returning to Pond Inlet on the third. He didn't appear, and on the fourth morning I went off to look for him. I flew his planned route to the first gas cache. The drums were unopened. I gassed up and flew to the second cache.

Here too, the drums were still sealed. The weather was clear so I flew back along his route, keeping fairly high, hoping to pick up a flash from his signal mirror. While I'd been away, Denny Lamb had returned from a supply trip in the Beaver. We both set off to look for the helicopter, one a few miles to the right of his intended course, one a few miles to the left. Neither of us found him, so the following day we radioed for help from Search and Rescue. An R.C.M.P. Otter joined us, and we were told an R.C.A.F. DC-3 was coming up from Edmonton.

That evening, after a fruitless day of searching, we were having a hasty supper before going out again, when we heard the other helicopter coming in to land. It wasn't easy to work out what had happened. Something had been wrong with the helicopter, so he had landed and then waited for me to find him so that I could bring an engineer out. I had flown several times over the place he claimed to have landed at, yet neither he nor his passenger had seen me. After five days, he'd decided he'd better risk trying to fly back to base. Mysteriously, the problem he'd had with the helicopter had cleared up.

I didn't pursue the matter. Instead, I went and had a drink with the Hudson's Bay manager and got on the radio to call off the search. By this time news of the missing helicopter had hit the newspapers down south, and there were a lot of worried relatives to be informed. We didn't do any more fly-camp traverses after that.

We had been out now for over four months, and I was getting twitchy. For several days I had to cross the channel from Pond Inlet to Bylot Island, and I must confess I didn't enjoy it. There was a strong tide in the channel which carried a mass of ice floes out to sea at an alarming speed. Occasionally a largish iceberg would sail by, reminding me of how quickly I would be swept out to sea if the engine failed.

There was about ten miles of channel to cross, so I never bothered to climb — I just took off and chugged across a few feet above the water. On one occasion I was looking to my left at a rather impressive iceberg. When I turned back, a huge blue-grey mass stretched ahead of me. It was so large I couldn't bring myself to believe at first that it was a living thing. Then, as I swung out and around to keep watching it, a majestic plume of spray rose into the air. It was a blue whale, fully 60 feet long. It really was an awesome sight.

By the middle of August, apparently to the customer's astonishment, we had completed everything they set out to do. The helicopters were to be ferried out, all the way back to Ottawa. We got as far as Igloolik, on the Melville Peninsula, on the first leg, and spent the night in the Hudson's Bay manager's house. He had just returned from a vacation in Scotland. He had some whiskey more delicious than any other I have tasted. Unfortunately, it was one of those blends which are not exported.

We spent the next night in Eskimo Point, just south of Chesterfield Inlet. Greg Lamb had flown with us this far, landing to give us gas when we needed it. Now he put out the last cache on the way to Churchill, and left us. I had intended to cut across country once we left Churchill, through Oxford House, God's Lake and then down through Fort Hope on the Albany River to pick up the railway at Nakina. I had come out that way the previous year. But the company said no; we must, in the interests of safety, follow the railway down to Winnipeg, and then turn east along the C.N.R. Their solicitude would have been touching if I hadn't known that they were interested only in the extra revenue hours we would pick up on this much longer route.

When we reached Nakina, in northern Ontario, I ran into a snag I had never encountered before. Since our company was still in undischarged bankruptcy, we could not use credit cards to buy our fuel; I had to carry cash. A cheque for $750 had been waiting for me in Winnipeg. I didn't want to cash it until I had to, but by the time we reached Nakina I needed money to buy gas. Unfortunately, having been in the bush for five months, I had forgotten that other people had statutory holidays. This, presumably Labour Day, was one of them, and I couldn't find anyone to cash my cheque.

When you are going home, a delay of even one day assumes the proportions of a calamity. I was sitting at the coffee bar of the motel in which we were staying, complaining bitterly to the girl behind the counter, when a very large woman, wearing a mackinaw at least three sizes too large for me, came in. She was a taxi driver, and the girl behind the counter suggested I should ask her.

"How much's the cheque for?" she asked.

"Seven hundred and fifty bucks."

She stirred her coffee thoughtfully. "Sure; just let me finish my coffee. I'll get it cashed for you."

We drove to the outskirts of town and pulled up in front of a dilapidated little shack. I found it hard to believe that the owner

200

could muster up $50 in cash, let alone $750. But when the owner answered the door, and the taxi driver had explained the problem, he didn't bat an eyelid.

"You got I.D.?" he demanded.

I started to reach for my wallet, but he turned away. "That's okay, just as long as you got it. Gimme the cheque."

He glanced at it, went inside for a couple of minutes, then came back and slapped the money, nearly all of it in hundred-dollar bills, into my hand. He turned to look at the taxi driver. "You don't get no commission on this one, Susie," he remarked tartly.

I had to choke off a giggle. Susie was a marvellously inappropriate name for that huge woman. "Fuck you, Ernie," she said amiably, and we drove back to the motel.

"Who the hell was that?" I asked.

"Ernie? He's the bootlegger."

I left her a handsome tip, and bought her another cup of coffee before she drove me out to the airport. When we reached Ottawa two days later I felt a huge elation, and a huge sense of relief, of course, that I had survived the season. But no one in Ottawa was impressed. They had been hoping for a lot more revenue hours from us. I tried not to let it bother me. In fact, the operation hadn't been all bad. I'd had a lot of fun with the Lamb boys who, as usual, had replaced each other several times during the season. When we were working out of Pond Inlet, Jack Lamb, for reasons I have since forgotten, had to make a trip to Thule, in Greenland. We promptly emptied our wallets so that he could bring back some duty-free booze. He came back with half a Beaver load of liquor, among it a case of Schnapps.

That evening we made serious inroads into the Schnapps, and at about three o'clock in the morning we ended up on the verandah of the Hudson's Bay store, while Jack, with his arm around the Hudson's Bay manager's shoulder, sang his version of the ballad Tennessee Ernie Ford made famous:

> "Sixteen hours,
> You fly sixteen hours, and what do you get?
> Another day older and deeper in debt;
> St. Peter don't call me, 'cos I cain't go
> Oh, I owe my soul to the Hudson's Bay sto'. . . ."

CHAPTER 21

British Columbia and the Yukon

AS IT TURNED OUT, THE SEASON WASN'T OVER FOR ME YET. The people in Ottawa were more or less openly contemptuous because I hadn't earned enough money for them; but, by a nice irony, they still needed me. There was a boom in mining exploration in the Yukon that fall. A machine was sitting in Calgary with no pilot to fly it. I enjoyed that negotiation. I had made enough to get me through the year but, with a new house to pay for, a couple of months of extra salary would help. I made them raise my salary, give me ten days at home and pay my air fare back and forth. They were unhappy people, but they were also greedy; the thought of a machine sitting in a hangar, earning no revenue, was too much for them.

By a stroke of rare good fortune, I arrived back in Victoria just as it was time to move into the new house. I went back to Calgary with a sense that everything was in good order. When I got there, the western manager, Jim Lapinski, insisted that I do a five-day course of mountain training. Since I had been flying the mountains of Baffin Island for the past several months, it seemed a little redundant to me; but since it also meant five days in the hotel at Lake Louise — about as far as you could get from a tent on an icecap — I didn't argue.

I had been told in Ottawa that every machine but one was committed. The one left, the one I got, was the bottom of the barrel. It was a D model which didn't even have hydraulic controls. I found it hairy going back to the old mechanical linkage, which allowed every thump of turbulence you hit to be transmitted right back to your arms. But it was in good condition and, as long as I didn't run into any hot weather — which was unlikely in September — it was a much better machine to fly in the mountains than a J.

I was supposed to go up the Alaska Highway, all the way to Whitehorse; but when I reached Watson Lake, just north of the British Columbia-Yukon border, there were so many potential customers that I phoned Calgary and suggested working out of Watson. Jim agreed, and I put in a couple of hard months of flying for various mining exploration companies. It wasn't an unpleasant stint, because the Yukon at that time of the year is quite startlingly beautiful. The upper slopes of the mountains are covered with dwarf willow, and in the fall the colours are almost as spectacular as they are in Ontario.

For the first month, I worked right out of Watson Lake, living in the only motel in town. Sheldon Luck, a pilot whose experience reached right back into the early days of bush flying, was operating a DC-3 out of Watson and whenever possible I used to wait for him to get back in the evenings and fly him from the airport to our motel. He was known as Pappy Luck, and I spent many pleasant evenings with him, drinking beer and learning what it had been like flying this country in the 1920's and 1930's. Somehow it relieved my anxieties. I was getting my first taste of flying heavy loads out of drill camps in the surrounding mountains.

Then, at the beginning of October, I moved out of Watson to work at a drill camp up above the Liard River. The "show" we were working on was in a cirque at about the 5,000-foot level, and it looked very promising. The ore was very heavy and, to the unpractised eye, it looked like solid silver. The exploration company had been into this particular cirque in the spring; but then the snow was still on the ground and the geologist had seen nothing to get excited about. He had, however, left his pocket compass behind when he left. It was an expensive instrument and three months later, when he was passing the cirque, he asked the helicopter pilot to land, finding not only his compass but a very promising show of lead-silver ore beneath it.

I had to fly up the camp food and supplies — they already had a diamond drill working when I arrived. The geologist in charge was very enthusiastic about the find, which led me to believe that it was simply one more of the little pockets of rich ore you so often find in the Rockies. My experience was that if the find really was a significant one, the geologists were as talkative as clams. In any case, we set out to stake the area, carrying bundles of stakes on the rack beside the passenger, who would lean out of the door and try to drop them onto ledges along the side of the mountain. I noticed with interest that the stakes in at least one of the bundles had my name on them.

Two weeks later the snow began to fly in earnest and we pulled everything out of the camp. A B.C.-Yukon Airways Beaver brought everyone back from a nearby lake to Watson. That night there was a knock on the door of my motel room. The party chief had come to see me, bringing a bottle with him. After we'd had a drink or two, he produced some forms for me to sign. They were release forms for the claims which had been staked in my name.

"What claims?" I asked innocently. The geologist's laugh was a little forced. I kept him on the hook for quite awhile, exacting several more drinks while he in turn threatened and pleaded with me. As it turned out, he needn't have worried. The claims never amounted to anything; and shortly afterwards a supreme court judgement prohibited the dropping of claim stakes from the air.

Except for some time I had spent around Chibougamau, in Quebec, during my first year of flying, this was my first real exposure to mining exploration companies. The majority of their employees, I soon discovered, were very unscrupulous people and, since Spartan Air Services was now run by mining promoters, I had no trouble deciding when I got home that season to change companies. As a matter of fact, I had already done so before I got home. There was a memorable drunk in Calgary early in November. The hotel we were staying at had a tank full of live lobsters in the foyer of its restaurant. Garry Fields poured a couple of glasses of créme de menthe into the tank to liven them up. We were thrown out of the hotel, but some time during the evening I made arrangements with Garry for a flying job the following year.

The company I joined was called Capilano Helicopters, and it was based in Vancouver. For the past three or four years Alf Brenner, the president, had owned his own helicopter and worked for other companies on a lease arrangement. Now he had expanded, buying another two helicopters and taking on several ex-Spartan pilots and engineers to operate them — including Garry, who recommended me to Alf. The contract I went out on the following spring was with the inventories division of the British Columbia Forest Service.

The inventories people had been using helicopters for a number of years and by a stroke of luck my first year with them was the year they covered the most southerly forests in the province. There was none of the isolation of the previous operations, and I found it a very refreshing change. Our first camp was at Rock Creek, which is hardly a metropolis, but a far cry from, for instance, the Barnes Icecap.

There was another most refreshing change that year — the type of helicopter I was to fly. For the first time it was to be a turbo-charged machine, and the improvement was spectacular. Now, when you had to land above 5,000 feet, the landing technique was no different from a sea-level landing. Instead of having to pick a spot from the air you knew beyond doubt would do — and one, moreover, from which you could jump over the edge of a cliff to pick up speed for a take-off — you could go in to try a landing, backing away if it turned out to be unsuitable. This took a great deal of the anxiety out of mountain flying.

The machine I started with, however, was a 47-G3. It had the old Franklin engine in it and the turbo-charger was ungoverned. I picked it up from the hangar at Pitt Meadows and flew it for the first time on the ferry flight to Rock Creek. It was a disconcerting experience because now one had yet another gauge to watch: the manifold pressure gauge. I found it extremely hard to cope with this extra co-ordination. Needles seemed to be swinging in all directions. After two weeks, when I was just beginning to master things, Doug Dunlop, the pilot I had flown with three years before on the Geodetic Survey operation, brought me a brand new G3B-1. This, at the time, was undoubtedly the Rolls Royce of light helicopters.

It was supposed to have been ready for the beginning of the operation, but there had been a delay in delivery from the factory. And then, of course, it had taken a few days in Calgary to equip it for the bush — to fit cargo racks, radio and emergency equipment. That was one of the smoothest machines I had ever flown. You no longer had to worry about co-ordinating the manifold pressure; it was hydraulically governed. But the biggest improvement, it seemed to me, was that the bubble was nearly a foot wider than the one on the old machines. It was heaven not to have to sit with your left elbow jammed against the door when there were two passengers.

The job itself turned out to be a rather demanding one. First we had to put out sample crews — two-man student crews who camped out for four or five days at a time, putting in random sample plots, recording the numbers, species, ages and heights of every tree in the plot. This was fairly straightforward flying, except that the students, with all their food and camping gear, had to be moved in one trip; and to begin with, it was very hard to persuade them that they couldn't enjoy the luxury of taking cases of canned fruit juice in their packs because these items were just too heavy. Evidently they had been conditioned by Anita Bryant advertisements to believe that their health would rapidly break down if they didn't consume vast quantities of fruit juice. They were leaving the food behind and substituting juice. A couple of hungry weeks passed before they began to smarten up.

Once the sample crews had been put out, I would take the "classifier" and do an inventory traverse from the air. The classifier would map out his traverse on aerial photographs, marking in plots every two miles or so. He had a tape recorder on the seat beside him, and as we flew over the plots he would call them, estimating the numbers, species, heights and ages on tape. The difficulty was that we were flying some 50 feet above the tree tops, and from this height it is very hard to navigate. While the classifier was calling his plot, I would have to look ahead for the next recognizable feature. If I missed, we'd have to climb up and circle back to find ourselves, wasting a good deal of flying time.

This called for some fairly intense concentration, and after about an hour we would land on the shore of a lake, or in a swamp, beside one of the plots he had called, so that he could check his estimates from the air with actual measurements on the ground. The classifier would slosh off into the trees and leave me to speculate about why God decided at the same time to create something as beautiful as an Indian paintbrush in flower, and as ugly as a mosquito.

The form was to spend about three weeks with one crew, then move on to the next one — in this case a crew working out of Fernie, in the southeast corner of the province. Fernie, at the time, was a sort of ghost town. The underground coal mines at Michel and Natal had ceased to produce; Kaiser Resources had not yet started their huge open-pit mine. The wide main street of Fernie had once boasted more than a dozen thriving hotels. Now they, and nearly all the shops between them, were boarded up. It was a depressing sight, but even at that, it was not nearly so depressing as the twin towns of Michel and Natal, crouched in the Crow's Nest Pass and looking just like one of the more bleak and poverty-stricken Welsh coal-mining villages. Even the sheets hanging on the clotheslines were grey with coal dust.

The engineer with me this year was Jack Hardock. We had worked together on the Mid-Canada Line several years before, and he was an ideal companion. He was a good engineer, full of energy, and he always made the social best of things wherever he found himself. At first blush, Fernie didn't seem to have much to offer on the social side. Most of the residents left behind after the mines closed were Italians who, for obvious reasons, were in reduced circumstances. The forestry people had set up their camp in the park, more or less in the centre of town. It was an odd feeling to be living in a tent smack in the middle of town, but there was at least one advantage: the soccer pitch was right next to us and we could watch all the matches. One in particular, I remember, was between a team from Kimberley, consisting almost exclusively of Austrians, and the local Italian team. There really wasn't much soccer to watch, but the fights were spectacular.

When we arrived in Fernie, the forestry crew had been there for about a month. Many of them were university students on summer jobs, and they were complaining bitterly about the lack of what they called action in Fernie. A day or two after we arrived, I had put two sampling crews out in the morning and for some reason I wouldn't be flying the classifier until after lunch, so Jack Hardock put a sling on his arm and had me drive him down to the clinic. Jack walked up to the nurse at her desk.

"Yesterday," he said, lifting his arm in its sling well above his head, "I could get my arm right up to here. Now," he said, lowering it to the level of his chest, "I can only get it up to here."

The nurse studied him for awhile; then she stood up. "I think it's rabies," she said. "If you'll follow me, I'll start you on a course of injections."

Jack removed his sling and retreated to the door, ready to make a break for it. We explained to her the social problems the young people in our camp were experiencing. It turned out that the young women in Fernie were experiencing the same disappointment. The result was a successful party the following Saturday night, attended by nurses, schoolteachers, a dental receptionist and two or three stenographers. When Jack and I turned up, the students wanted to know what two old men like us were doing, trying to crash their party.

From Fernie we moved to Shuswap Lake, and here for the first time I was able to have my family with me on a flying operation. The forestry people provided camping equipment and we set up camp on our own. It made a world of difference to my morale, and my two young sons had the time of their lives.

But the operation was not without its problems. One of them was the avgas. A dealer had hauled a stack of drums into our Shuswap camp which he had originally assembled for an operation five years previously. They had never been used and he was delighted when we came along. Unfortunately, five-year-old gasoline begins to break down and we promptly ran into plug trouble. I found myself back in the bad old days of the Franklin engine and the 6V4 fuel. Spark plugs had to be changed two or three times a day.

We soon analyzed the problem, but the dealer, who reluctantly admitted that the gas he had given us might be a little old, needed two weeks to get in a fresh supply. We soldiered on, changing plugs, but one night, returning to camp at the end of the day, I found myself out of spare plugs, with the engine becoming rougher and rougher. I had to put down in a clearing beside a logging road. Before I did so, I asked on the radio for Jack to drive the 15-odd miles to where I was and bring me some new plugs.

Jack was on his way within minutes, but by the time he reached me we were running out of daylight. We didn't want to leave the machine out overnight, so we did a lightning plug change. In my haste I forgot to button down the cooling shroud round the fan after I had finished. The result was, of course, trouble. The heavy canvas shroud, with its metal snap-on studs, chewed up the cooling fan severely. We got the machine back to camp and phoned Alf Brenner for a new fan. He sent it off by bus the next day. The bus didn't pass where we were until nearly half-past three the following morning, at which time Jack and I stood sleepily at an intersection on the highway waiting for it. When the bus appeared, it showed no signs of stopping. We had to get right out on the road, waving like maniacs, before the driver reluctantly pulled over.

He opened the door, looked at us, and then suddenly burst out laughing. "I left your parcel in Kamloops," he said. "I didn't think anyone'd be stupid enough to come out for a parcel at this time of night." Then, still laughing, he shut the door and drove off.

We phoned the bus company after breakfast. It was the driver's fault, they assured us. The parcel would definitely be on the bus at half-past three the following morning. We suggested they warn the bus driver not to stop if it wasn't, because we'd kill him.

But it was a good season. About once every three years, I was finding, I went out on an operation that was more or less an unqualified success. This year was for me. I put in something over 500 hours of flying, and everyone went home happy that winter. Our company was happy, the customer was happy and so was I. So I suppose it was inevitable that the following spring things would go wrong.

Because I had had such a successful season, I naturally assumed that Alf Brenner would want me to fly for him the following summer. In the middle of May, he phoned me. He was sorry, but there wouldn't be a job for me this season after all. It was a particularly nasty blow because, by that time, most companies had hired the pilots they needed for the season's operations. For the first time, I had to start phoning around the country to ask for a job. To make it worse, 1963 turned out to be a recession year for the helicopter industry — even Okanagan had trouble that year. It was a thoroughly unnerving experience. We had just taken on a new house, and there was no way we could manage unless I got a flying job that summer.

Ironically, I had been offered a job by Vancouver Island Helicopters earlier that year, but of course I had turned it down because I thought I was committed. There was still, however, a faint hope. They had put in a bid for a forestry contract; if they got it, I would get the job. On May 28, which happens to be my birthday, Bob Taylor, the manager, phoned to tell me they had won the contract. I was over the hump for one more year, but now I decided that it was time to think seriously about getting out of flying. The present was insecure and the future seemed to have little to offer. In the meantime, I spent another summer with the forestry people, learning a good deal about trees but getting, to be honest, very bored with the job. We moved further north this year, up into the central part of the province, starting at Little Fort, some 70 miles north of Kamloops, and then moving west to the Chilcotin country, working out of Alexis Creek.

Later I had my first experience flying the west coast. The weather was remarkably pleasant for the whole three weeks of this phase of the operation, so it was another year or two before I discovered how tough coastal flying could be. In this case, we were operating off a scow which was towed behind a sizeable launch. The scow made an ideal pad for the helicopter, but the boat was much too small for the job, and we would have been horribly cramped if the weather had been bad and we had had to stay inside it. We joined her at Bella Coola, and it was fun — a sort of aircraft carrier. The boat would steam up an inlet while I flew the sample crews up into the mountains. After I had flown the classification traverse, I would pick up the crews, return them to the boat and we would tie up to the shore for the night.

It sounds simple enough, particularly in good weather, but I ran into an unexpected problem — one which proved how remarkably strong our conditioned reflexes are. When I came in for my first landing on the move, I lined up above the scow, only to find that I couldn't get the Collective down to land. The scow was only a foot or two wider than my skids, so that I couldn't fail to see the water rushing by, and I had been so conditioned to stopping all movement before I touched down that nothing would persuade my left arm to go down. I hovered there for so long that my passenger turned to look at me, wondering what was going on. In the end, I had to shut my eyes before my left arm would respond. When I'd landed I opened my eyes to find my passenger still looking at me. His eyes were opened very wide indeed.

That season was far less enjoyable than the one before. One of the continuing problems with a government contract was that most civil servants fancied themselves as logisticians; they spent the entire winter trying to work out schedules that were more efficient. In this case, the fly-camp syndrome took over, and I spent most of the season working out of a pup-tent or a filthy and abandoned logging shack, eating food fried up at the last minute by a student who had never in his life before produced a meal more ambitious than a peanut butter and jelly sandwich.

It was particularly irritating because we were moving from camp to camp; thus the forestry people seldom spent more than a week or two in these conditions, whereas the helicopter crew spent virtually the entire season in fly camps. The following year, my last with the forestry service, we went one step further in the economy kick; we went back to using a G2 instead of a turbo-charged machine. The argument was that the job had been done in the past with a G2; thus there was no point in paying for the more expensive machine. In that case, I suggested, why not abandon helicopters altogether and go back to using pack horses? My sarcasm provoked a much stronger reaction than I anticipated. The truth was that one of the party chiefs had planned to do just that — and it turned into a hilarious fiasco. The packer he hired had little or no experience with horses. Loads were dumped all over the mountainside on their first sortie and a helicopter had to be brought in to salvage the equipment. Thank heavens it wasn't me. I would have injured myself, laughing.

It was time to move on, and that winter I made the necessary arrangements to enrol as a first-year education student at the University of Victoria. This seemed the wise thing to do because computer predictions insisted that there would be a severe shortage of qualified teachers well into the 1970's. Yet when I graduated four years later, there was an unmistakable surplus of teachers. The only jobs available were in places like Telegraph Creek or Wonowon, on the Alaska Highway. By then, though, I had changed direction, graduating with an English rather than an education degree.

In the meantime, I was very much what is called a mature student, and I found it a disconcerting experience to be competing against the bright young things just out of high school. Fortunately, there was a balancing factor; most of the young people were confident they could become successful without a degree if necessary; besides which, there were so many social distractions for them, so few for me. I survived without too much humiliation, but it was no picnic. When I had written my final exams that spring, I had to do three weeks of practice teaching at an elementary school in Sooke, which meant not only a long day of concentration but a 30-mile drive, morning and evening.

I finished my practice teaching on a Friday evening. On Sunday morning I was on my way to Golden in a helicopter to start work with the Geological Survey of Canada again. On the way there we stopped to refuel in Revelstoke and met a helicopter crew who had worked for the G.S.C. in British Columbia the previous year. What they had to tell us was not encouraging. "When you fly over your first camp, you'll see four or five big, luxurious trailers; then you'll see two pup-tents down near the garbage dump. Those'll be for the helicopter crew."

It wasn't quite as bad as that, but nor was it very satisfactory. The camp was in a gravel pit about four miles west of Golden, along the highway, and we found ourselves occupying the top bunks in a tiny room at the end of the stores trailer. Our room-mates were the cook and his assistant. This may have served to show us what our status was, but it was a silly and impractical arrangement. The cooks got up before five o'clock every morning to prepare breakfast. They went to bed at about eight in the evening. Since this was too early for us, we invariably woke them up when we went to bed; and they enthusiastically retaliated before dawn the following morning.

The engineer with me that year was all for walking out on them and going into a motel in town, but I was reluctant to get involved in such an overt confrontation so early in the season, and we stuck it out. The next camp we moved to was a blessed improvement; a tent-camp on Bowron Lake. The party chief was an extremely pleasant character, and there were no class distinctions this time. From there we moved to Revelstoke, then to Takla Lake in the Chilcotin country, and finally back to Golden to finish the season. It became obvious in time that hostility between the G.S.C. people in the west and their helicopter crews had been building up for several years. There really wasn't much you could do about it.

But one good thing to come out of that season was that I finished my apprenticeship as a mountain pilot and became a journeyman. While the geologists didn't necessarily want to land on the highest peaks of the mountains, they did want to land on the high, narrow shoulders joining them. These shoulders were usually so sharply rounded that they wouldn't accommodate my skids; thus I would have to balance on the apex of the ridge while the geologist climbed out and propped up the back of the skids with flat rocks. It was a nerve-wracking process, but it was the only way to get them where they wanted to go — unless you dropped them on the hover, landed somewhere down in the valley and returned later to pick them up; something I did fairly frequently if the weather was really good.

It was a tough job, both for the pilot and the geologist. The geologist would sit with sketchbook, his back propped against the skid, in what was almost invariably a cutting wind, trying to produce a comprehensive drawing of the chaotically folded and faulted formations of the Rocky Mountains. I soon began to understand how the hostility had developed; it was a product of the job, not the people involved. First thing in the morning, I would have to put out two crews of two students each to do traverses high in the mountains. They would cover three or four miles, plotting the geology and collecting rock samples, and I would pick them up and return to camp in the evening. Unfortunately, some of the students had adopted the attitude of their superiors; they thought that the helicopter crew belonged in the category of servants, and consequently they paid little attention to the arrangements for a pickup spot, moving in whatever direction they found interesting. They were not going to be bound by any instructions from me. I didn't mind too much if the weather remained fine — I could usually spot the fluorescent red signal panels they carried from a long way away. But when the weather closed in, I often had a frightful job finding them.

This put a heavy strain on me because it would have been very dangerous if two inexperienced students had had to spend a night or two out in the mountains. In fact, I never did have to leave any-one out overnight, but I suffered through some grim evenings flying in rain and hail, looking for people who were four or five miles away from where they should have been. There were other com-plications, too. One day, two students tried to cross a ridge that turned out to be too precipitous for one of them. He had frozen. Fortunately, I was able to land about a hundred yards away. The other student climbed across to tell me what had happened. I locked the controls and climbed back along the razorback ridge with him. It took us some 20 minutes to get the other lad moving, one of us on either side of him. I had thought that once he saw the helicopter so close to him, he would move back to it very quickly. Instead, less than halfway back, he froze again. I had left the heli-copter with its engine running and now, 30 minutes later, it was still running.

But I was behind the student. There was a more or less sheer drop on either side of the ridge and no possible way I could climb past him. In the end, after a great deal of shouting and pushing, he began to move again. Agonizingly slowly, we crawled back to the helicopter. When we got there, we put him on the seat between us. He sat there, his face the colour of old snow, his eyes tightly closed, until we had landed back in camp.

Nervous strain, however, wasn't the only thing that made people edgy on that operation; there was also the enormous boredom. After putting out the two student traverse crews in the morning, I would take one of the geologists out for the day. Usually I would fly for about ten minutes and he would call for a landing on a ridge. Once this was accomplished, I would have to sit for at least an hour, sometimes two or three, while the geologist did his sketching and interpretation. There was seldom room, perched as we nearly always were on a sharp ridge, to walk more than a few feet from the helicopter. Then, two or three hours later, we would fly for perhaps five minutes and land on another, identical ridge — to sit for another two or three hours. The days passed very slowly.

When at last it was over, and I was back in Victoria, I advised Bob Taylor to forget that particular contract. It was a high risk, low yield operation; we never exceeded 70 hours of flying in a month. But when the following spring came round, things were still slow and the company bid on the contract again. They got it, with the stipulation that I would not be the pilot. Bob gave me a severe dressing down, but his heart wasn't in it because really he knew that I was right. It wasn't the pilot or the customer who was at fault; it was the nature of the job. He turned the contract down, and I went on to some of the most interesting and enjoyable years of my flying career.

There were no more government contracts; instead I became for that year the relief pilot. The company had established a base in Prince Rupert, and the base concept was proving very successful. Charter flying held none of the disadvantages of the contract. When you had finished flying for the day, you did not have to eat your meals and spend all your waking hours with the customer; you went home, even if home was only a motel, and forgot him. Besides which, there was constant variety. If a job was tedious, you knew it would only last for a day or two. That summer I didn't work from any particular base; I moved to wherever there was some activity. Business was picking up again after the doldrums of 1963, and I was never short of work. I flew for any number of mining exploration companies; I did some work on Hydro construction lines; I flew biologists on game counts; I helped install a fish weir. I even spent some time that summer flying out of Victoria. Life was fun again.

It was fun because now I was working for a company I both liked and trusted. Vancouver Island Helicopters had been founded by a pilot called Ted Henson. He had been killed in a flying accident in 1957 and his widow, Lynne, kept the company going with Bob Taylor as manager. Alf Stringer, who with Carl Agar had founded Okanagan Helicopters, married Lynne the year after I joined the company and became its president. From my point of view, he was an ideal employer. His experience with Okanagan had turned him against the cult of rapid growth and expansion; he enjoyed running a company he could control without having to create a bureaucracy. The company had some nine or ten machines when I joined it; there were still only 12 when I gave up flying 12 years later. And in all that time I never had to have anything in the way of a written contract with the company. I was paid what

I thought I was worth, and when the summer came I never had to worry about a job. I could leave university and go straight back to work. In an industry that was notorious for its sudden shifts of policy, its abrupt lay-offs, I was remarkably lucky to enjoy such stability.

CHAPTER 22

Geological Exploration

BY 1966, THE RECESSION WAS OVER FOR THE HELICOPTER industry; things were thriving again and I spent another summer as a roving pilot. Burns Lake and Smithers were hot that year, and I spent most of my time in one or the other, flying for mining exploration companies. Towards the end of the season I went on a three-week contract — quite the most enjoyable contract I'd ever flown. The man I worked with, Will Tompson, was an American geologist who had settled in Canada. He had been involved in the discovery and development of at least two producing mines. What I liked most about him was that he believed in travelling first class. He failed to see why the people who actually discovered minerals shouldn't enjoy the same standard of living as the many who made profits out of the discovery. His camps were always provided with the best equipment and he didn't subscribe to the dawn-to-dusk rat race in the bush. On this occasion, he was investigating coal deposits at the headwaters of the Skeena River.

Will and his partner flew into Kluayaz Lake by fixed-wing, with all the camping gear, food and avgas for the helicopter, and I joined them there, flying in from Prince Rupert. There had been very little activity in the area since the turn of the century; perhaps because of this, there were at least two errors on the map sheet and it took me some time to find the lake. I was relieved to hear that the fixed-wing pilot had had the same problem. But once there, we settled down to an almost idyllic existence for the next three weeks.

Will had become interested in the area when he came across some records of mining exploration undertaken more than 50 years before. In 1910, a mining engineer with the imposing name of Ronald Campbell Campbell-Johnston had been commissioned by a Montreal financier to investigate what came to be known as the Groundhog Coalfield. We had his reports with us, and it was fascinating to be able to retrace his steps the easy way. He described the area as a "Large Tract of Coal-Lands Extending Over More Than Sixty Thousand Acres — or Ninety-Five Square Miles Situated on the Headwaters of the Yetze Branch of the Stikine River, British Columbia."

The headwaters of the Yetze originate on the same height of land from which the Skeena begins its journey to the sea just south of Prince Rupert, and we took photographs of each other, leaping across the Skeena in one bound. The valley is so wide it really constitutes a small plain — a grassy plain, with one or two lakes but very little swamp. In the late summer, it is filled with caribou and it's quite remarkably beautiful.

What made the area more interesting was that for some 60 years practically nobody had been there. I suppose there was really no incentive. The mountains were of sedimentary rock; they contained no minerals. There was no gas or oil. None of the prospectors who passed through it on their way to the Klondyke had found any gold, and the place might have been ignored altogether if someone hadn't spotted little pieces of black float on the sand and gravel bars a few miles south of the height of land.

Then, when the Yukon Telegraph line was completed in 1900, it by-passed the headwaters of the Skeena, so there was no reason for anyone to go there. But a packer from the village of Kispiox, just north of Hazelton, remembered the black float and went back to stake claims. He sold the claims to Leon Benoit, a Montreal promoter.

Benoit hired Campbell-Johnston to go and assess the property, and Campbell-Johnston left Vancouver on September 14, 1910, travelling by steamer to Prince Rupert, by riverboat up the Skeena to Hazelton, and then by pack train — under the guidance of Georges Biernes, the packer who had originally staked the claims — to what came to be known as the Groundhog Coalfield. It came by its name simply enough: all the groundhog burrows were surrounded by coal instead of soil.

But Campbell-Johnston had to overcome some minor difficulties before he could get away from Hazelton. The Indians recruited by Biernes from their village at Kispiox were unenthusiastic. The Telegraph Trail, which they would have to follow for two-thirds of the journey, was a notoriously difficult one and the season was well advanced — too well advanced, they complained. But Campbell-

Johnston was a Scot with aristocratic connections; a man obviously accustomed to overcoming the timidity and apathy of the lower classes. He spoke with the brisk assurance of someone belonging to a nation which had colonized half the world:

The Telegraph Trail was followed by us from Hazelton past the fifth cabin to the Indian village below the outlet of Blackwater [now called Damdochuck Lake]. This route by the wire is one hundred and thirty-five miles, but by the trail one hundred and fifty-five, over and under fallen trees, through and round bogholes and muskeg swamps, across creeks some with, some without rickety bridges, over poison and S.O.B.! mountains, up to 3200 feet elevation and down to 1000 feet again and again, irrespective of grades, mountains, rivers and morasses, forest or meadows. In its original route any old Indian trail was followed, and the location had never since been bettered.

To the engineer, these were minor problems. "All this," he remarked tersely, "must and can easily be remedied." But the Indians were still being awkward:

At Blackwater the Indian captain of our packtrain refused to take the horses further even to the base of Ground Hog Mountain, another twenty miles. Discretion and diplomacy had to come into play to prevent the Indians deserting us and returning alone to their village at Kispiox, and also to fatten up the packtrain on good pasturage against the return through snow and so starvation through want of grass, as our journey had been inadvertently delayed until too late in the fall of the year, and was commenced and undertaken against the advice of over careful old timers among the white settlers, and also the wiseacres and weather prophets among the Indians. "Witch" Mabel with uplifted hands warned us at Blackwater of certain death for the whole packtrain, and so slow starvation for ourselves.

Discretion and diplomacy must have prevailed, because Campbell-Johnston and George Biernes made "a hasty start up the north fork of the Blackwater [Snomaldo Creek] with three dogs to pack full loads, so as to give all the time required to make a thorough examination of the property." They traversed the Groundhog Pass at an elevation of 5,700 feet, and spent six days, "actually in the valley [of the Skeena] to study the geology, coal-bearing measures, outcrops and exposures, local conditions and environments." There were people at the time who hinted that six days on foot, with the freeze-up imminent and the snow flying, were scarcely sufficient for such a comprehensive survey; but Campbell-Johnston wasn't given to understatement. "The examination and result of our search," he advised the financier, Benoit, "are most successful by proving the existence of high class steam coal in ample quantities. By means of the excellence of this coal and the certain future facility and ability for the cheap winning and transportation so a splendid profit can be harvested."

This was heady stuff for an engineering report. But it worked, and the following year he went back, this time with a "large force of miners with pack trains to convey food, explosives and all supplies necessary to carry on a continuous campaign of development and research by reconnaissance from June to November." And this time, though he doesn't mention it in his report, he took his wife with him. I think Esther Campbell-Johnston was the first white woman to visit this country.

After completing this season's work, he was offering his financial backers an estimate of no less than "Twenty eight hundred and fifty millions of tons . . . of high class anthracite coal. This at a daily output of 30,000 tons or 9,000,000 per annum affords a supply for 300 years, that is beyond the dreams of avarice."

Unfortunately for Campbell-Johnston, the dreams of avarice never materialized. The Royal Navy switched from coal to oil at about this time, and the deteriorating political situation in Europe may have made the financiers cautious. Whatever the reason, except for a few surveyors, nobody went back into that country until we did, nearly 60 years later. And this made it fascinating for us. Most of the tunnels dug by the miners had caved in, but their cabins were still standing and they were still full of tools and utensils, rifles and shotguns, kerosene lamps, Sheffield cutlery, bottles, bibles and sewing kits. And we had the time to browse among all these interesting relics.

Will Tompson had the most relaxed schedule I've ever enjoyed on a helicopter operation. When we got up in the morning, we would ease into the day, lighting a fire and sitting round it to drink coffee before we began to cook breakfast. After breakfast, when everything had been washed up and put away, we would stroll over to the helicopter and set off to fly over the gently rolling uplands between Kluayaz Lake and the valleys of the Nass and the Skeena Rivers, looking for the old workings left by Campbell-Johnston's crew. We had time to stop and examine all the old cabins and campsites. Our working day ended at about five o'clock. After I had tied the helicopter down for the night, refuelled it and done an inspection, Will dug out his bottle of Scotch and we sat around the fire for an hour, discussing the day's discoveries. Two drinks, and the bottle would be put away while Will cooked the supper. He was a very good cook, and I was happy to accept the lesser responsibility of washing up. It was one of the very few times I worked in the bush without deadlines to meet. I think we were there for a little over three weeks, and for once I was genuinely sorry to leave a job.

We went back the following year for a four-month season. This time it was with a full geological exploration crew of about twelve people. I would put out two, two-man crews to traverse the ground on foot, then go out for the rest of the day on aerial reconnaissance with Will or one of the other geologists. As often as not we would spend an hour or two digging for artifacts in one of the old cabins. Occasionally we managed to land at one of the Telegraph cabins. They were always interesting because here, even more than in Campbell-Johnston's cabins, it was obvious that when people left in the 1930's they thought they were going to return; the cabins were always rich in artifacts. The one thing I never found, though, was an actual telegraph key. Apparently people treasured these as a very personal possession, and they always took their key with them when they moved.

In one cabin we found a rifle under the floorboards. It was a .30-30 Winchester, packed solidly in grease and then wrapped in gunny sacking. One of the crew cleaned it up. It was still in working condition. There were other such finds. A complete set of wood-working tools, still bright and shining once the grease had been removed. But from my point of view, far the most interesting find was that of a cabin, tucked high up on the east bank of the Skeena, just below the tree line and some ten miles north of the junction of the Kluatantan River.

I'll have to go back to a little history again. In June of 1906, an Indian trapper from Kispiox brought his furs in from his trapline and sold them to the Hudson's Bay post at Hazelton; then, not sur-prisingly, since he had just come back from the bush, he went to a party and did some drinking. His name was Simon Gunanoot, and during the course of the party a miner called Alex McIntosh made some derogatory remarks about Simon's wife. The following morn-ing, Alex McIntosh was found lying dead on the trail from Hazelton to Kispiox. He had been shot in the back. After this, the story be-comes confusing. Two miles further down the trail another man called LeClair was found dead. He, too, had been shot in the back. Gunanoot became an obvious suspect in the murder of McIntosh, but when the Provincial Police went to question him, they found he had gone. They sent out a patrol to search for him. The search lasted for 13 years, and Simon Gunanoot became British Columbia's most celebrated outlaw. He never was caught; he gave himself up in the end and was acquitted when he was tried in Vancouver.

Officially, of course, no one knew where he was during those 13 years. In fact, many of Campbell-Johnston's crew met and spoke with him, as did the packer, George Biernes. He was hiding out in that country and I am convinced that he spent a good deal of his time in the cabin we found. There were lots of animal bones around it, but virtually no artifacts. The only thing we found was a packet of rusty needles. Besides which, what trapper would build his cabin in such an inaccessible spot, way up the side of a mountain? The main trail from Blackwater to Telegraph Creek ran along the west bank of the Skeena. If you stepped out of the trees around the cabin, you could see for miles along it in either direction. I am convinced Gunanoot stood and watched many a police patrol slogging along it in their search for him.

One day I landed wtih Will Tompson on the rolling height of land between the Skeena and Nass Rivers. We had spent some time examining a show of coal along the banks of a stream, when we heard what at first we thought was a pack of coyotes. They were coming in our direction; then, just as the noise seemed to be all around us, it ceased. We climbed cautiously up the bank of the stream and came face-to-face with a family of wolves, standing immobile, some 30 yards away. The parents were big, grey timber wolves; their four offspring were all jet-black and no more than three months old. We stood for two or three minutes inspecting each other before the wolves moved off, silent now and suspicious.

For the remaining three months of that season I kept an eye on the family. They became so accustomed to the helicopter that I could land no more than a hundred yards from them, then sit on a hillock and watch the pups playing or trying to dig out a ground-hog, while the mother lay beside them glancing lazily over her shoulder every now and again to make sure I was still there. On one occasion, a groundhog suddenly burst from its burrow and dashed right through the middle of them. The pups were so surprised they stood frozen for a moment — then they all turned and collided with each other as they tried to chase it. By this time, the groundhog had disappeared safely down another burrow.

I had to leave that operation before the season ended to go back to university. About three weeks before I left, two youngish men from Vancouver flew in to Kluayaz Lake to occupy a cabin on the shore opposite our campsite.

Will Tompson had gone south for a few days on business, so it seemed reasonable to me that I should hop over after supper and see what they were up to. But just as we were finishing supper, the two men appeared in our cook tent. One of them asked which of us was the pilot. When I identified myself he said, "We'll be needing the helicopter for a day or two."

"I'm under contract," I told him. "So you'll have to wait until Will Tompson, the party chief, gets back. What is it you want to do in the helicopter?"

"We're setting up a guiding outfit," he said, "and the first thing we gotta do is to get out there and kill all the goddam wolves before they kill our caribou."

I had discovered a long time ago how angry people become if a helicopter pilot showed signs of being an eco-freak; if he mentioned things like the balance of nature. So I didn't — even though this area was a superb example of it: all the caribou were in perfect condition, and so were the dozen or so wolves whose territory it was.

I shrugged and told them we were pretty busy. They never did get a shot at a wolf while I was there. But I heard later that the pilot who replaced me when I left took them out and they shot every wolf they could find from the air — including the family I had watched over all summer and who had grown so accustomed to the helicopter that they scarcely bothered to look up when I flew slowly by them to see how they were getting on.

The sad part of being a helicopter pilot, I was discovering as time went on, was that you almost inevitably became the vanguard of destruction. First the animals went; then, if in this case an open-pit coal mine had been developed, the country went. I envied the earlier bush pilots, who never seemed to have experienced this unease.

But I enjoyed that season much more than I did the one that followed. I went out for the summer on a contract with a commercial exploration company subcontracted to do the job by the Japanese, who were by then becoming more and more involved in supervising the extraction of our raw materials.

We were camped at a small lake, whose name I have forgotten, some 50 miles northwest of Finlay Forks. The operation was run on a shoestring and, for the first time, I was putting students out in the bush on their own. I put them out one at a time at the top of drainages, and they would work their way down to the main valley, taking soil samples as they went. Then I would repeat the process as we worked our way along the valley.

I was very unhappy about this because it was a dangerous practice. If one of them fell on a creek bed, in amongst the trees, it would take a very long time to find him — even longer to get him out to where the helicopter could pick him up. But there was no law against it, so I couldn't change things. I noticed, though, that when one of the Japanese executives visited us and I suggested leaving him on his own, he promptly declined; he made me take him back to camp while I moved the crews.

The only real excitement we had that season was caused by forest fires. Because it is a relatively dry area, the Stikine country burns well nearly every year; and that year in particular was a bad one for forest fires.

Late one evening, a lightning strike started a fire two or three miles along the valley to the west of us. As usual on that operation, our radio was on the fritz; the batteries were flat, the generator in pieces as the engineer tried to repair it. So I flew, very early the next morning, to a much larger exploration camp some 30 miles away and called the forest service to report the fire. I borrowed two fully charged batteries from them and returned to our camp. I felt sure we were going to need our radio during the next few days.

Just before noon, three water bombers appeared and set to work on the fire. But by then it was too late; the wind was blowing strongly and the fire took off. The water bombers gave up after a couple of hours and flew off. I had no doubts in my mind that it was time for us to do the same thing, and I went to the party chief, a youngster still in graduate school, and told him so. The same company had another camp near Dease Lake, about 100 miles to the west of us; we could move there and come back later if the fire didn't wipe out our camp. He got on the radio and tried to get permission from his superiors to evacuate the camp. They were loathe to spend the money it would cost to evacuate the camp.

That night, when the wind died away, the smoke settled right down on us: our eyes smarted, we found it difficult to breathe, and everything was covered in a thick film of wood ash when we got up in the morning. By ten o'clock the smoke above us was so heavy we were in a brownish-yellow gloom, with a visibility of no more than half a mile. The fire was close enough for us to hear the crackling of the flames. The party chief was still dithering because he hadn't received clearance from his superiors to move us out, so I went to the radio and managed to get hold of an Otter pilot who was just going in to land at Dease Lake. He dropped his load there and came straight out to pick up our crew. The visibility was so bad he had to come in from about four miles along the valley to the east of us, flying just above the tree tops.

Only two days after we left, the weather changed. Heavy rain fell for at least 36 hours, and when we returned to our camp a week later, we found the fire had stopped a mere two or three hundred yards away. Most of the tents had holes burned in them by falling cinders, and the paint on the gas drums had bubbled in the heat. The acrid smell of the burn hung over us for the three weeks before the operation ended. But the fire was the only real excitement we had that season.

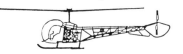

CHAPTER 23

A Fixed Base

FOR THE NEXT TWO YEARS I WORKED VERY, VERY HARD; BUT those were the most satisfying years of all for me. I operated out of a base and I had my family with me. In 1968, I went up to Alice Arm, which is on the west coast, north of Prince Rupert. A new molybdenum mine had opened there in the spring, and an exploration rush was on in the surrounding area.

Dan Dunn, the pilot who had started the base there, was swamped with work, so I was sent up to help him out. We had an old shack down on the tidal flats as a base office, and we rented two of the old houses which were vacant in the settlement. The principal family in the community, Mr. and Mrs. Peterson and their two sons, ran the place as expeditors, manning the radio and looking after all movements in and out by Pacific Western Airlines, as well as the unloading of the weekly supply ship, the *Northland Prince*.

Apart from the Petersons, there was one other woman and about 10 or 12 permanent residents, all men and all more than 70 years old. Originally, they had come to the area as miners, working in the copper mine at Anyox, an island some 30 miles away. Anyox had closed down after a long and bitter strike in the 1930's, and these few people had stayed on in Alice Arm, living on heaven knows what. They had interesting names — Jimmy McGee, Maurice, The Colonel, Preacher Smith, Yorkie — and they were all delightfully eccentric, even though some of them smelled like polecats.

They were tough old birds; they had survived many a lean year. But now they were having the time of their lives. Each of them had a "property" staked somewhere out in the surrounding mountains. For all these years they had backpacked into these claims every summer, working on them just enough to satisfy regulations and keep their claims alive. Maurice had an adit — a horizontal tunnel into the side of the mountain — he had begun 20 years before. Every summer he would pack in with a hand drill and a few sticks of dynamite and blast a foot or two more out of his "mine."

This year, none of them had to pack in. There was a constant stream of geologists from the big multinationals — companies like Kennco, Rio Tinto, Inco, Falconbridge and Noranda — and the old-timers would climb into the helicopter with the geologists to fly up and examine their claims; proud, propriety expressions on their faces. All of them were convinced that the lean years were over. Their own property would become a mine, their future some sort of undefined bliss.

Their optimism was understandable because that is how the new mine across the inlet had come into being. Inge Fevre, one of the old-timers in Alice Arm, had persuaded one of the large companies to come and look at his property two years previously. Now he was reputed to be a millionaire. And his brother, with the delightful name of Gunn Fevre, ran the only store in the settlement and he, too, was reputed to be making a fortune out of the exploration companies who were pouring into the area.

It was sad in a way, because nothing came of it in the end. No new mines were developed, and over the next few years I kept hearing that Yorkie had died, or that Maurice had passed on, or that the Colonel had gone to the great gold mine in the sky. Meanwhile, our company had a remarkably profitable season. I have never been situated quite so strategically. Some twelve exploration drill camps were spread out in a semi-circle, radiating perhaps 20 miles around our base.

We would go from one to the other, taking in food and equipment, slinging diamond drills to new locations, moving people in and out, bringing out drill cores. In the four months I was there, I logged over 550 revenue hours; and Dan Dunn considerably more than that. We were both tired by the end of the season, but there was a gratifying sense of accomplishment as well.

However, the perfect season doesn't exist, and I had my problems that year. The machine I was flying, a G3B-1, wasn't pulling the load it should. Normally, if the gas tanks weren't too full, you could get away with eight or nine hundred pounds on the hook. I was down to something like 650 pounds as a maximum. The engineer could find nothing wrong. It was one of those cases when nothing showed, and the engineers were understandably sceptical when this happened; so I had to resign myself to it for that season. What made it hard to take was that Dan Dunn was one of the better pilots I've met. He was also very competitive and my performance was bound to look shabby by comparison to his. Just before Christmas the following winter, Art Johnston, the company's chief engineer, told me they had found out what the problem was with the machine. The wrong valve had been put into the hydraulic system which governed the turbocharger: the engine was developing only three-quarters of its potential power.

One day I had to move a drill camp some 30 miles to a new location. The old camp was in a very tight clearing cut out on the brow of a cliff. Because the drillers had stacked all their equipment on the helicopter pad, I couldn't land there — I had to go in, drop them some nets, then wait until they had a load ready before I could return to hook up. This didn't bother me because I had worked with the crew for some weeks and I was confident they knew what they were doing.

When I came in for the first load, the hook-up seemed to take a long time. But finally the driller who was doing it came out from under the helicopter and signalled me away. I lifted the load off, backed out and swung away. The trip to the new camp took about 15 minutes, and when I got there I went in without hesitation. The clearing was in a swampy area, down among the trees. I had looked at it before; it was small, but we could cut some trees down later. In fact, if they took down a dozen or so trees, I would be able to swing out over the main valley of the Kitsault River.

In any case, for the moment I would be able to climb out vertically without any load. I put the net down gently, took the weight off it and punched the hook release button on the Cyclic. The lanyard didn't drop off. I tried punching the button several times, without success, then reached down to yard up on the manual emergency release. Still nothing happened and I began to perspire a little. I could never lift that load out vertically if I couldn't get rid of it.

I spent some five minutes trying to snap the load free by hauling up into the air with full power while I held the release button down. Next I tried putting the load down and backing away from it so that I could land behind it. But the lanyard wasn't long enough. The front of my skids propped themselves on the load, tilting the tail down, and I knew I would wipe out my tail rotor if I went down any further.

By now I was soaked in sweat and trying to remind myself that I mustn't panic; I must think. Unfortunately, my thoughts kept dissolving into a futile rage because this was one of the very few times I had ever put a sling load in without first putting somebody in on the ground — somebody who could come and cut the load free if necessary.

In the end I managed to pull myself together and start making some rational decisions. The only acceptable one I could come up with was to back as far into one corner of the clearing as I could, and then run at the trees to see if I could force the load through the tree tops and out into the main valley. The trees were swamp spruce; the tops looked scrawny. At the most, I would have about 200 feet in which to get up speed before the load hit them. I had trouble forcing myself to start; but it worked. The net load crashed around in the tree tops for what seemed an eternity, and when I finally burst out into the clear, the load was flailing around like an erratic pendulum — and I was feeling several years older.

I flew straight back to base, where the engineer came out and liberated me. The cargo hook is mounted on a bar, which in turn is bolted laterally to the underside of the main frame. The driller who had hooked me up had decided it would be safer to take a couple of turns with the lanyard around the bar before snapping the ring into the hook. There was no way I could ever have got rid of that load without help from the ground.

On the whole, though, that was a thoroughly enjoyable season. The next one, 1969, was even more so. Utah Mines had announced during the winter that they were going to open a copper mine just outside Port Hardy, on the northern end of Vancouver Island. This would almost certainly provoke another flurry of exploration and claim staking, just as the new mine in Alice Arm had the previous year. So Dan Dunn went back to keep the base going in Alice Arm, and I was sent up to establish a new one in Port Hardy.

I had at least one serious problem facing me when I got there. Okanagan Helicopters, who were very much larger and better known than my company, already had a machine based there. Thus the first two or three weeks were depressingly unproductive. What business there was all went to Okanagan. I tried some hard-sell tactics, taking the senior B.C. Hydro man out for a free demonstration, and then the local MacMillan Bloedel manager. But this didn't do any good; and so far, the anticipated rush of exploration geologists had been a mere trickle. This was the first time I had been entrusted with the task of establishing a new base, and it was beginning to look as though it would be a fiasco.

Because we had nothing better to do, I would stand with Don Borden, the engineer, in the airport terminal watching the twice-daily influx of people from the Pacific Western Airlines scheduled flights. I knew that there were probably people coming in who would need a helicopter, but I couldn't quite bring myself to solicit work like an eager cabby.

One morning after the sked had come in, Don and I were sitting dejectedly in the airport coffee shop, watching the Okanagan helicopter take off with a customer. The two P.W.A. stewardesses off the flight came in for a coffee and we invited them to join us. They had about an hour to kill before their plane took off to return to Vancouver, and when we'd finished our coffee one of them asked if I would give them a ride in the helicopter; they had never been in one. I agreed readily enough; they were both attractive young women, and I had nothing better to do. I showed off a bit — gave them some razzle-dazzle — then flew slowly along the beach for some miles before returning them to the airport.

I have met very few people who don't find their first helicopter ride an exciting experience, particularly if the weather is half decent. These two young women were no exception. Their eyes were sparkling when I dropped them off on the tarmac by their Convair. The consequences should have been predictable, but still I was taken aback; we got a steady stream of requests for helicopter rides from the other stewardesses on the route. We even got some from other routes who had swapped with our regular stewardesses so that they could come to Hardy for a helicopter ride.

I won't pretend I didn't enjoy all this; at the same time, I couldn't help wondering what my boss Alf Stringer's reaction would be if he found out that this was my principal occupation at the moment. I am sure he must have heard about it eventually, but by then he wouldn't have minded too much. For the moment, it suddenly occurred to Don Borden and me that we might be able to capitalize on our unexpected popularity with the P.W.A. stewardesses. We asked them to canvass their customers on the way in to Hardy and if they found one who was going to need a helicopter, to steer him our way. We suggested they should avoid any mention of our company name — just tell the potential customer that they would point out the helicopter crew to him after he had disembarked.

We struck pay dirt right away. Almost the day after we had asked the first two stewardesses to do this, a geologist with a staking crew of eight men came in on the afternoon flight. While he and his crew were waiting for their luggage and equipment to be unloaded, one of the stewardesses introduced me. The geologist in charge was a little confused — he thought I was the Okanagan pilot — but he had a lot on his mind and I didn't feel it would help things to comment on this. Although we didn't know it at the time, this was the beginning of the real rush. He knew that other crews were on their way. He wanted to be first, and he had come in such haste that he hadn't even booked accommodation for his crew in the one and only hotel in town. Don Borden leapt for the telephone and got the last remaining room; but even with hide-a-beds, that would only provide for four of them. I was able to reassure him. We could get some mattresses and his crew could put down their sleeping bags in our office, which was not only heated, but boasted a washroom as well. They could store all their equipment in the hangar, and in the morning I would fly them all out to the first campsite he had planned.

Don Borden drove our old pickup round onto the tarmac and we loaded them all into it and drove to our hangar. It wasn't until we reached it and the geologist saw our logo on the office door that he began to realize that something was amiss. Apparently he had made some commitment to use Okanagan before he left Vancouver. I assumed what I hoped was an expression of pained astonishment when he told me this; but by then I wasn't very worried. We had him boxed in.

That was not only the first sizeable job we landed, it was also the best one. We put his main camp out the following morning. It was about 50 miles north of Hardy, in the area to the east of Cape Scott. I would fly out to this camp first thing every morning, put his crews out in the bush, then fly back to work on other jobs. In the evening, I would return to bring his crews back into camp. I had a steady three or four hours of flying practically every day. And once you become busy in a situation like this, that in itself seems to attract other customers. Before long, I had to plan carefully and work very hard to keep people satisfied.

An exploration rush is always fun, and this one was no exception. The principle of confidentiality is vital, but it has interesting ramifications for the helicopter pilot. Every geologist expects you to keep his activities absolutely confidential; yet at the same time, he is convinced that he has the right to know what every other customer of yours is doing. I developed a repartee of gross exaggeration to deal with this problem. I would claim that other geologists were making startling mineral discoveries right in the gravel parking lot of the Port Hardy supermarket. This irritated them at first, but gradually they caught on and abandoned their attempts to pump me for information.

On one occasion, I put a staking crew into the bush on one side of a large, bare hill known locally as Old Baldy. I flew them in from the end of the road by the Holberg Radar Station. Then I went off to the camp of the crew I have been talking about and put them out to stake claims on the other side of the hill, some five or six miles away. The foreman at the camp was suspicious. He had heard a helicopter over on the other side of the hill, and he wanted to know what I had been doing there. "Must have been another machine — Okanagan, perhaps," I replied blandly.

Late that afternoon the two crews came face to face with each other, more or less on the crown of Old Baldy. When they discovered that I had put both crews out, they were infuriated. Several days passed before I could reason with them, convince them that I had done the only thing possible; anything else would have violated the confidentiality of one or the other.

I did a little of almost everything that season. I worked with the exploration companies and the lumber companies, forestry, hydro and highways, as well as some land survey crews. There were a number of accidents in the woods, and I landed many times on the lawn in front of the only hospital in the area at that time — the hospital at Alert Bay. I even went back in time to the early days of aviation and did some barnstorming, giving five-minute rides for a dollar a minute at the Port Hardy and Rumble Beach summer fairs.

For want of business, Okanagan pulled their machine out of Hardy in the middle of July, and my season was made. In fact, that summer was the crest of the wave for me. My machine, appropriately registered with the initials of the company, VIH, would pull a superb load. My own confidence had reached its peak. I could afford to play around a little without sacrificing any safety margin. I still have pleasant memories of the two attractive young stewardesses sitting beside me in the helicopter as I prepared to take off from the tarmac in front of the hangar. Both wore expressions of studied nonchalance — they were, after all, flying people themselves. But when I hauled up on the Collective I didn't bother to use any rudder to counteract the torque. As the helicopter spiralled up into the air, the young women abandoned their nonchalance; they squealed loudly and grabbed at my arm for protection.

Oh yes, it was a good season. And no doubt because of this the few that came after tended to be anticlimactic. The following year I was sent up to Stewart, on the British Columbia-Alaska border, to open up another base for the company. This was the toughest area I have flown in; everything goes just about straight up from sea level to about seven or eight thousand feet. Every time I had to go anywhere, it seemed to me I had to grind up over a high glacier or a narrow, windy pass. In my first few trips with passengers who knew the area, they were constantly pointing out to me spots where this or that aircraft had crashed. In spite of this, I did well and put in a lot of hours for the first two months of the season. Then the weather turned sour for the next month — really sour — and when that happens the best pilot in the business invariably loses his stripes.

I made some trips through those high passes, bucking wind and rain and snow, but still the customer grew more and more dissatisfied as the days passed and the work they wanted to do didn't get done. But the flying I did during the early part of the season was interesting, because Stewart is an interesting place. Since the turn of the century, the area around it had been the scene of countless mining ventures, most of them unprofitable. The mountains were dotted with derelict mineshaft headgears and the sad remnants of ore tramways and ropeways. They must have been incredibly hard to put in, and in some cases you could see the tortuous trails zigzagging up an almost sheer sidehill to them. Only two mines had really succeeded for more than a year or two: the Premier silver mine, which had folded in the late 1940's; and the Granduc copper mine, which was still in production while I was there.

I visited several of these old mine workings with geologists and mining engineers, and this gave me an insight into just how unscrupulous the penny stock promoters were. I landed at one with a consulting engineer. It was on a high ridge, and the buildings, such as they had been, had long since collapsed. All that was left was a caved-in shaft and the remains of a wire ropeway. The engineer stretched when he got out of the helicopter, walked a few paces to relieve himself, then sat down on a rock and had a smoke. We talked for a few minutes of the difficulties the old-timers must have had getting their equipment up onto a high ridge like this one before there were any helicopters to do it for them. While we were talking, a wolverine suddenly appeared on the sidehill below us, loping up in its peculiar gait right towards us. The engineer jumped to his feet with a cry of alarm and the wolverine stopped and looked up for the first time, only about 15 feet from us. It let out an inscrutable hiss before turning to lope off down the hill again.

About a month later, I read the report by that consulting engineer on the property we had visited, in a Vancouver newspaper. He claimed he had conducted a thorough examination of the property, and of the area surrounding it; he mentioned all sorts of mineralization he had seen, and ended the report by recommending an extensive program of diamond drilling. It didn't surprise me to read a few months later that the reputation of both the mining industry and the Vancouver stock exchange had sunk to new lows.

My season in Stewart was not a distinguished one, but by then I was no longer suffering much anxiety over my reputation as a pilot. I had finished my education and I was working full time during the college year as a teacher; I was flying in the summer only to try to restore a bank balance which had been sadly depleted by the student years. My only regret was that I didn't earn very much money for a company which had treated me very well for the past several years.

And after that I ran into an odd but I suppose understandable phenomenon: I can remember very clearly the first few years of my flying career, yet the last two or three have already faded from my memory. But the last season, 1974, I do remember because I had made up my mind it was to be the last. In May, Nina and I went with our neighbours to their cabin in the Chilcotin for the first summer holiday I had taken in 20 years. The lake by which the cabin stood was delightfully isolated; there was only one other cabin on its shore. I think this was because the lake was shallow and filled with weed, and most people look for clear, sparkling depths when they decide to build a cabin.

If the weeds kept people away, they didn't bother the fish. The lake was teeming with rainbow trout and an occasional dolly varden. Over the years I had stopped fishing because it was invariably too easy. But this was fly-fishing, and any fish we couldn't eat, we could smoke in the smokehouse my neighbour, Howie Routh, had built, and take it back home with us. Howie and I drank a little whiskey, too, and it was marvellously peaceful to be out in the bush with no helicopter to worry about — and no importunate customer, either.

When we came out, with great reluctance on my part, our first contact with other people for nearly a month was with the Bliss family, who own a ranch-cum-resort on the highway, about half-way between Williams Lake and Bella Coola. They had a gas pump — one of the old manual ones — and I was filling our car when Mrs. Bliss came out with a message for me. It was from Alf Stringer. He wanted me to phone him at once; there were hints of urgency and emergency. I phoned him when we reached Williams Lake. A pilot, newly trained the previous winter, had had an accident; Alf needed me to replace him on a contract as soon as possible. I learned later that Alf had very nearly chartered a fixed-wing to fly into the lake and bring me out.

Three days later I was on my way in a new machine from Victoria to Terrace to start work on a timber inventory with a commercial consulting firm. We worked our way from Terrace up the Nass Valley to a point somewhere past Mezziaden Lake. The job was a familiar one — putting out sample crews and then timber cruising from the air — but because of the accident, the whole crew was horribly nervous. The pilot I was replacing had gone into a sand bar on a creek to drop a net load of fly-camp equipment, and ran into the same problem that I had in Alice Arm: he couldn't unhook his load. He had lost control and swung himself into the trees. The machine caught fire and he was badly burned. It was a sad business because Paddy had distinguished himself as a fixed-wing bush pilot; he had for many years flown a Grumman Goose for Trans-Provincial Airlines on the notoriously difficult Prince Rupert-Stewart run. He recovered from this accident, but only a year later he tried to go in for a landing through a gap in the trees. The gap was too small, and this time he was killed.

For the moment, though, my problem was to restore confidence among the forestry crew I was working with. Fortunately, I had a gimmick which worked rather effectively. By this time I was teaching English at the British Columbia Institute of Technology, and I had managed to get a modest grant to make a movie on helicopter flying; a training film for forestry students to show them how to use a helicopter safely and efficiently. I carried a 16-mm Bolex and a tripod on the rack when I flew. And of course, I had to get my passengers to help; they had to act as cameraman as often as not, and this took their minds off the dangers of flying. My grant dwindled as time went on, so the film never rose much above the level of a good home movie; but it was fun making it.

Somehow it seems unfair to me that my flying career ended without any excitement or drama. But the truth is that it ended very tamely during the Labour Day weekend. Alf called me on the Saturday morning and asked me to go out and fight a Mac and Blo slash-burning fire which had got away on them in the hills overlooking the San Juan River on Vancouver Island. I worked through the weekend, landed for the last time in front of the hangar in Sidney at half-past ten on Sunday night. The following morning I caught the seven o'clock ferry to head back to my classroom in Burnaby.

CHAPTER 24

Customer Management

IN ALL MY READING ABOUT THE EARLY DAYS OF BUSH FLYING, one thing has always intrigued me: nobody ever appeared to have any social problems; there was no hint of friction, let alone conflict, between flying crews and the people they worked for. Yet even in the 1950's, when helicopters were still unreliable and we encountered all kinds of maintenance problems, as well as the problems of unfamiliar terrain and vicious weather, I never regarded these as more than about a third of the total. The other two-thirds were caused by people: people who were bored and needed some conflict to brighten things up; people, particularly in our case, who were filled with resentment at what they considered the high cost of renting a helicopter, and whose resentment would focus on the helicopter crew. They seemed to feel they could redress the balance, somehow, by making life hard for us. Thus we had to fight some stern battles in those early days to establish reasonable working and living conditions.

One of the most obvious ways in which a customer could attempt to recoup the money spent on the helicopter was to provide as little as possible in the way of food and camp equipment. One such customer, working in Newfoundland and Labrador, reduced its crew to the sort of diet the early explorers had to survive on: flour, sugar, tea and such meat as they could shoot. It was a very large and wealthy international consortium of mining companies, and this parsimoniousness infuriated Harry, the pilot who had been picked to go on this contract. One night, after being served a supper of boiled seal meat, Harry reacted vigorously. He sent a telegram to the Department of Transport complaining that malnutrition was causing his health to deteriorate and he was concerned about the possibility of an accident. At the same time, he sent a similar telegram to the New York head office of the multinational corporation he was under contract to, hinting very strongly that, if nothing was done about it, he would contact the press. Two days later, a de Havilland Otter arrived at their camp with a full load of fresh meat and vegetables.

But there was another customer who became much more notorious among helicopter crews in the middle 1950's. He was a consultant who undertook exploration contracts for large mining and oil interests. He had no difficulty winning contracts because of the remarkably economical rates he quoted; and he made no secret of the fact that he intended to compensate for the high cost of helicopters by providing his crews with minimal living standards. The tents he provided were tiny, cotton hiking tents. For a cook tent he supplied a tarpaulin, small two-burner Coleman stoves and the nest of little tin saucepans mountaineers carry in their packs. Dehydrated food was just coming on the market at the time, and it was even more unpalatable and lacking in nourishment then than it is now. The crew would be provided with enough dehydrated food to last them for three or four months, and then left without fixed-wing resupply for the rest of the season. His crews would return from an operation looking gaunt and emaciated.

After two or three years of this, helicopter crews could neither be persuaded nor coerced into going out on one of his operations. He was known, clear across the country, as the Beast of the Boondocks, and people just blankly refused. Spartan resorted to a by now familiar solution: they hired another pilot from Texas. When he arrived early in the spring, he heard from the gossip around the hangar what he was getting himself into, but he appeared undismayed. He loaded up his helicopter and set off for the camp. It so happened that when he got there, the Beast of the Boondocks was there to see that the operation got away to what he considered a good start.

The pilot's name was Bud, and Bud was a sportsman. Since this was his first visit to the Canadian wilderness, he had come prepared to deal with any kind of fish or game. In the cockpit with him he had two fishing rods, a shotgun and two different calibre rifles. When the Beast walked up to the helicopter to meet Bud, and saw this array of sporting equipment, he flew into a rage. "What the hell do you think this is," he demanded furiously, "a vacation camp ... or a dude ranch, perhaps?"

Bud sat in the helicopter, the door propped open with his foot, looking up at him calmly. "Waal, Mr. ——," he said, in his rich Texas accent, "they told me back in Ottawa that ah might have to shoot you."

The Beast left shortly after Bud's arrival, and Bud was dissatisfied when he went to inspect his quarters and found that they consisted of a pup-tent which he had to share with his engineer. Next he walked across to watch a student, squatting under the tarp, preparing their evening meal on two tiny Coleman stoves. Bud picked up one of the packages of dehydrated food, looked at it for a moment and shook his head. Then he went to find the party chief, a young and rather nervous graduate geologist, and asked him if he, the party chief, really expected Bud to play boy scouts all summer. The party chief shrugged and said that that was all the equipment and food they had.

But Bud, like Harry, was a resourceful person, and he reacted even more positively than Harry had. He strolled back to the helicopter, started up and took off to fly to the nearest town, some 50 miles away. There he proceeded to assemble the tents, stove, propane bottles and other equipment he felt was necessary to run an acceptable bush camp — billing it all to the customer. The story is that he spent more than $3,000, and made some six or seven trips to fly all the gear in — charging all the flying, once again, to the customer. Then, and only then, did he turn his attention to the business at hand: geological exploration.

The Americans at that time had a certain confidence that some of the rest of us lacked (though we learned quickly), and in the end nothing happened to Bud. The bills for the equipment and food he was buying did not turn up at the Beast's head office for more than a month. When they did, the Beast's reactions were predictable. Within minutes he was on the phone to Ottawa, shouting threats at Spartan's management — demanding that Bud be fired forthwith. But Spartan was able to tell him quite truthfully that no other pilot in the company would go out on one of his jobs — so it was Bud or nothing. And as for the money spent on food and equipment, the Beast could sue Bud for that if he chose — but they suggested that he would be unwise to do this because by now stories had begun to circulate rather widely about people in his camps suffering from malnutrition by the end of the season. The publicity of a court case might dig up some ugly skeletons. So, for the rest of the summer, Bud made regular supply trips, picking up fresh food and all sorts of delicacies which had never been heard of before in one of the Beast's bush camps.

Of course, these are exceptional cases I have been talking about, and they tend to give the impression that all customers were ogres and all helicopter crews saints. The truth is that although many of the party chiefs on the spot did try to provide reasonable living conditions, in the early days of helicopter flying they were often overruled by their superiors in Toronto or New York, people who fully expected us to sleep on the ground in pup-tents and eat beans all summer — we were, after all, mere hewers of wood and carriers of water. So we had to work in our own ways to establish minimum standards of living in a camp. I never duplicated Bud's rather dramatic solution to this problem, but I did on several occasions insist on flying out for a load of fresh food, on the threat of pulling out altogether unless I was allowed to. As more and more helicopter crews adopted this attitude, standards began to improve.

Another problem, one which I suspect will never be resolved, was the frequent power struggle which developed between the pilot and the party chief. In the early days particularly, party chiefs tended to adopt a purely authoritarian approach. They would not discuss with the pilot what it was they wanted to do, and leave it to the pilot to arrange the most suitable flying program; they would draw up rigid schedules and issue commands, many of which were impractical and unattainable. But in any case, the authoritarian approach was doomed to failure. Pilots, I suppose by virtue of what they do, are nearly always inclined to be a little arrogant. After all, much of the time you are looking down on a foreshortened world; you have an omniscient view, and this by itself engenders a sense of superiority. In a helicopter this sense is enhanced by the fact that you can go virtually anywhere you want to. And when it comes down to it, the power lies very literally in the pilot's hands. He, and only he, can fly the helicopter; and if the party chief becomes too demanding, too domineering, there are a host of technical reasons, a mass of flying regulations, the pilot can invoke to slow things down.

But in the early days, people were slow to realize this and the tendency was to demand a replacement as soon as they felt any dissatisfaction with the pilot. And the helicopter companies responded to begin with, making complicated and expensive exchanges of pilots from one job to another — only to discover, in most cases, that the customer was more dissatisfied with the new pilot than he had been with the old. This was hardly surprising, of course, because when such an exchange took place, the two pilots concerned would invariably have a chat — and the new pilot quickly made the old one look like a paragon of productivity by comparison.

In fact, using odious comparisons between pilots working for them now, and other pilots who had worked for them in the past, was a favourite ploy with many customers. And this sort of gamesmanship could be very dangerous if the new pilot was inexperienced and insecure. He might try to meet fictitious standards of skill and daring, and easily get into trouble. As an example, on one occasion I replaced a pilot for a few days who had to return to Ottawa because one of his children had been injured in an accident. On my second day on the job, one of the geologists asked me to make a landing on the side of a hill. There were two very good reasons why I could not land in the spot he indicated — the slope was much too steep, and there simply wasn't room to fit the blades in amongst the trees in the clearing. But the geologist insisted that my predecessor had landed there several times. I went back for a second look, and then told him he was mistaken; no pilot could land there.

He was very insulting. He didn't hesitate to accuse me of incompetence or cowardice. Thus when the original pilot returned, some ten days later, the first thing I did was to whisk him and the geologist into the helicopter and go back to the spot. When we got there, the other pilot began to laugh. All three of the geologists on the crew had wanted to land there; there was something about the rock outcrop just above the clearing which excited them. He had told them that if they really did want to land, they would first have to walk in, cut down some trees and build a landing pad. The geologist with us merely shrugged; he refused to apologize or make any comment.

Okanagan Helicopters responded to this particular problem rather effectively, I thought. For several years all their machines carried a plaque in the cockpit, mounted where the passengers could not fail to see it. The text was a simple one: "Yes, I know that the last pilot you had flew into smaller clearings with heavier loads in worse weather than I do."

For me, though, the most irritating situation would occur when we were visited by VIP's — senior executives from New York or

240

Chicago or Europe, or even occasionally Toronto. Almost without exception they would want to go fishing as soon as they arrived. But unlike the mandarins on the Mid-Canada Line, these ones were governed by the puritan ethic; it was impossible for them to fish during working hours — they had to do this in the evenings. I can recall on many occasions sitting down to a late supper at around eight o'clock in the evening, after having flown more or less continuously since 7:30 that morning. I would be looking forward to lying down for half an hour after supper before strolling out to have a chat with the engineer, when three or four plump, pink-cheeked executives would come into the cook tent and sit down with me, their brand new bush clothes creaking, their rimless spectacles gleaming with excitement. After exchanging civilities for a few minutes, one of them would invariably say something like this: "Well, we've got a treat for you tonight — we're all going fishing."

At first, when this happened, I used to sigh to myself and accept it as a necessary part of what was called good customer relations. But in time I began to lose my patience. In the north, in the summer, daylight lasted at least until midnight, and these incongruous outdoorsmen would either catch absurd numbers of fish — in which case I would have to make extra trips, more or less in the dark, bringing their wretched catch back to camp — or they would stay until the bitter end when the fish were not biting, determined not to return empty handed.

Fortunately, there were a number of ways of discouraging this sort of thing if you thought about it. One of the most effective, I found, was to twist around in my seat to look over my shoulder as we neared the lake or river we had chosen as a fishing spot, and let out a grunt. When asked what was the matter, I would shrug and say: "Not sure whether it was a grizzly or a black — but it was a big son of a bitch." Then when we reached our destination, I would circle around, searching the ground carefully and advising my passengers that I was just making sure there weren't any bears around — that bears came out in the evening, and if they smelled fish they could be troublesome. This always seemed to dampen the fishermen's enthusiasm to a remarkable degree, and as a rule I didn't have to wait too long before they wanted to get back to camp.

Another very successful tactic I used — before it was used too often and became known — was to get hold of an empty whiskey bottle and fill it with cold tea. I would drop it down by the Collective and then, as soon as we had settled down to fly to our destination, pick it up, holding the Cyclic between my knees while I unscrewed the cap — allowing the helicopter to flounder around with some abandon — and take a healthy slug; then I would let out a sigh and say: "By God, a man needs a good belt to unwind at the end of a long day." My passengers would lick their lips nervously. And after we had reached our destination, I would stand at the water's edge, making sure that everyone could see me taking frequent swigs at the bottle. This, once again, seemed to have a remarkably inhibiting effect on sportsmen. All at once they would decide that they had better not keep me up too late; they realized that I had to go to work again early in the morning. Then they would watch me out of the corners of their eyes, surreptitiously and with profound anxiety, as we flew back to camp. I resisted the temptation to overdo it by wandering all over the sky, but I did permit myself the luxury of an occasional hiccup.

The answer to the inevitable conflicts and frictions of bush life was, of course, motherhood stuff — co-operation rather than confrontation. But at that time the concept that big was better was very much in vogue, and it was difficult to get people who were working for large corporations, and who felt that by association they had great power and authority, to appreciate this. They were convinced that someone like myself, who worked for a relatively small company, was vastly inferior to them. I could never bring myself to subscribe to this point of view, and I resisted it tenaciously.

But a friend of mine who had been flying all summer to supply an oil-drilling rig, told me a story the following winter which still stands for me as the perfect parable of labour relations in this context. They were in the Swan Hills field, I think, and the hole they were drilling was a deep one: it was down some 4,000 feet. One day the crew had to pull the rods to change the diamond drill bit. While tightening the new bit onto the rod, one of the members of the crew had slipped, and dropped the 16-inch Stillson wrench he was using right down the drill hole.

From time to time such accidents do happen, of course, and there is a method of retrieving stray objects from the bottom of drill holes. It is not easy; a complicated grapple has to be used, and on this occasion they spent an entire week, three shifts every 24 hours, trying to get the Stillson out of the hole. The cost of having a drill rig shut down for this length of time is formidable, and tension mounted as they sweated and cursed, shift after shift. Twice they very nearly got the wrench to the surface, only to have it slip and drop down to the bottom of the hole again. By a coincidence, when they finally managed to get it out, the same crew was on shift as had been when the wrench was first dropped. The "Push," or foreman of the rig, grabbed the Stillson when at last it emerged from the collar of the hole and turned to the roughneck who had dropped it.

"Here," he said, "you can have this for a souvenir — you're fired!"

The roughneck stood for a moment looking at the Stillson in his hand. "Fired, eh?"

"Yeah, you got it — fired!"

"Oh well, in that case I don't need this no more then, do I?" he shrugged, and turned to drop the wrench down the hole again.

What I have been describing are merely variations of the conflicts and tensions that occur on any job. In the bush they are a little more focused, a little more intense. People who have to spend all their waking hours for months at a time with the same small group of companions invariably tend to become aggressive and uncompromising. Conflict brings some relief from the tedium of life in a bush camp. For the pilot, though, the unpredictable, often irrational, behaviour of people when they were around a helicopter usually kept him from becoming either bored or complacent.

When I was on a Forest Service contract in northern Ontario, we had to leave the helicopter in more or less public places in the small towns and communities we worked out of. As a rule, people were very good; they seldom if ever opened the door and tried to climb into the helicopter, and for the most part they would not even touch the machine. There were two exceptions. First, absolutely everyone found it necessary to kick the floats. Second, virtually everyone was seized with an urge to rap on the bubble with their knuckles. The kicking of the floats didn't bother us too much, but the rapping on the bubble did. Some burly logger or truck driver could easily rap hard enough to crack the plexiglass. We tried hanging a sign on the bubble: "Please do not touch — fragile." But this was merely an invitation to people to find out just how fragile it was.

I could think of no solution to the problem, but in the end Paddy Reilly, the engineer with me, came up with the answer. Being an Irishman, perhaps he understood the forces of paradox more clearly than I did. He began by drawing the outline of the sole of a boot on the outside of each float in white paint. Then he drew arrows pointing to them, with the caption: "Kick here to test." On the passenger side of the bubble, he drew a small red circle, once again with an arrow pointing to it and the words: "Tap here to test." I don't pretend to understand it; I can only record that after that nobody but very small children, who couldn't read, ever kicked the floats or rapped on the bubble again.

However, this was merely perplexing behaviour; there were other types which brought a different kind of excitement to the pilot. The old cliché that bush flying is hours and hours of grinding boredom, punctuated by sudden brief moments of sheer terror, has a good deal of truth to it. Let me give just one example before leaving you.

Noel Dodwell, an Australian who had emigrated to this country in his 20's, was working on a forestry contract in the west. He had to put out sample crews in the mountains every few days. These two-man sampling crews would take enough food and camping equipment with them to stay out for a week or ten days, doing their sampling, before returning to main camp to replenish their supplies before being moved out to the next area. On this occasion, Noel had dropped the crew's food and camping gear in a clearing on the bank of a creek. Then he took off again to drop the two students some three or four thousand feet up the mountain, near the tree line, so that they could put in two samples before walking back down to set up their fly-camp. He couldn't find a landing site where they wanted one and he decided to prop one skid on a steep bank of scree, holding the helicopter in a semi-hover while they jumped off.

Before doing this, he explained to them very carefully the importance of leaving the helicopter one at a time, and of not lingering on the cargo rack before jumping because he could not hold the helicopter level for more than a few seconds in this unbalanced condition. Finally, satisfied that they understood, he settled the skid on his side of the machine firmly on the scree and nodded to the student on the outside to go. Unfortunately, the student was still wearing sneakers; he had tied the laces of his boots together and he was carrying them in his hand. When he got out on the rack and looked down at the jagged scree, some four or five feet beneath him, it occurred to him that he should be wearing his boots before he jumped, and he calmly sat down on the cargo rack to change into them.

Noel, fighting to keep the machine from turning over, shouted to the student still sitting beside him to tell his companion to please get off the rack (or words to that effect). As the second student moved over to do so, Noel finally lost control and the helicopter rolled down the slope, thrashing itself to pieces as it did so.

Astonishingly, no one suffered anything more serious than minor scratches and bruises; but the people in main camp, more than ten miles away, claimed afterwards that they heard profanities couched in an Australian accent echoing among the mountain tops for several minutes.

If you could keep going after that sort of thing without losing your nerve, being a helicopter pilot was fun.

Epilogue

AFTER I HAD BECOME A HISTORY CURATOR AT THE B.C. PROVINCIAL
Museum (now the Royal British Columbia Museum) in the mid-
1980s, I teamed up with a colleague, Bob Turner and, as a part of
the Museum's outreach programme, we toured the province twice
a year giving slide talks — he on the history of sternwheelers and I
on the history of helicopters. We rationalized that they belonged together because both were driven by something that rotated. The
evenings were for adults, and the programmes were not only enjoyable, they also often led to meeting with experienced aviation people
who had stories to tell. During the days, whenever possible, we gave
talks in schools and I was more than a little complacent when I discovered that a bush pilot had rather more prestige amongst the young
people than academics and other professionals.

I would start my talk by asking what made an aircraft fly, to give
some impression of the function of a wing and its shape — and then
go on to tell them that the rotors on a helicopter were wings and they
simply rotated to give lift, instead of being pushed or pulled through
the air. This worked well until we arrived in Hudson's Hope and
found ourselves in a gymnasium facing more than a hundred students,
ranging from junior high to grade 12. The usual response to the first
question was speed. I would point out that cars, especially racing cars,
travelled at speeds up to 200 miles an hour, and they didn't fly. One
tall young man, leaning against the gym wall, heaved himself up-
right and said, "They will if you open the doors." The entire room
exploded with laughter and I never really did re-establish any of the
quiet dignity and authority which all pilots strive for. There were
times when a damp sleeping bag and the mosquitoes didn't seem so
bad after all.

Yet another venture of mine ended in something of a humiliation.
Bob Turner had constructed a model sternwheeler, complete with
steam engine to drive the paddlewheel. In addition, he had a model

steam locomotive. Both were a resounding success in the schools. We noticed that even the six-foot seniors, who usually wore an expression of some disdain on their faces, leaned forward eagerly to watch the locomotive chugging across the gymnasium floor. This demonstration became a highlight of our programme. I must confess I was a little miffed to be upstaged like this, and I decided that I needed a similar attention-grabber; so I bought a radio-controlled model helicopter driven by a battery pack.

I have talked earlier in this book about my difficulties in mastering actual helicopter flying. I am now in a position to say that it is twice as hard to fly a model one. To begin with, power was marginal; secondly, the controls were astonishingly sensitive: in short, you need the hands of a surgeon and the reflexes of a grand prix racing driver. The thought of trying to demonstrate my short, faltering flights in a gymnasium full of students, which had seemed so promising in concept, made me shudder. A helicopter pilot who couldn't fly a model helicopter would surely be the ultimate irony — and, in any case, I have had to suffer any number of patronizing comments from Bob Turner.

Several years later, I gave the model to Eric Cowden, a helicopter engineer who had taken to flying models as a hobby. It did something for my bruised ego to be told that the model was not only under powered, but the control system was so unsophisticated that nobody in the hangar could fly it — but I still have lingering daydreams of dazzling those young audiences with my skills.

Another, far more satisfying project was born in another hangar. On one of our speakers' circuits in the late 1980s, we visited an old friend, the late Jack Nicolson, President of Alpine Helicopters in Kelowna. Surrounded by modern turbine helicopters, I glanced up at the rafters in the hangar and spotted the familiar trelliswork of one of the early Bell helicopters of my day resting on them.

Driving back to Victoria, we discussed the possibility of restoring, or at least reconstructing, one of the early models as a museum exhibit. The idea took hold, and when I got back I started to work on Dave Parker, another colleague with whom I had co-authored *Helicopters: The British Columbia Story* in the early 1980s. Dave liked the idea. We agreed that it would be impracticable to go for an airworthy machine, so we settled on a static display of the second model in the long Bell 47 series: a 47D1, circa 1950. Then we went to work. The Friends of the Provincial Museum, who support such projects, made a grant of $7,500. Not much, but enough to encourage us and I began to phone old friends in the business and, after some nudging, most agreed that they probably had some parts tucked away in dark corners of their hangars — parts they were prepared to sell for a nominal sum or donate to the project.

Soon we began to assemble what we needed: a mainframe and basket were available for a reasonable sum in Edmonton; a tailboom was available for a song from Conrad Busch in Delta, as well as a very serviceable Plexiglas bubble; a gas tank was available for nothing from Canador College in North Bay, Ontario; Alf Stringer of Vancouver Island Helicopters (VIH) in Sidney donated the expensive transmission, as well as many other parts. The Coast Guard found a set of skids and had them flown across the country for us. We felt confident enough by now to start looking for someone to assemble the helicopter.

Eventually, we approached Chuck Roberts, instructor in helicopter maintenance at the B.C. Institute of Technology hangar on Sea Island in Richmond. Chuck's students could work on the reconstruction as part of their training. Chuck was understandably cautious but, when we assured him that we would do all the hunting and grovelling for the many parts we still needed, he agreed.

The first year of this project was often frustrating but ultimately very rewarding. Feeling like something between detectives and remittance men, we gradually tracked down and scrounged more and more of the parts we needed. Ken Mizera, an old friend from my flying days, who runs a helicopter operation in Calgary, contributed a cabin section, as well as a host of parts from the original control system that were almost invariably thrown away when newer models appeared on the market. Particularly rare were irreversibles — ingenious mechanical devices to limit the feedback from the rotor system to the stick — which preceded hydraulic systems.

Because this project was an addition to the training curriculum at BCIT, progress was understandably slow; but, after eight months, Chuck and his students had accomplished more than half the difficult work on the restoration — and contributed such vital parts as the Franklin engine and a set of wooden main-rotor blades. Now we had to move the helicopter to the Island to complete the detailed work.

At this stage two veteran air engineers, Eric Cowden and Ian Duncan, took over. VIH's Chief Engineer, Barry Hewko, gave us permission to use the hangar in off-work hours — but this turned out to be impractical because the machine was constantly having to be moved to allow the regular fleet to be serviced. The next move was to Nils Christensen's Viking Air, which had unused space across the road from his main hangar. Nils is one of aviation's natural gentlemen and he turned a blind eye to a little pilfering — locking wire, cotter pins and the like.

Given this environment, Eric and Ian brought our machine to within something like 85% of completion. They worked in an unheated hangar during the cold winter months without complaint (or at least, no more than you can expect from any helicopter engineer), and the result was nothing short of first class. We had adopted the registration of Okanagan Air Service's first machine, CF-FZX and, after much heated discussion, decided on the exact shade of blue used in the original livery. The paint job glittered and only the bubble needed polishing — but that, of course, was the pilot's job.

Now came the final and sometimes exasperating 15% to completion. Ian Duncan had donated a set of wooden tail-rotor blades — blades that almost never became time-expired because they were so vulnerable to damage. Yet still, there seemed to be a multitude of small parts needed for completion. We made a final move to the basement of the Museum, and now the late Art Johnson, for many years chief engineer for VIH, took over.

The most challenging task during this last phase was to make doors — we had found just one, but so badly battered that it served only as a pattern. After some experimentation, we discovered that old aluminum ski poles provided the perfect dimensions for the frame and went to work. Pat Scott, the Museum's expert in plastics, formed the convex Plexiglas, but it turned out to be very tricky getting an exact fit in our frames. We went through more than one prototype before Art's skill and patience triumphed.

By a happy coincidence, not long after we had finally come to the end, the Museum was putting on a temporary exhibit about the oil and gas industry in B.C. It was the perfect setting: we brought in a load of rocks and set the helicopter on them in front of a mural depicting a mountain scene. Then we found the necessary props: a canvas packsack, a clipboard, an old wooden-handled geologist's pick, maps and aerial photographs; and, thanks to Bruce Payne, formerly chief pilot at VIH, but then flying for MacMillan Bloedel, we even had some of the old square, four-gallon fuel cans which he had found in an abandoned logging camp.

Opening night for the exhibition was a happy occasion. Many of the now senior oil executives who attended had been young geologists or mining engineers in the early '50s and for them it was a piece of pure nostalgia — their early adventures in helicopters were being recounted in every corner of the gallery. Their pilots were losing revs, dinging their blades or they, the geologists, were jumping down onto mountain ridges all over the place. It was a very enjoyable evening, and now we have a valuable artifact preserved; one that will become even more valuable as the years pass.

Unfortunately, once the temporary exhibit was over, we had no space in our Museum for the helicopter; consequently, it is now on a long-term loan and on display at the British Columbia Aviation Museum, in Sidney.

P. C-S, 1995

Other

Sono Nis Press

Aviation History Titles

by

PETER CORLEY-SMITH

BARNSTORMING TO BUSH FLYING
1910-1930

BUSH FLYING TO BLIND FLYING
1930-1940